RESTRUCTURING MATERIAL THINKING

RESTRUC-TURING

Material and Data
in Architecture and
Urban Scales

Michael Hensel
Bob Geldermans
Defne Sunguroğlu Hensel
Milica Vujovic

Birkhäuser
Basel

MATERIAL THINKING

TABLE OF CONTENTS

A growing body of literature is highlighting the rapidly increasing interest in the role of data in architectural design (Deutsch, 2016; Petrova et al., 2018; Sunguroğlu Hensel et al., 2022), urban design and planning (Batty, 2013; Kitchin, 2015; Kitchin et al., 2018; Chokhachian et al., 2022; Bokolo, 2023), urban management (Engin et al., 2020), and metropolitan and regional planning (Ramos and Silva, 2003; Altafini et al., 2024). This literature includes interdisciplinary and multi-scale perspectives (Hensel and Bier, 2022; Chokhachian et al., 2022). This book examines the transformative impact of the rapidly developing relationship between material and data in architecture and at larger scales.

In today's context of digitalization and Big Data, new potential arises from the evolving relationship between material and data. Data science focuses on extracting patterns from large datasets, frequently with the aim of supporting decision making, and plays an increasingly pivotal role in numerous disciplines (Kelleher and Tieney, 2018), including materials science. Data are increasingly a key resource in the field of materials science, serving the purpose of knowledge discovery for materials. This is especially the case for materials for which very large datasets already exist which are too large for human reasoning, thereby requiring advanced computational methods (Himanen et al., 2019). In general, data and data-driven computational methods can serve the purpose of discovering novel materials and advanced material performance, as well as understanding and instrumentalizing material flows. This development offers considerable potential for planners and designers who are confronted with increasingly complex planning and design requirements that arise in the context of diminishing resources and environmental degradation, and that involve questions of material sustainability, resilience, adaptation, life cycles, circularity, flows, etc. In general, increasingly complex planning and design requirements require an interdisciplinary and trans-scalar approach that is progressively framed by the intersection of sustainability science, urban science, and architectural science (Hensel, 2022), where questions of material performances and material flows play a pivotal role.

Over the last three centuries industrialization has transformed agricultural societies into industrial ones at a global scale (Turner II et al., 1990). As part of this transformation, industrialization dramatically changed the way humans gain knowledge about materials. This implied a shift away from a vernacular logic of tacit knowledge gained by direct experience and instruction towards the application of industrial and scientific methods and knowledge to design and systematically test materials, acquire and use data, develop computational methods for design and manufacturing, and assure accountability for material resources, material use and material flows.

The emergence of industrially produced materials, building parts and systems required a new way of systematizing and disseminating the required information on materials. This led to the emergence of a broad range of material catalogs that were not at first coordinated, neither in content nor in format. In 1906, *Sweet's Indexed Catalogue of Building Construction*, which was published in the United States, began to address the gap in systematized information on materials. Andrew Shaken points out that "*Sweet's Catalogue* [...] arose [...] in response to what architects called the 'catalogue problem.' Besieged by thousands of catalogues of irregular size and format, the architect or builder could scarcely keep up with the proliferation of building materials in the emerging national economy, let alone organize and read the trade catalogues generated by a building industry stoked by the emerging field of advertising. *Sweet's* systemized the chaotic lines of communication between architects, builders, engineers, and manufacturers, regularizing the typography and size of trade catalogues, and binding them in one large reference book with an index. By 1912 [...] the idea of the compilation catalogue shifted from an attempt to reign in the unruly business of advertising, to a progressive era attempt to rationalize and manage the larger industry for architects and builders." (Shaken, 2005, p. 28)

According to Joachim Krause, this development constituted a major shift from *architecture to information architecture* (Krause, 2011). Under the editorial leadership of the architect Knut Lönberg-Holm, Director of the Information Research Division at Sweet's Catalogue, and under the artistic directorship of the Czech graphic designer Ladislav Sutnar, Chief Designer in the Information Research Division, an approach to information display was developed that focused on information organization and retrieval. Lönberg-Holm and Sutnar revolutionized catalog design at Sweet's (Lönberg-Holm and Sutnar, 1950). Their work paved the way for information graphics and its spread into mainstream literature. One example of this is the Atlas of Globalization published by Le Monde Diplomatique, which is available at newsagents across Europe, illustrating how a broad general readership has grown used to reading and understanding information graphics. This shows that data and data graphics have become everyday items in the popular press. Krause elaborated that "the catalogue was hence positioned between design and construction as an information technology device that opened up access to all industrial products relevant to construction [...] This increase in building information in the twentieth century indicated not only the industrialization of building [...] but also the spread of 'American' construction methods and the corresponding building typologies across the globe. Even in a highly industrialized country like Germany, attempts were made to organize building knowledge differently: as a system of measurements (Neufert) or as a compendium of 'building materials'. Both must be seen as complementary approaches to a design and construction practice that was largely still craft-based and influenced by local building practices." (Krause, 2011, pp. 23–24, our translation) In this context, Richard Neutra stated that "'raw materials' are no longer raw, but themselves end products of long drawn-out and widely scattered manufacturing processes. The new builder and designer quarried his material from *Sweet's*, the great annual building material catalogue. And Sweet's began to stand on shelves in Mexico City, Shanghai, Melbourne, and Johannesburg. [...] The building market had become cosmopolitan." (Neutra, 1954, p. 51)

The shift towards obtaining information on materials from specialized sources ushered in the development of a multifaceted relationship between data and material described in this book. Alongside systematized information on materials in print format, material libraries emerged that provided broad ranges of material samples often particular to a specific sector. Large companies, material laboratories, and universities began to establish materials libraries. Additionally, universities started to include in their curricula courses on material knowledge and selection for a given task or set of requirements.

Digitalization and the internet underpinned the next major step of the evolution of the relationship between material and data. Sweet's Catalogue, for instance, evolved into Sweet's Products Database. Today there are numerous online material collections, including Altair, materiO', MCX Material ConneXion, M Material Bank, and Total Materia. Many of these online material collections soon expanded to include material consultancy services, today frequently offering advanced material property visualizations, data format conversion and high-resolution data suitable for use in various types of computational simulations. In other cases, property visualization has been integrated into software packages and advanced simulation tools. One prominent example is the *Ashby Material Property Charts* that provide a comprehensive visual representation of material properties and their interrelationships (Ashby, 1989; Ashby, 2011) (see Chapters 1.2 and 2.2).

Material libraries and databases provide valuable information but can be limited in scope, when focusing on only a specific part of the full range of available materials. Vincent et al. pointed out that while "the database of technical materials is comparatively well known [...] that of biological materials is due almost entirely to the efforts of Wegst (Wegst and Ashby, 2004) and is as yet unavailable generally" (Vincent et al., 2006, p. 478). This points towards underlying preferences based on specific approaches to the understanding and use of materials, and thereby to specific configurations of problem and solution spaces that are strongly tied to engineered industrial materials. Moreover, while the unfolding relationship between material and data has clearly set the scene for restructuring material thinking in architecture, and on urban and larger scales, this cannot fully take place without a broadening of the current approach to include on the one hand all available materials, and, on the other hand without recognizing the role of experimental design efforts and methods that have begun to explore knowledge discovery in relation to material performance that combines tacit and scientific modes.

A key question in the field of materials science concerns the ability to design and engineer materials. David Ball has written that "in the past 200 years, our ability to manipulate and even design matter with specific properties has dramatically increased and, in so doing, has had a substantial impact on progress" (Ball, 2015, p. 1). Ball explained that the properties of matter arise from the interaction between various "components of the universe," among which he examined more specifically the interaction between matter, energy, and entropy, and the way properties arise from these interactions. Furthermore, Ball showed that this applies to existing natural materials as well as new human-made materials, which can be designed to exhibit specific desired properties (Ball, 2015). The possibility of designing matter based on desired properties raises the following questions: (1) from which perspective or worldview shall one address this possibility, (2) how does one in consequence understand and frame the problem and solution space, (3) which alternative approaches exist or can be put into motion, and (4) what is required if the solution to a given problem is indeed the design of materials with desired properties?

In this context, the differences between technical solutions and biological solutions to a given problem are of interest. Vincent et al. selected six key parameters for the analysis of technical and biological solutions: (1) information, (2) energy, (3) space, (4) structure, (5) substance, and (6) time, utilized across scale-range from nanometer to kilometer (Vincent et al., 2006, p. 478). Their research demonstrated that technological solutions predominantly rely on energy, space, and substance as primary resources. In contrast, biological solutions rely predominantly on information, structure, and time. Figure 1 shows the results of the research by Olga and Nikolay Bogatyrev in 2004–2006 and assembled and presented by them with the help of Julian Vincent at the University of Bath. The researchers summarized the results as follows:

The salient features of the 'technology' graph are:

- Energy is important at the micrometer (μm) level, probably due to materials processing.
- Substance (probably raw materials) is of considerable importance.
- Information is obliterated at the μm level, while increasing slightly at larger sizes.

The salient features of the 'biology' graphs are:

- The parameters remain relatively constant across the size range.
- Substance is much less important than in the 'technology' graph.
- Energy is the least important parameter.
- Structure is of vital importance across the size range.
- Information is increasingly important as size increases.

Vincent et al. also pointed out that when "faced with an engineering problem, our tendency is to achieve a solution by changing the amount or type of the material or changing (usually increasing) the energy requirement. But in biology the most important variables for the solution of problems at these scales are information and space [...] This comparison between the few materials of biology and the many materials of technology has been made commonly, but never explained functionally [...] It appears that biological systems have developed relatively few synthetic processes at low size at which the contribution of energy is significant; but the main variety of function is achieved by manipulations of shape and combinations of materials at larger sizes achieved by high levels of hierarchy, where energy is not an issue. This is a very subtle biomimetic lesson. Instead of developing new materials each time we want new functionality, we should be adapting and combining the materials we already have." (Vincent et al., 2006, p. 478)

Fig. 1
Engineering solutions arranged according to size/hierarchy (top). Biological 'solutions' arranged according to size/hierarchy (bottom) (Vincent *et al.*, 2006, p. 478). Courtesy of the Royal Society, London.

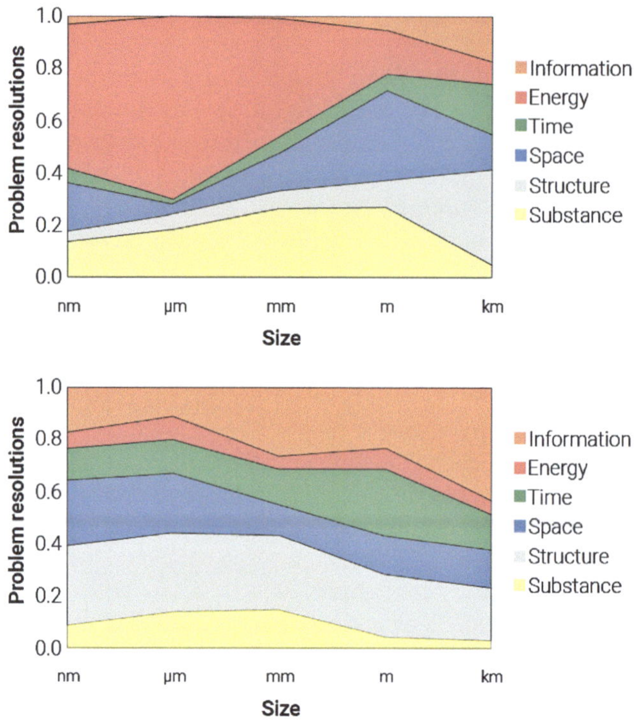

Fig. 1

Michael Ashby explained that "the technical designers' instinct is for methods that are systematic and deterministic [...]. Selection via deductive reasoning is now a well-developed route to meeting technical design requirements and powerful software and databases exist to support it. [... However,] it limits the approach to a subset of well-defined problems and well-established rules. [...] There is more to creative selection than this [...]. The method of synthesis, by contrast, has its foundations in previous experience and analogy. [...] The path to material selection exploits knowledge of other solved problems [...] that have one or more features in common with the new problem, allowing new, potential solutions to be synthesized and tested for their ability to meet the design brief." (Ashby, 2014, p. xxi)

The choice or design of materials for a particular application in architecture and engineering can also be informed by material-flow thinking and contextualization, taking account both of global resource challenges and local resource opportunities (Fig. 2). In this respect, suitability must be understood in a more integrative way, incorporating design factors that can unlock innovations that can go beyond technology-centric solutions.

Fig. 2

Fig. 2
Local reuse-driven design materialization of a balustrade in a bookshop in Brussels, Belgium. Photography: Bob Geldermans, 2023.

Different approaches are not necessarily contradictory. However, they may place emphasis on different aspects, thereby fostering divergent inroads to the understanding of and research into materials and prompting divergent framings of problem and solution spaces and the way material consideration may play out within them. This can happen along established divisions into separate disciplines and knowledge domains or, alternatively, along inter- and transdisciplinary trajectories. Moreover, this may either take place along established divisions of spatial scales that typically separate planning from design, or along multi- or trans-scalar perspectives that engage questions of material performances and flows across spatial, temporal, and functional scales. From this realization three questions arise:

/ What are the key topics along which the transformative relationship between material and data can be traced in a meaningful and future-oriented manner?
/ What are the spatial, temporal, and functional scales in which the relationship between material and data plays out?
/ Which prospects do these developments point towards?

To address these questions, we selected six themes which are addressed in individual chapters: *data*, *agency*, *time*, *flows*, *ubiquity*, and *Industry 4.0, 5.0, ...*

Chapter 1 examines the intersection of materials science, data science and innovative technologies, and shows how materials science and engineering use data resources and repositories to drive research and development efforts. These resources provide a significant amount of data on material properties, material behavior, and material performance, thereby facilitating improved utilization of existing materials, as well as discovery and design

Fig. 3
Material data repositories collect data on material properties and apply novel technology to structure and synthesize data.

of new materials and material technologies (Fig. 3). The continuous cycle of data acquisition, integration, and utilization, underscores the importance of material data across various industries, and more specifically in the architecture, engineering, and construction (AEC) sector. Material data are typically sourced from scientific literature, patents, and experimental measurements, and are curated, standardized, and organized into searchable databases. Data collection typically involves researchers from academia and industry and is aided by software tools for automation. In the AEC sector, material data are used for selecting building materials, evaluating different properties, and increasingly also for assessing environmental impact. Furthermore, material data contributes to cost estimation, site management, and maintenance planning, optimizing construction processes and ensuring safety, energy efficiency, and environmental and economic sustainability.

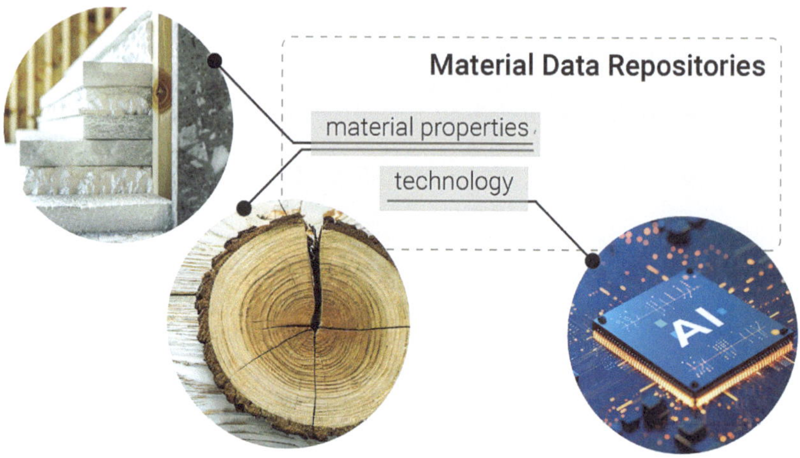

Fig. 3

Material data resources and repositories enable researchers to access large amounts of data, thereby driving innovation in materials science and engineering across spatial and temporal scales. Information modeling and material ontologies support material selection. *Smart buildings* and *smart cities* use advanced materials and sensor technologies to improve performance. *Smart materials* integrated with sensors offer real-time monitoring capabilities for structural integrity, energy efficiency, and environmental performance. Building Information Systems (BIS) employ digital materials and Building Information Modeling (BIM) to streamline design, construction, and maintenance processes, optimizing building performance and sustainability. The role of data in future innovations is reflected in the capacity of the researcher to inform material design, predict performance, and guide material development processes by analyzing large datasets. This chapter also examines advances in nanotechnology, materials science, artificial intelligence (AI), and data analytics that are driving the development of advanced multifunctional and adaptable materials for tailored interactions with the environment.

Fig. 4
Materials science leverages data science components, including data acquisition and analysis, data integration, and data utilization, to enhance Building Information Modeling (BIM) and the development of smart materials

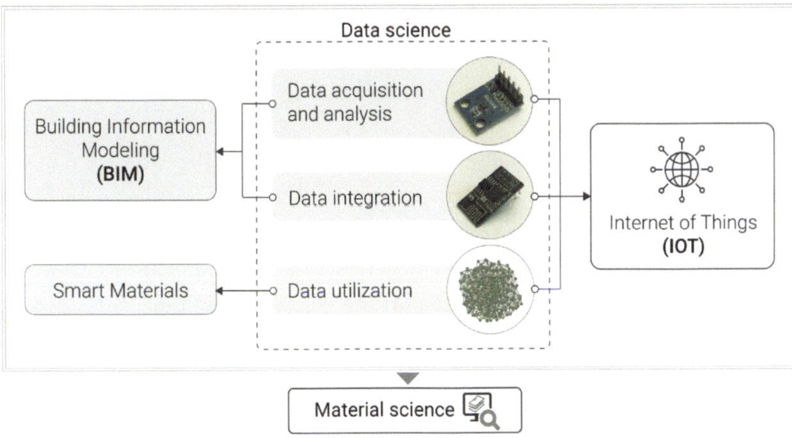

Fig. 4

Chapter 2 examines the topic of *material agency*. Materials are characterized by specific sets of properties. When subjected to changing conditions in the surroundings the interaction between material properties and external conditions can lead to material behavior, such as dimensional changes caused by fluctuation in ambient temperature or humidity. Differentiated (i.e., anisotropic) materials display different behaviors in different spatial directions, thereby requiring more data to describe their behavior. Thermodynamic properties of materials are of fundamental importance in this context. While data is available on material properties and behavior, designers frequently view material behavior as negative and seek to constrain it. However, differentiated and heterogeneous materials and material behaviors represent a largely untapped potential for exploitation across various industries, and especially in the AEC sector. From this understanding, the notion of material *performance* developed. This means that design purposefully takes advantage of material behavior. In a dynamic context this requires an understanding of performance ranges, not just of single materials, but also of material assemblages and

Fig. 5
Time sequence of the thermal performance of dry-stone walls from 8:00 am to 22:30 pm in a high-altitude terraced vineyard in Lamole, Tuscany. Courtesy of the Department for Digital Architecture and Planning at TU Wien and LamoLab Research Center, 2019.

material systems. Ranges and critical limits related to specific material performances are linked to spatial, temporal, and functional scales, and can occupy different extents on scale ranges. Therefore, producing different combinations of material performances is not only a question of a static configuration, but also an unfolding in time. This chapter shows that while this approach paints a complex picture, data can enable planning and designing material performances in an instrumental manner. For this purpose, observational data, as well as projective data (i.e., data generated by simulations, etc.) are required.

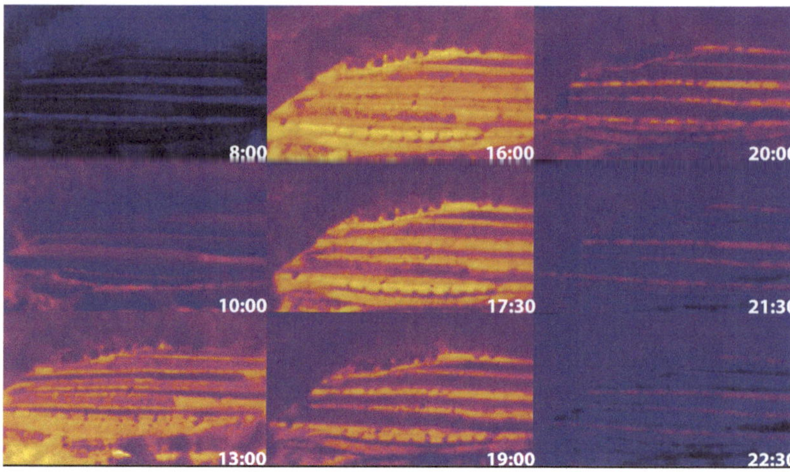

Fig. 5

Chapter 3 considers the relationship between materials and time in urban environments, which are always subject to change at faster or slower paces. Focus is placed on the role of time in the performance of the built environment, and how to understand cities and architectures as dynamic and adaptive. This has significant implications for the associated data, as material data needs change over time. This commences with examining the need for spatio-temporal data and multi-scalar data and their role in facilitating time-based planning and design. The importance of contingency is explored, looking at dynamic principles and design approaches from the viewpoint of complexity. Furthermore, the concepts of resilience, adaptation, and designing for change are discussed. Designing for change focuses on *shearing the layers* that comprise a building, each with a different service lifespan. This relates to the '*ecology of production*' as a metaphor for distributed control over materials and products. These materials and products are part of the shearing layers, thereby connecting with circular building strategies, a topic that is further addressed in Chapter 4 on Materials and Flows. Attention is then placed on technology advancements and the evolution of material data, looking at how innovative imaging techniques have taken the place of time-consuming and resource-intensive methods for material characterization and data collection. This is followed by an examination of the concept of *regeneration* which extensively depends on instrumentalizing the time dimension. Finally, the outlook suggests various trajectories of development when linking the introduced concepts and further foregrounding the time dimension.

Fig. 6
'Ecology of production' diagram visualizing distributed control of parts (over time, space, and actors), pinpointing connections between technical building systems and interrelations in the building and manufacturing sectors. Adapted from Kendall, 1990, and Geldermans, 2020.

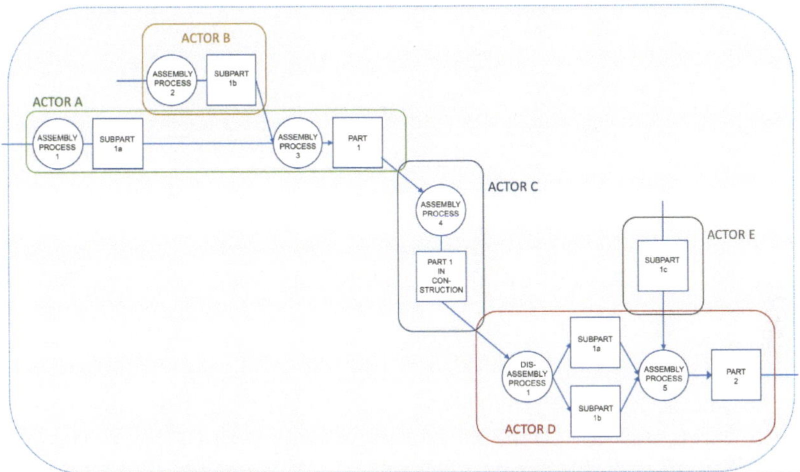

Fig. 6

Chapter 4 focuses on the geographical distribution of resources in general, and explores resource flows associated with the architecture, engineering, and construction (AEC) industry. Next, specific attention is given to material stocks and material flows in the built environment, distinguishing between fast human-induced flows and slow natural flows, while outlining the role of Material Flow Analysis (MFA). This is further reflected upon by addressing recent developments regarding MFA and its related data requirements. Furthermore, the urban metabolism metaphor is examined, taking a closer look at macroeconomic data-processing. The discussion then focuses on the human scale and vernacular architecture, exploring the linkages between architecture and local conditions. The subsequent section delves into the non-linear movement of substances through human societies, unraveling the notion of *circularity* through various concepts, notably circular economy and circularity in the built environment. Focus is placed on the spatial and territorial implications of global resource flows in relation to circular economy propositions. The notion of value is highlighted, looking at product design with its associated business models and networks of decision making. Subsequently, material tracking techniques are discussed, pinpointing multiple facets and criteria that are at stake in this domain. Finally, the outlook explores new innovations and developments around the topic of material flows, space, and circularity, specifically considering ways to better measure, monitor and understand systemic complexities.

Fig. 7

Fig. 7
Building materials at end-of-use stage, deconstructed for further utilization. Associated data for optimal value-retention of such materials concern, for example, origin, composition, manufacturing details, operational processes, transport & logistics, storage requirements, and reuse scenarios. Photography: Bob Geldermans, 2024.

Chapter 5 addresses the topic of *material ubiquity*. While various natural material resources are diminishing fast due to urbanization and construction, an increasing number of materials in urban environments can be reused. This implies that material resources need not originate from outside of cities, but instead can be recycled from buildings that have reached the end of their life cycle. In this context, contemporary thinking in waste management has come to the fore. This includes an approach known as *urban mining*. Furthermore, there is another type of ubiquitous material in urban environments that is beginning to be recognized as a key material resource in urban planning and architectural design for significantly advancing green city and green architecture approaches. These are materials that are typically not considered a part of the built environment, but instead a part of the surroundings. However, a closer integration of architecture and surroundings for the purpose of overcoming negative environmental and ecological impact, places attention on materials such as rock, soil, water, air, and biomass that serve to sustain life. This suggests that future nature-integrated approaches to planning and design require knowledge and data on such materials, as well as their interactions and their impact on urban environments and ecologies.

Fig. 8

Fig. 8
Vegetation/biomass integration into urban fabric, New York, USA. Photography: Bob Geldermans, 2023.

Chapter 6 examines innovative technologies that promise to or are in the process of further fundamentally changing the way materials are thought of, designed and experienced, particularly during design processes. Currently, humanity is in the process of progressing to a stage of industrial evolution that has been termed the *Fourth Industrial Revolution* or *Industry 4.0* (4IR). The German Federal Ministry for Economic Affairs and Climate Action defines Industry 4.0 as "the intelligent networking of machines and processes for industry with the help of information and communication technology [...] For Industry 4.0, it is not the computer that is the core technology, but rather the Internet. Digitalizing production is gaining a new level of quality with global networking across corporate and national borders: the Internet of Things, machine-to-machine communication and manufacturing facilities that are becoming ever more intelligent are heralding a new era: the fourth industrial revolution, Industry 4.0." (Federal Ministry for Economic Affairs and Climate Action – Platform Industry 4.0, 2024) Combined with a set of novel technologies this constitutes a new paradigm shift. Klaus Schwab, who introduced the term Industry 4.0, stated that humanity stands "on the brink of a technological revolution that will fundamentally alter the way we live, work, and relate to one another. In its scale, scope, and complexity, the transformation will be unlike anything humankind has experienced before." (Schwab, 2015) As Industry 4.0 unfolds, it will exert a significant impact on the AEC sector. The question is how material thinking, material design and material engineering will evolve accordingly. This involves the development of networking technology via the internet, the Internet of Things, and the role of various technologies that enhance design and manufacturing in the context of 4IR. A key question is how materials and material data are experienced and instrumentalized in planning and design processes in terms of material flows and material agencies. The chapter examines innovative technologies that have emerged that promise to play or are in the process of playing prominent roles in the field of materials science, and the way planning and design instrumentalizes material flows and material agency. These technologies include Extended Reality (XR), including virtual, augmented, mixed reality, the provision of haptic feedback in Extended Reality, as well as gaming and gamification. The development of Industry 5.0 parallels the implementation of Industry 4.0, foregrounding the transition to a human-centric and sustainable industry.

Together, the six chapters trace the interlinked developments that shape the relationship between material and data, thereby restructuring not only materials science and material engineering, but also material thinking and design in architecture and at urban and larger scales.

CHAPTER

1

DATA

This chapter explores the intersection of data science and innovative technology in materials science and examines how materials science and material engineering depend on data resources and repositories to drive research and development efforts. These resources provide a significant amount of information on material properties, material behavior, and material performance, thereby facilitating advanced utilization of existing materials, as well as discovery and design of new materials and technologies. The continuous cycle of data collection, data integration, and utilization underscores the importance of material data across industries, and specifically in the architecture, engineering, and construction (AEC) sector (Fig. 9). Data for material databases are sourced from scientific literature, patents, and experimental measurements. They are curated, standardized, and organized into searchable databases. The data collection process involves researchers from both academia and industry and is aided by software tools for automation. In the AEC industry, material data are instrumental in selecting appropriate building materials, evaluating different properties, and assessing environmental impact. Furthermore, material data contribute to cost estimation, site management, and maintenance planning, optimizing construction processes and ensuring safety, energy efficiency, and environmental sustainability. Material data resources and repositories enable researchers to access large amounts of data for their studies and collaborations, driving innovation in materials science and engineering across spatial and temporal scales. Smart cities use advanced materials and sensor technologies to enhance urban infrastructure and services. Integrating smart materials with sensors offers real-time monitoring capabilities for a broad range of purposes, including structural integrity, energy efficiency, and environmental performance. Building Information Systems (BIS) and Building Information Modeling (BIM) streamline design, construction, and maintenance processes, and optimize performance and sustainability. The role of data in future innovations lies in informing material design, predicting performance, and guiding development through data analytics. Advances in nanotechnology, materials science, artificial intelligence, and data analytics drive the growth of sophisticated, multifunctional materials, enabling continuous advancements in adaptable materials that reshape environmental interactions.

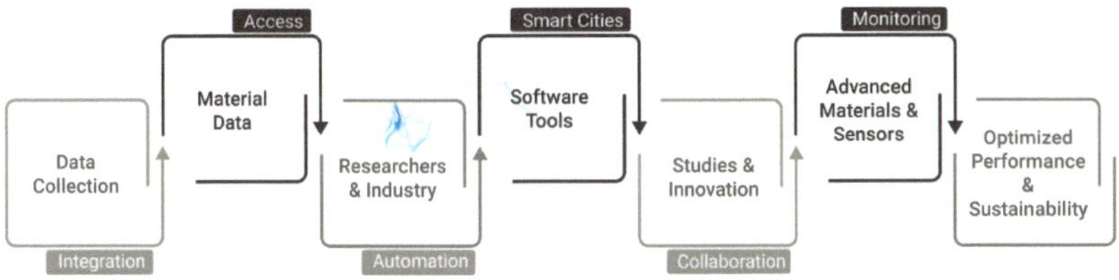

Fig. 9

Fig. 9
Process of automatic material data collection, monitoring, and application to optimize performance and sustainability.

This fast-evolving, data-driven approach enables continuous advancement in creating adaptable materials that reshape interactions with the environment. For instance, integrating machine learning and materials science can contribute to further developing materials with tailored properties, such as materials that adapt to changing environmental conditions. Similarly, data analytics can help optimize material selection and usage, reducing waste and environmental impact. With data collection and analysis methods improving, the potential for materials science and materials engineering breakthroughs is vast, with far-reaching implications for fields such as construction, energy, and environmental sustainability. The following subchapter explains how material data resources and repositories are essential for materials science and engineering, providing information on material properties, behavior, and performance, which aids in developing new materials and supports informed decision-making in the architecture, engineering, and construction (AEC) industry.

1.2 DATA RESOURCES

Material data resources and repositories are crucial to materials science and engineering research. These resources and repositories provide scientists and engineers with information on material properties, material behavior, and material performance and play a key role in the development of new materials and technologies. Figure 10 illustrates the continuous process of data collection, organization, and utilization in AEC processes, and the impact on various aspects such as design, construction, environmental considerations, and maintenance planning. It emphasizes

Fig. 10
Material data lifecycles in the AEC sector depend on data collection, integration, software tools, curation, standardization, material databases, access, and collaboration between researchers and practitioners.

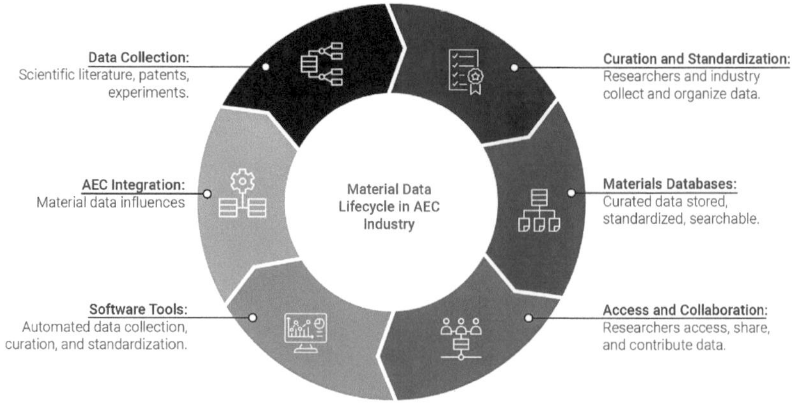

Fig. 10

how material data flows through stages and ensures informed decision-making and efficient construction practices in the AEC industry.

Data for materials databases are typically collected from a variety of sources, including scientific literature, patents, and experimental measurements. They are typically gathered by researchers and scientists working in academia or industry and may include information on the properties, structure, and synthesis of a wide range of materials. These data are then curated, standardized, and organized into searchable databases, which can be accessed by researchers and scientists looking for specific information on a particular material or class of materials. Some databases enable users to upload their own data and may have collaboration tools to make it possible for researchers to share information and collaborate on projects. Additionally, there are several software tools that can automate the collection, curation, and standardization of data for materials databases (Fig. 10; O'Mara et al., 2016; Hill et al., 2016; Yuan et al., 2018; Lv et al., 2021; Rumor and Andrade-Campos, 2022; Hearley et al., 2023).

In the architecture, engineering, and construction (AEC) industry, material data play a crucial role in the design and construction of buildings and other constructions. The selection of appropriate building materials is a critical aspect of the design process, and material data can provide valuable information to architects and engineers regarding the properties, behavior, and performance of different materials. One area in which material data are used is in the calculation of structural properties (Bigdeli and Monfared, 2021). This information is necessary to ensure the safety and integrity of structures and to satisfy the requirements of building codes and regulations. Material data can also be used to evaluate thermal properties of building materials, to achieve energy efficiency goals, and to control indoor temperatures (Rumor and Andrade-Campos, 2022; McMasters and Schlussel, 2023). Finally, the availability of detailed material structure, properties and source references is essential for proper use of material data (Fig. 11; Jain et al., 2013).

Fig. 11
Detailed information on Materials - The Material Project database. Courtesy of The Materials Project, 2024.

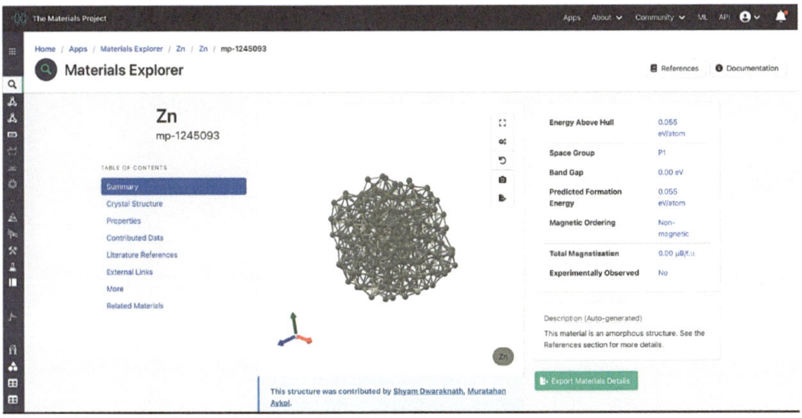

Fig. 11

Material data can also be used to evaluate the environmental impact of different building materials (Bajpai et al., 2020). This can include evaluating factors such as the embodied energy of a material, its potential for contributing to indoor air pollution, or its impact on the surrounding ecosystem. By analyzing this information, architects and engineers can make informed decisions about the materials they use and contribute to sustainable building practices. Furthermore, material data can also be used for other purposes within the AEC industry such as cost estimation, site management, and maintenance planning (Wentker et al., 2019; Gao et al., 2019). Material data can provide information on the cost of materials, their availability, and the time and resources required for installation and maintenance. This serves to optimize budget, schedule, and the construction process. Therefore, as material data constitutes fundamental information for decision making, optimization of designs and processes, and for ensuring that the final design fulfills all set requirements, access to this information is crucial (Fig. 12).

To address current needs of the materials science community, the *Materials Data Facility* (MDF) provides Cloud-based services for publishing and discovering material data (Blaiszik et al., 2016). With increased demands for material data management,

Fig. 12
Example of a Material Database – Crystallography Open Database (COD)

replicability, and handling large datasets, MDF provides open data sharing, as well as advanced data search capacities. Therefore, MDF offers two distinct actions: 1) data publication, which allows researchers to store data securely, assign identifiers, and include detailed metadata and 2) data discovery, which provides advanced tools for searching and analyzing datasets. MDF allows researchers, projects, and institutions to publish datasets of any size, generate custom metadata, interact with data through APIs, and access a data discovery for further research.

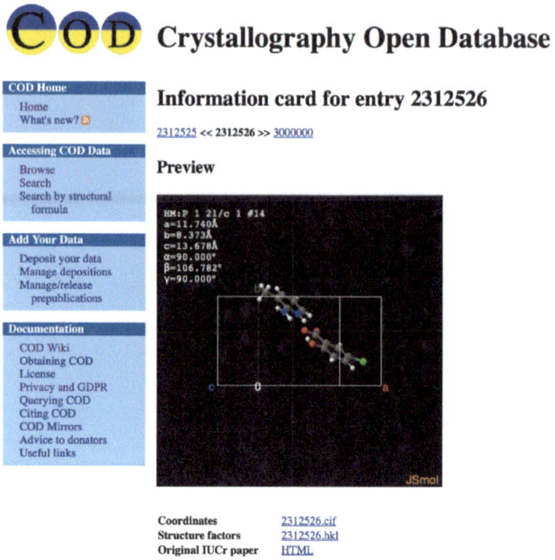

Fig. 12

Table 1 lists examples of material databases. One of the most widely used materials data resources is the *Materials Project*, which is a public and open-source repository of material data (Jain et al., 2020; Ye et al., 2018; Himanen et al., 2019). The Materials Project contains information on over 100,000 materials, including properties and performance-related data (Fig. 13). This information is derived from experimental measurements and theoretical calculations and is accessible through a Web interface (Jain et al., 2013).

The *Ashby Material Property Charts* are another resource in the field of materials science, providing a comprehensive visual representation of material properties and their interrelationships (Ashby, 1989; Ashby, 2011). They condense large amounts of material data into intuitive graphs, thereby enabling researchers and engineers to compare and select materials based on specific property requirements. By plotting material properties such as strength, stiffness, density, and cost on logarithmic scales, the *Ashby Material Property Charts* facilitate informed decision making in material selection, design optimization, and innovation. These charts offer a structured and accessible framework for exploring a large range of material properties and aid the advancement of materials research and development efforts.

Fig. 13
Example of an Ashby material property chart, correlating yield strength and density of a variety of materials. Image taken from the Ansys Education Resource "Material Property Chart Collection". Chart created using Ansys Granta Edupack™ software. Copyright ANSYS, Inc.

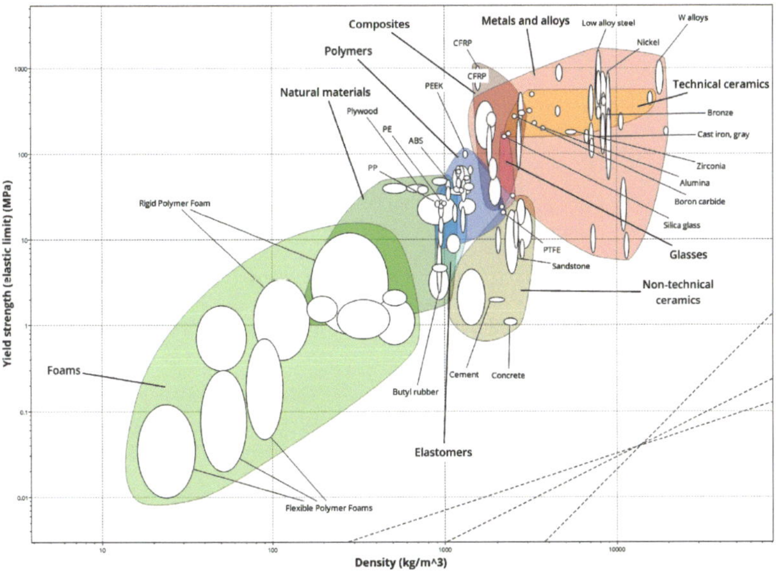

Fig. 13

The *Novel Materials Repository* (NOMAD) is an open-access repository for storing and sharing data related to materials science generated by the scientific community (Sbailò et al., 2022). It contains vast quantities of data collected from different scientific studies and is openly accessible to promote scientific collaboration and transparency. NOMAD also offers tools for analyzing and visualizing material data, which makes the analysis of material properties easier. It can be further integrated with other material databases, which allows researchers to access more information indirectly. Therefore, NOMAD makes it possible for scientists to conduct complex analyses more efficiently. It can also be used as an educational tool, providing data and resources for training and research in materials science. Furthermore, NOMAD is the only materials science database recognized by Nature Scientific Data. It accepts and stores all the data files for at least ten years after the last upload and provides a DOI so the data can be easily cited.

Table 1
Examples and descriptions of material databases

MATERIAL DESCRIPTION	MATERIAL DATABASE
Materials Project	An open database of calculated material properties, including crystal structures, energetics, and electronic structure.
Ashby Material Property Chart	A collection of charts that display the relationships between various material properties, used for materials selection and design.
Crystallography Open Database - COD	An open database that stores information about the atomic and molecular structures of different materials, such as chemicals, minerals, and compounds.
NIST Materials Resource Registry (MRR)	A collection of materials-related information and tools, maintained by the National Institute of Standards and Technology (NIST) which includes databases, software, and other resources
International Centre for Diffraction Data (ICDD)	A non-profit group that provides reference data and databases to help identify what materials are made of. They use special X-ray and neutron powder diffraction techniques to create these references.
American Elements	Database with information on various advanced and specially made materials, such as metals, ceramics, plastics, and composite materials.
Organic Materials Database (OMDB)	A free, publicly available database containing information about the material properties of organic crystals.

Table 1

The *Crystallography Open Database (COD)* (Vaitkus et al., 2023) is a public repository of crystal structures (Himanen et al., 2019; Zagorac et al., 2019). COD contains information on over 900,000 crystal structures, including their crystal system, space group, and unit cell parameters. This information can be used to identify new materials with specific crystal structures, as well as to better understand the relationships between crystal structure and material properties (Fig. 15). The *NIST Materials Resource Registry* (MRR) is another key resource for finding and sharing information about materials and their properties (Abreha, 2019; Ma et al., 2023). The *MRR* contains information on over 100,000 materials, including data on their composition, structure, properties, and performance. This information is derived from a variety of sources, including experimental measurements, theoretical calculations, and literature reviews.

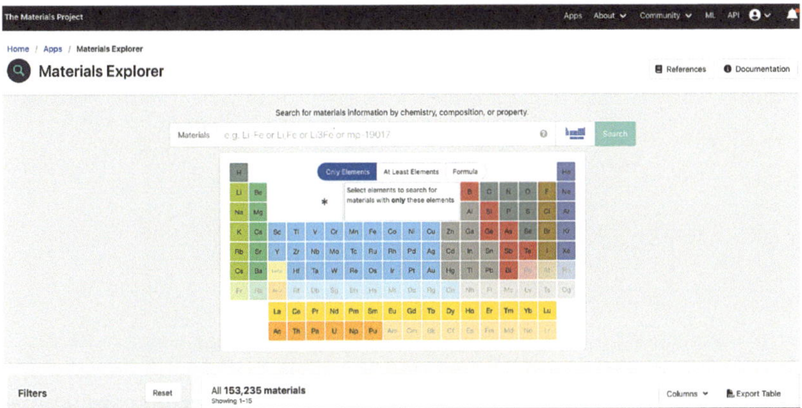

Fig. 14

▾ Structure parameters

Common name	2-Amino-3-methylpyridinium 5-chlorosalicylate
Chemical name	2-Amino-3-methylpyridin-1-ium 5-chloro-2-hydroxybenzoate
Formula	C13 H13 Cl N2 O3
Calculated formula	C13 H13 Cl N2 O3
Title of publication	Synthesis and structural investigation of salts of 2-amino-3-methylpyridine with carboxylic acid derivatives: an experimental and theoretical study.
Authors of publication	Balasubramanian, Hemalatha; Ashraf, Aarifa Muhammed; Karuppannan, Srikanth; Poomani, Kumaradhas
Journal of publication	Acta crystallographica. Section C, Structural chemistry
Year of publication	2024
Journal volume	80
Journal issue	7
a	11.7399 ± 0.0002 Å
b	8.3731 ± 0.0001 Å
c	13.6779 ± 0.0002 Å
α	90°
β	106.782 ± 0.001°
γ	90°
Cell volume	1287.27 ± 0.03 Å^3
Cell temperature	293 ± 2 K
Ambient diffraction temperature	293 ± 2 K
Number of distinct elements	5
Space group number	14
Hermann-Mauguin space group symbol	P 1 21/c 1
Hall space group symbol	-P 2ybc
Residual factor for all reflections	0.0389
Residual factor for significantly intense reflections	0.0353
Weighted residual factors for significantly intense reflections	0.1038
Weighted residual factors for all reflections included in the refinement	0.1067
Goodness-of-fit parameter for all reflections included in the refinement	1.045
Diffraction radiation probe	x-ray
Diffraction radiation wavelength	0.71073 Å
Diffraction radiation type	MoKα
Has coordinates	Yes
Has disorder	No
Has F_{obs}	Yes

Fig. 15

Fig. 14
The Material Project database. Courtesy of: The Materials Project, 2024.

Fig. 15
Crystallography Open Database - material structure parameters. Courtesy of: Crystallography Open Database, 2024.

The *International Centre for Diffraction Data (ICDD)* is a further resource for materials data (Gates-Rector and Blanton 2019; Hayashi et al., 2019). The ICDD maintains the PDF-4+ database, which contains information on over 500,000 inorganic and organic compounds, including their X-ray and neutron diffraction patterns. This information can be used to identify unknown materials, as well as to better understand the relationships between crystal structure and material properties. Another important materials data resource is *American Elements*, which is a data repository for properties and applications of a broad range of materials. *American Elements* provides detailed information on the composition, structure, properties, and performance of thousands of materials, including metals, ceramics, polymers, and composites. In addition to these resources, there are also several specialized materials data repositories that focus on specific types of materials or applications, such as the Organic Materials Database (OMDB; Geilhufe 2019; Khan et al., 2023).

1.3 METADATA

Access to data is becoming increasingly important across scientific disciplines including materials science. However, it has been pointed out by various experts that while access to scientific data, as well as computational methods and tools for data-analysis and integration holds the promise of fundamentally advancing material science, this point has not been reached. Hill et al. stated in this context that "the materials community faces serious challenges to bringing about this data-accelerated research paradigm, including diversity of research areas within materials, lack of data standards, and missing incentives for sharing, among others. Nonetheless, the landscape is rapidly changing in ways that should benefit the entire materials research enterprise." (Hill et al., 2016, p. 1) Materials informatics brings together data science with materials science and materials engineering, and with large amounts of data already being available (Grassi et al., 2018) material informatics has considerable impact on the interpretation and utilization of data for different material systems (Rickman et al., 2019), Given the large and rapidly increasing amount of data in "the data-centric era" (Hey et al., 2009) it is indispensable to annotate data so that they can be found, accessed, managed and utilized (Grassi et al., 2018). These 'data about data' are called metadata, which is key to the effective use and management of materials data. Metadata provide context such as the origin, structure, and conditions under which material data was collected, ensuring its accuracy, reproducibility, and interoperability. Properly managed metadata enable researchers to understand the reliability and relevance of data, facilitating better comparison and integration across different studies and databases.

Ghiringhelli et al. found that "the need for storing and characterizing data by means of metadata is determined by two main aspects, related to data usage. The first aspect is as old as science: *reproducibility*. In an experiment or computation, all the necessary information needed to reproduce the measured/calculated data (i.e., the metadata) should be recorded, stored, and retrievable. The second aspect becomes prominent with the demand for *reusability*. Data can and should be also usable for purposes that were not anticipated at the time they were recorded. A useful way of looking at metadata is that they are attributes of *data objects* answering the "wh- questions": who, what, when, where, why, and how. For example, "Who has produced the data?", "What are the data expected to represent (in physical terms)?", "When were they produced?", "Where are they stored?", "For what purpose were they produced?", and "By means of which methods were the data obtained?". The latter two questions also refer to the concept of *provenance*, i.e., the logical sequence of operations that determine, ideally univocally, the data. Keeping track of the provenance requires the possibility to record the whole *workflow* that has led to some calculated or measured properties" (Ghiringhelli et al., 2023, p. 2).

Open-access indexed repositories are key to ensuring data availability and reproducibility. Electronic lab notebooks such as *Jupyter Notebooks* enable data analysis and provide accessible and reproducible computational research. However, currently there is no way to combine open-access indexed repositories and materials science specific electronic lab notebook applications (Brandt et al., 2020). Brandt et al. pointed out that such a combined system "should support researchers throughout the entire research process, starting with the generation and extraction of raw data, up to the structured storage, exchange and analysis of the data, resulting in the final publication of the corresponding results [...]. In an interdisciplinary field like materials sciences, there is a special need to model the [...] heterogeneous workflows of the researchers (Hill et al., 2016, p. 1). For this purpose, the research data infrastructure Kadi4Mat (Karlsruhe Data Infrastructure for Materials Sciences) is being developed at the Institute for Applied Materials (IAM-CMS) of the Karlsruhe Institute of Technology (KIT) [...] The aim of the software is to combine the possibility of structured data storage with documented and reproducible workflows for data analysis and visualization tasks [...]. Instances of data infrastructure have already been deployed and show how structured data storage and data exchange are made possible (Brandt, 2020). Furthermore, the source code of the project is publicly available under a permissive Apache 2.0 license." (Brandt et al., 2020, p. 3)

The combination of data-driven methods and tools with open-access indexed repositories results in more available data for the purpose of data mining. Material data mining (MDM) is key to developing and utilizing criteria for material design and for models serving the purpose of predicting material properties, whether for known or new materials (Lu et al., 2017). Various tools for mining material data are currently under development. *Matminer*, for instance, is an open-source platform for analyzing and predicting material properties (Ward et al., 2018). Metadata facilitate data mining (Thuraisingham, 2000) and other approaches and methods of material discovery.

1.4 MATERIALS INFORMATICS AND MATERIAL ONTOLOGIES

Today, a broad range of materials science data, models and software tools for computational modeling, simulation and prediction exist. However, the wide range of different databases with different data models and other computational resources that frequently diverge in format, terminology and concepts used, complicate working across resources and locating useful information for material evaluation and material design. A relatively new discipline, materials informatics comprises data management, data curation, data integration, and data analysis. Cheung et al. pointed out that "materials informatics is defined as the high-speed robust acquisition, management, analysis and dissemination of diverse materials data [...]. Critical requirements include: persistent unique identifiers for materials science resources; metadata standards for describing samples, processes, properties; common semantic models/ontologies to enable mapping between database schemas, information integration and semantic interoperability; laboratory information and provenance capture systems that capture the processes both in the laboratory as well as in the post-processing of the data." (Cheung et al., 2008, p. 1)

A computational ontology is "a formal description of knowledge as a set of concepts within a domain and the relationships that hold between them. It ensures a common understanding of information and makes explicit domain assumptions." (Ontotext, 2024) Computational ontologies have been developed in the field of artificial intelligence to enable the sharing and reuse of knowledge and facilitate knowledge representation, management, and engineering (Fensel, 2001). This includes formal representation of domain knowledge to improve data availability and interoperability across different computational workflows and systems (Li et al., 2020), thereby making relevant knowledge available in a way that is specific to user requirements, through knowledge representation and interactive query and feedback generation facilitated by computational ontologies (Munir and Anjum, 2018).

In general, there exist different types of computational ontologies for different purposes. In the context of materials, domain ontologies that capture domain specific knowledge are of particular interest. A domain ontology is a "computer readable concept map [...] which describes concepts and relationships among the concepts in materials science and engineering" (Ashino, 2010, p. 1). Domain knowledge contained in ontologies can be queried by way of competency questions, which are "natural language questions outlining the scope of knowledge represented by an ontology. They represent functional requirements in the sense that the developed ontology or an ontology-based information system should be able to answer them; hence contain all the relevant knowledge." (Wisniewski et al., 2018, p.1) As Glick pointed out, "addressing the complexity of materials science ontologies requires a significant departure from traditional database and semantic web ontology approaches, including the use of neural networks that are capable of implementing methods for modeling context, relevance, complex systems, and human expertise" (Glick, 2013, p. 147). Baas et al. explained in the context of material science "the growing complexity and interdisciplinary nature of [...] research demand efficient data management and exchange through structured knowledge representation. Domain-Level Ontologies (DLOs) for materials science have emerged as a valuable tool for describing materials properties, processes, and structures, enabling effective data integration, interoperability, and knowledge discovery." (Baas et al., 2023, 120372)

Numerous domain ontologies on materials and material design have been developed or are currently under development. For instance, *EMMO (European Materials & Modelling Ontology)*, developed by the European Materials Modelling Council (EMMC), "is an ontology to provide a formal way to describe the fundamental concepts of physics, chemistry, and materials science. *EMMO* is designed to pave the road for semantic interoperability providing a generic common ground for describing materials, models and data that can be adapted by all domains." (EMMO, 2020) Li et al. developed the Materials Design Ontology (MDO), "which defines concepts and relations to cover knowledge in the field of materials design. MDO is designed using domain knowledge in materials science [...] and is guided by the data from several databases in the materials design field." (Li et al., 2020, p. 212) Another example is the *Material-Ontology (MatOnt)* developed by Sunguroğlu Hensel and Vincent, which aims “to provide a general framework and common data standard for comparison and integration of biological and architectural data, spanning various levels of complexity, for systemic analysis, integration, and systematic transfer of knowledge. This information can be harnessed to develop material-based structural systems with multi-functional and adaptive properties [...], which can be adapted for locally specific architectural applications.” (Sunguroğlu Hensel and Vincent, 2015, p. 129)

In summary, materials informatics and material ontologies present a powerful trajectory of research and development leading to advanced levels of data utilization and knowledge modeling in materials science and the use of materials across numerous industry sectors.

1.5 SENSOR-BASED DATA ACQUISITION

Sensor technologies significantly contribute to data collection across various fields, emerging as a cornerstone in the fast-developing domain of sensors. Sensorics, the science and technology of sensors, encompasses the design, application, and integration of sensors to collect data with precision and efficiency. Sensors are devices that detect various types of physical inputs from the environment, such as temperature, light, pressure, or chemicals, and convert these inputs into readable signals for monitoring or controlling systems (Fig. 16). This field has witnessed rapid advancements due to innovations in materials science, miniaturization, and connectivity (Plageras et al., 2018).

Modern sensors, such as light sensors, sound sensors, optical sensors or bio sensors detect various physical, chemical, and biological parameters, enabling real-time monitoring and data-driven decision-making. The integration of sensors into everyday objects and environments, often called the Internet of Things (IoT), has expanded data collection capabilities, facilitating more intelligent and responsive systems across industries, which use microcontrollers to control the sensors (Fig. 17; Plageras et al., 2018). These advancements are vital for enhancing performance, safety, and sustainability of various applications, including environmental monitoring, healthcare, and industrial automation.

Fig. 16

Fig. 16
A light sensor is a device that detects and measures light intensity, converting it into an electrical signal. Photography: Milica Vujovic, 2023.

In architecture, biosensors are a cutting-edge application of sensor technology, providing new opportunities for creating healthier and more efficient built environments. Biosensors, which detect biological molecules and processes, can be integrated into buildings to monitor air quality, detect pathogens, and assess the presence of harmful substances (Turner, 2013). This capability is crucial for maintaining indoor environmental quality, especially in public spaces such as hospitals, schools, and office buildings. Furthermore, biosensors can contribute to energy efficiency by optimizing HVAC (heating, ventilation, and air conditioning) systems based on real-time occupancy and indoor air quality data.

Fig. 17

Fig. 17
Microcontroller (left) with light sensor (center) and sound sensor (right). Photography: Milica Vujovic, 2023.

Fig. 18
Microcontroller suitable for IoT application - a compact integrated circuit designed to process sensor data and enable communication between devices, facilitating real-time monitoring, control, and automation.

These sensors often require sophisticated control and integration into the Internet of Things (IOT) (Fig. 18). By incorporating biosensors into the design and management of buildings, architects and engineers can create spaces that respond dynamically to the needs of occupants and promote health and well-being.

Fig. 18

The synergy between biosensor technology and architecture exemplifies the transformative potential of sensors to enhance the functionality and sustainability of the built environment. Furthermore, data collected by different sensors can provide valuable insights into the performance of building materials under various conditions. These material data are essential for developing new, more resilient, and sustainable construction materials that enhance the longevity and efficiency of architectural designs.

1.6 MATERIALS FOR SMART BUILDINGS AND CITIES

Smart cities are urban areas that utilize technology and data to improve citizens' quality of life (Ismagilova et al., 2020). A crucial aspect of smart cities is the use of advanced materials that can make buildings, infrastructure, and transportation more

Fig. 19
Diagram: mechanical properties and sensing capabilities of smart concrete.

energy-efficient, durable, and sustainable (Camero and Alba, 2019). Smart cities integrate advanced technology and data analytics to improve efficiency and sustainability of urban areas (Kirimtat et al., 2020; Ghazal et al. 2021). Research into materials for smart cities typically involves the development and testing of new materials and technologies that can be used to improve various aspects of urban infrastructure and services (Kirova et al., 2020; Zhao et al., 2021). One area of research involves the development of new types of sensors and sensing materials that can be used to monitor and collect data on various aspects of the urban environment, such as air and water quality, traffic patterns, and energy usage (Akhter et al., 2019; Alablani and Alenazi, 2020). Another area of research involves the development of new types of building materials and construction techniques that can be used to create energy-efficient and sustainable buildings (Belussi et al., 2019). This can involve the use of advanced insulation materials, solar panels, and other renewable energy systems, as well as new building techniques that can reduce the amount of energy required to heat and cool buildings (Pásztory, 2021; Abdalazeem et al., 2022). Finally, research into smart cities also involves the development of new types of transportation systems and infrastructure, such as electric and self-driving vehicles, intelligent traffic management systems, and smart bike-sharing programs (Shen et al., 2022; Yu, 2022).

One example of an advanced material used in smart cities is smart concrete (Fig. 19; Demircilioğlu et al., 2019; Makul, 2020; Li et al., 2022). Smart fibers in cement, often referred to as fiber-reinforced concrete with embedded sensors, enhance the material's mechanical properties while integrating sensing capabilities. These fibers can detect and transmit data about changes in strain, temperature, and load conditions within the concrete structure, enabling real-time monitoring and providing valuable insights into the structural integrity and performance of the construction. Furthermore, smart concrete can be embedded with sensors that can monitor the structural integrity of buildings and bridges (Ding et al., 2019). In the event of a disaster or extreme

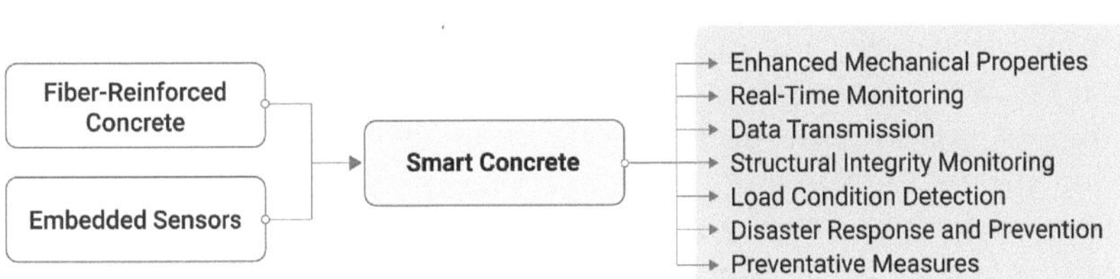

Fig. 19

Fig. 20
Diagram: Graphene, used with different materials, can improve material characteristics and performance.

weather event, the sensors can alert officials to potential damage, allowing them to take preventative measures before a collapse occurs. Smart concrete can also be used to collect data on traffic and pedestrian patterns, helping city officials to optimize the flow of vehicles and people.

Another advanced material used in smart cities is graphene (Fig. 20) (Kirova et al., 2020; Li et al., 2022). Graphene is a single layer of carbon atoms that is incredibly strong and conductive. When added to traditional building materials like concrete and steel, it makes them stronger and more durable. Graphene can also be used in the construction of solar panels and batteries, making them more efficient and longer lasting. Smart glass is another advanced material that is used in smart cities (Nguyen et al., 2020). This type of glass can change its opacity in response to changes in light and temperature, reducing the need for artificial lighting and air conditioning. Smart glass technology comes in various forms, such as electrochromic, thermochromic, and photochromic glass, each utilizing different mechanisms to achieve the switching effect (Aburas et al., 2019; Maiorov, 2019; Badour et al., 2023). While smart glass can have higher initial costs than traditional glass, the long-term energy savings, enhanced comfort, and design versatility often justify the investment. As this technology advances, it is poised to reshape how people interact with the built environment and optimize living and working spaces.

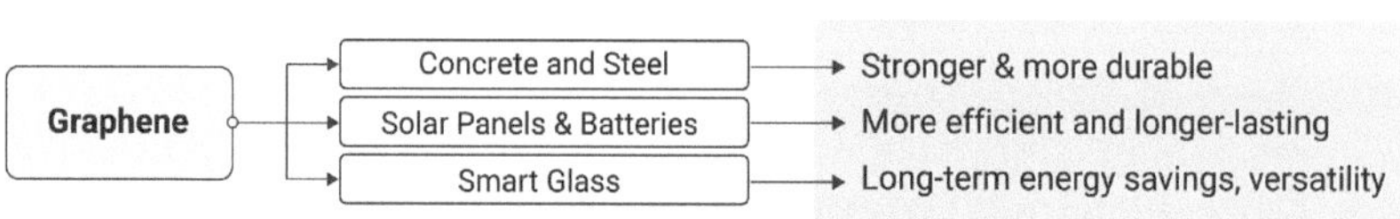

Fig. 20

Research into materials for smart cities is a multidisciplinary field, involving contributions from materials science, materials engineering, computer science, and other fields. Sensor-collected data are crucial in designing and operating intelligent buildings and cities by providing real-time insights into air quality, energy consumption, occupancy patterns, and infrastructure health. These data enable architects and urban planners to create more efficient, sustainable, and responsive spaces to inhabitants' needs. Continuous monitoring allows for timely optimization and intervention, such as improving energy efficiency or enhancing structural integrity. Ultimately, data-driven approaches help develop smarter, more adaptive urban environments, enhancing sustainability, resilience, and livability. Therefore, the goal is to develop new materials that can support adaptive urban environments. In conclusion, advanced materials play a vital role in the development of smart cities. These materials have the potential to make our cities more livable and sustainable, by improving the quality of life for citizens and reducing the environmental impact of urban areas (Fig. 21).

Fig. 21
Applications of innovative materials in a smart city (smart buildings, intelligent transportation, smart infrastructure, graphene applications and smart glass integration) alongside data collection, multidisciplinary collaboration and sustainable practices.

Fig. 21

1.7 MATERIALS IN BUILDING INFORMATION SYSTEMS

Building Information Systems (BIS) are computer systems that store and manage information related to the design, construction, and maintenance of buildings (Dave et al., 2018; Lützkendorf and Speer, 2005). The materials used in BIS are typically digital, such as 3D models, blueprints, and specifications (Dave et al., 2018). These digital materials are stored in a database and can be accessed, edited, and shared by multiple users, such as architects, engineers, and contractors. The data in BIS are often stored in the form of Building Information Models (BIM), which are 3D digital representations of a building's physical and functional characteristics (Lee et al., 2006; Volk et al., 2014). BIM includes information such as the location of walls, floors, and ceilings, as well as the materials and systems used in construction. BIM models are created using specialized software and can be used to simulate and analyze various aspects of a building's performance, such as energy consumption, lighting, and acoustics (Abanda and Byers,

2016; Tan et al., 2017). The use of BIM in construction can improve collaboration and coordination between different stakeholders and can also lead to more efficient and sustainable building design (Cerovsek, 2011; Ali et al., 2022). BIM can also be used to improve the maintenance and management of buildings after they are constructed, by providing detailed information about the building's systems and components (Volk et al., 2014). Overall, a BIS is a digital means of storing, managing, and sharing data and information related to the design, construction, and maintenance of buildings, which can help improve the quality, efficiency, and sustainability of the built environment (Fig. 22; Lee et al., 2006).

Fig. 22
Components of a Building Information System that are used to store and manage data related to the design, construction, and maintenance of buildings.

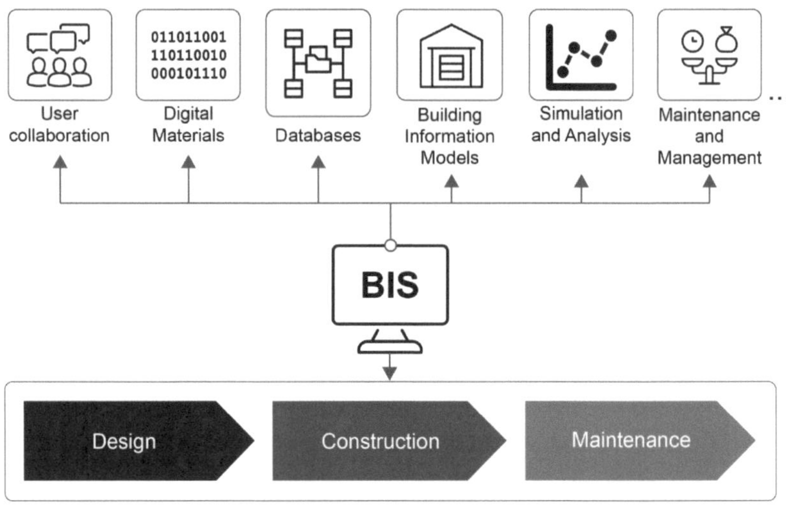

Fig. 22

Materials science in BIM involves the use of digital materials to accurately represent the physical and functional characteristics of a building's components and systems (Teng et al., 2022; Xia et al., 2022). These include the types of materials used, their properties, and their performance characteristics. In BIM, materials are typically represented using a Material Take-Off (MTO) which is a list of all the materials used in a building, their quantities, and cost (Gohil et al., 2022; Fig. 22). This information is used to estimate the cost of the building and to help identify any potential issues with the material choices (Fig. 23). The use of digital materials in BIM allows for more accurate and precise modeling of a building's performance. For example, the thermal properties of different materials can be used to simulate a building's energy consumption, and the acoustic properties of materials can be used to simulate its sound insulation. By using accurate material data in BIM, the energy consumption, sound insulation and other important features of a building can be optimized and improved (Abanda and Byers, 2016; Tan et al., 2017). Materials science in BIM also allows for more accurate and efficient construction. By using BIM, architects, engineers, and contractors can work together more effectively and can more easily identify and resolve any issues that may arise during construction. The use of accurate material data in BIM enables more accurate simulation and analysis of building performance and can improve the efficiency and quality of the construction process.

Fig. 23
Material take-off - list of all materials used in a building, their quantities, and cost.

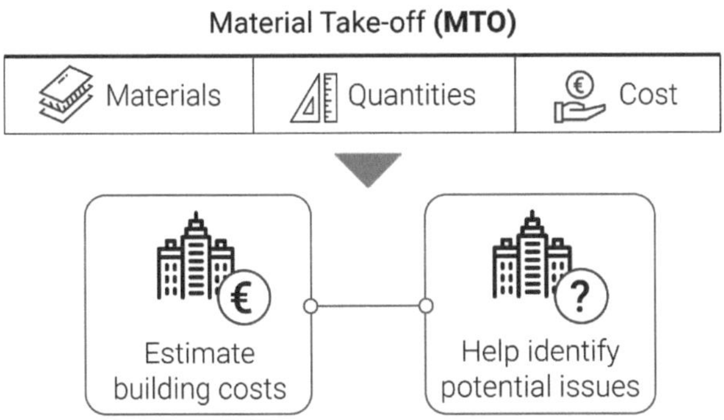

Fig. 23

1.8 MATERIALS AND THE INTERNET OF THINGS (IOT)

The Internet of Things (IoT) is a network of connected physical devices that communicate and exchange data over the internet, enabling real-time monitoring, control, and automation. It is used in various applications, such as smart homes, industrial automation, and smart cities, to enhance efficiency, improve decision-making, and create more responsive and adaptive systems (Plageras et al., 2018). Microcontrollers play a crucial role in the IoT by processing sensor data and enabling communication between devices (Fig. 24).

Fig. 24
Microcontroller used in IoT systems for communication between devices.

Fig. 25
Application of sensors integrated in materials for enhancing performance, functionality, and monitoring.

Fig. 24

At the forefront of modern engineering applications, IoT-integrated innovative materials with embedded sensors take center stage (Hassani et al., 2020; Napolitano et al., 2021; Hao et al., 2022). The choice of these materials and the configuration of sensors are pivotal, driven by the demands of specific applications. The latter refer to factors such as the required sensor durability, power consumption, compatibility with other system components, and the environmental conditions it will be exposed to. These considerations ensure the sensors provide reliable and precise data, which is essential for effectively monitoring and optimizing IoT-integrated innovative materials, also known as smart materials. The utility of smart materials and sensors extends across a wide spectrum of domains, including aerospace, automotive, biomedical, and structural engineering (Bahl et al., 2020; Spaggiari et al., 2019; Mahapatra et al., 2021; Siadkowska, 2021; Cai et al., 2022). The diverse nature of these fields necessitates the adaptability of smart sensors to distinct requirements (Fig. 25). This has led to the development of innovative sensor technologies that play a key role in enhancing the functionality and performance of systems they monitor.

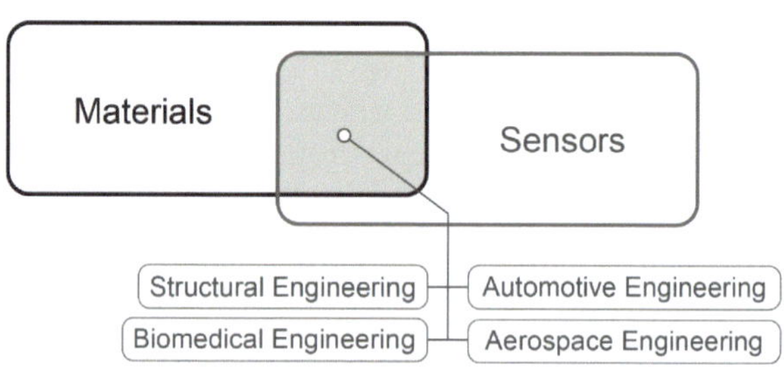

Fig. 25

Smart sensors play a particularly critical role in structural engineering. They are seamlessly integrated into the structure, and continuously monitor structural aspects (Chong and Garboczi, 2002; Oliveira et al., 2018; Mangalika, 2021). They are designed to track changes in structural integrity, stability, and performance over time, making them invaluable tools for ensuring the long-term safety and efficiency of buildings and infrastructure. Smart sensors used in structural engineering possess the capability to measure various parameters, including temperature, air pressure, displacement, strain, deformation or stretching of materials (Fig. 26). The real-time monitoring of such parameters provides engineers and architects with insights into the behavior and health of a structure (Sung, 2016; Mir, 2017).

Fig. 26

Fig. 26
Temperature and air pressure sensor for real-time monitoring of the behavior of materials integrated in structures.

Materials and sensors coexist within the Internet of Things (IoT) paradigm. They utilize the properties of specific materials to detect environmental changes and translate these into electrical signals (Fig. 27; Mahapatra et al., 2021). This process, termed transduction, describes how IoT technologies facilitate the interconnection of devices. For instance, in an IoT pressure sensor, a piezoelectric material produces an electrical charge when subjected to pressure, which is then amplified and processed by electronic circuitry to yield a measurable output, such as voltage or current, interpretable by IoT devices. Similarly, in an IoT temperature sensor, a thermistor, which acts as a resistor sensitive to temperature fluctuations, alters its resistance and thereby enables the electronic circuit to translate it into temperature data (Cai et al., 2022). Another application is shape memory alloy (SMA), wherein materials revert to predefined shapes upon receiving specific stimuli, such as changes in temperature (Jani et al., 2014). SMAs can serve as actuators in smart structures, converting electrical energy into mechanical motion. A common example is the self-adaptive wing flaps on aircraft, but SMAs can also be applied in architecture.

Fig. 27
Integration of sensors and various materials through IoT to create smart materials.

Fig. 28
Application of neural networks for early detection and diagnosis of issues in smart materials.

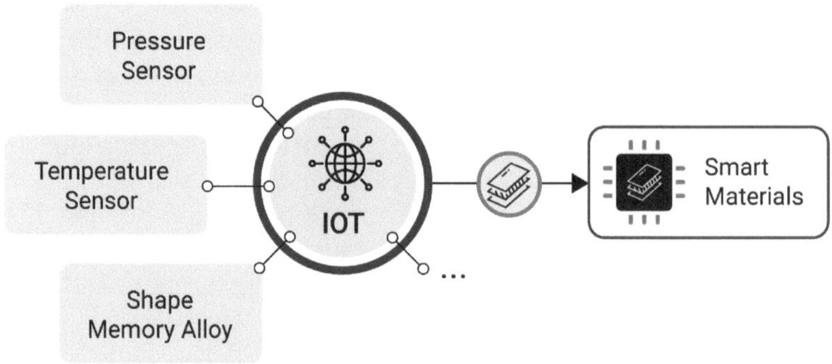

Fig. 27

Data gathered by IoT-enabled smart materials and integrated sensors facilitate predictive responses to varying loads and environmental factors, thereby optimizing structural designs (Sun et al., 2010; Sofi et al., 2022). Advanced signal processing and machine learning techniques analyze outputs from sensors to extract insights into structural behaviors, aiding in the early detection and diagnosis of issues such as material damage or fatigue (Khan et al., 2019; Fig. 28). In consequence, active measures can be taken to prevent catastrophic failures, ensuring structural safety and longevity through real-time monitoring and analysis.

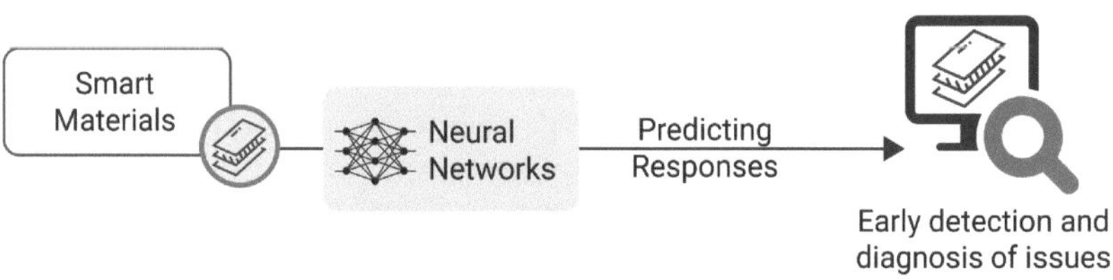

Fig. 28

Smart materials with integrated sensors in the context of IoT offer considerable potential for innovation and transformation, such as the development of advanced multifunctional smart materials to enhance sustainability, efficiency, and safety. Artificial intelligence, data analytics, and sensor technologies will likely render these materials more intuitive, adaptable, and predictive, further reshaping human interactions with the environment.

The integration of material data resources, advanced materials, smart sensors, and digital modeling technologies contributes to the further development of the architecture, engineering, and construction (AEC) industry. Material data resources and repositories are foundational for materials science and materials engineering research, offering valuable information on material properties, material behaviors, and material performance. Architects and engineers rely on this data to ensure safety, integrity, and energy efficiency, as well as to guide sustainable building practices. The concept of smart cities further highlights the importance of advanced materials and material data utilization, as they integrate technology and data to enhance living conditions, utilizing energy-efficient, durable, and sustainable materials to improve buildings and city infrastructure. Research focuses on developing materials such as smart concrete, graphene, and smart glass, which, combined with advanced sensors, enable real-time monitoring of environmental parameters, contributing to efficient city management and improved quality of life.

Building Information Systems (BIS) and Building Information Modelling (BIM) store and manage building-related information while facilitating collaboration among architects, engineers, and contractors, leading to more efficient and sustainable building designs. BIM models provide detailed digital representations of buildings, including material properties and performance characteristics, allowing for accurate simulations and analyses that optimize building performance. Furthermore, in structural engineering, integrated sensors monitor structural integrity and performance in real time, detecting changes in strain, temperature, and other parameters of materials. The data collected can be analyzed to model structural behavior, predict responses to different loads, and optimize design.

The continued integration of material data resources, advanced materials, smart sensors, and digital modeling technologies promises a transformative future for the AEC industry. Improved decision-making and effectiveness will likely result from the continuous flow of structured material data throughout the planning, design, construction, and reuse and adaptation processes. The use of advanced materials promises more sustainable and resilient constructions. Digital platforms such as BIM will foster improved collaboration and innovation, leading to adaptive building performance. Maintenance and safety will be achieved through real-time monitoring by smart sensors, ensuring the longevity and integrity of structures. These advancements promise a future where smarter, more sustainable, and resilient materials enhance the environment.

CHAPTER

2

AGENCY

Fig. 29
Front cover of the August 1967 issue of Progressive Architecture, entitled *Performance Design*. The approach to performance design portrayed in this issue of the journal evolved from systems theory and was mainly based on an engineering and hard systems approach, involving systems analysis, systems engineering and operations research.

In the 1960s the space flight program of NASA constituted one of the most complex and ambitious systems engineering projects. Sustaining life in outer space is essentially a question of engendering livable environments through technical and material performance. Paralleling this development, the question of performance emerged also in architecture, culminating in the August 1967 issue of the journal Progressive Architecture on the theme of *Performance Design* (Fig. 29). This approach to the notion of performance drew extensively on systems analysis, systems engineering and operations research, with a particular focus on mathematical modeling, optimization, and efficiency. This foregrounded a hard systems and quantitative approach to performance (Hensel, 2013) and further reinforced the perceived form and function division that limited architectural discourses for most of the last century, especially due to the focus on performance-oriented design. To overcome the engrained form-function dichotomy, Hensel suggested an understanding of performance that takes an integrative approach to form and function and utilizes both hard and soft systems approaches, thereby addressing both qualitative and quantitative aspects of performance (Hensel, 2010, 2013).

Fig. 29

In recent decades the notion of *performance-oriented design* (Hensel, 2010a, 2011, 2012, 2013; Hensel and Sunguroğlu Hensel, 2020) has been developed. Its aim is to overcome the prevailing *form* and *function* division that has divided the discipline and thereby delimited architectural discourse for the better part of the twentieth century. Questions of *material performance* (Hensel, 2009, 2010b, 2012; Hensel et al., 2008) emerged that hold the potential to redirect on a fundamental level the way designers and planners perceive and transform environments. This evolving discourse is closely linked to and driven by a research-by-design approach and methodology, a commitment to systems thinking (Sevaldson, 2022), and data-driven processes for planning and design (Sunguroğlu Hensel et al., 2022). At the same time, it has become more widespread in academia to explore materials as well as material systems and material assemblages through an experimental performance-oriented approach (Hensel and Menges, 2006), resulting in an emphasis on experimental *making*, the construction of full scale demonstrators, and data-driven computational design and analysis methods (Hensel and Menges, 2006; Menges, 2012, 2015) that use material experiments to derive potential for design and knowledge production with specific focus on *material agency*.

The anthropologist Tim Ingold explained that "we are accustomed to think of making as a *project*. This is to start with an idea in mind, of what we want to achieve, and with a supply of raw material needed to achieve it. And it is to finish at the moment when the material has taken on the intended form [...]. I want to think of making, instead, as a process of *growth*. This is to place the maker from the onset as a participant in a world of active materials [...]. The maker's ambitions, in this understanding, are far humbler than those implied by the hylomorphic model. Far from standing aloof, imposing his designs on a world that is ready and waiting to receive them, the most he can do is to intervene in worldly processes that are already going on." (Ingold, 2013, pp. 21–22) In this view, makers and materials are entangled and actively engaged in the processes that shape the world. Importantly, it is not only the maker that possesses *agency*, but also the materials and their surroundings. If the surroundings undergo changes, materials will respond to these changes. Likewise, materials bring about change in their surroundings and environments respond to these changes.

To begin with, it is useful to examine the notion of *agency*. Dwiartarma and Rosin stated that "actor-network theory (ANT) asserts that agency is manifest only in the relationship of actors to each other. Within this framing, material objects exert agency in a similar manner to humans. [...] ANT [...] asserts that any entity that exists within the social system is meaningful because of the network of relationships it shapes with others [...]. To account for this attribution of meaning, ANT uses the term actant to distinguish its conception of an actor as embedded within network relationships [...]. An actant is thus defined as 'an effect generated by a network of heterogeneous, interacting, materials' (Law, 1992)." (Dwiartarma and Rosin, 2014, https://www.ecologyandsociety.org/vol19/iss3/art28/)

Materials are characterized by their specific composition and the properties that derive from that. Materials may be homogeneous or heterogeneous in their composition and therefore respond differently in kind or degree to changes in the surrounding environment. When subjected to changing conditions the interaction between material and environment can result in *material behavior*. For instance, changes in ambient temperature or humidity can cause dimensional changes in materials. Homogeneous or isotropic materials display the same value of properties in different directions. It can therefore be assumed that such materials display not only the same kind of behavior in all directions but also to the same degree. Heterogeneous and differentiated (i.e., anisotropic) materials display properties of different values in different directions. It can therefore be assumed that such materials do not display the same degree of behavior in all directions, and perhaps not even the same kind of behavior.

In the context of *material agency* and *material behavior* the notion of *smart materials* has received significant attention and interest over recent decades. Addington and Schodek explained that "common uses of the term 'smart materials' do [...] suggest materials that have intrinsic or embedded quick response capabilities [...]. The implied notions of cleverness and discernment in response are not without interest [...]. The concept of the intelligent and designed response is a seamless quickness – immediate action for a specific and transient stimulus." (Addington and Schodek, 2005, p. 9) Furthermore, Philip Ball defined smart materials as "materials that replace machines – in other words, materials that can carry out tasks not as a consequence of signals or impulses passed from one component to another [...] but as a result of their intrinsic properties." (Ball, 1997, p. 103) In this context two questions arise. First, do materials separate into smart and non-smart ones? And second, is smartness a question of one-directional stimulus and response trajectories or of multi-directional interactions in which cause and effect relations switch? In response to the first question, Addington and Schodek argued "Most probably [not], as there is nothing a smart material can do that a conventional system can't" (Addington and Schodek, 2005, p. 9). This insight suggests a shift of emphasis away from engineering smart materials and towards designing smart multi-trajectory material and environment interactions (Hensel and Sunguroğlu, 2006). While large amounts of data exist on material properties and material behavior, this needs to be reassessed and expanded from a material agency and material performance perspective.

The prevailing framework of liability means that designers frequently view material behavior as negative and seek to constrain it. However, numerous experts and researchers have pointed out that material variability and behavior present a largely untapped opportunity for design and a range of industries. This chapter seeks to chart a way forward by approaching the discussion on material properties, material behavior, material performance, material systems and material assemblages from a performance-oriented design perspective, equipped with a systems-thinking approach, and linking this to an examination of data-related methods and tools that are already or could in future support this approach at an instrumental level.

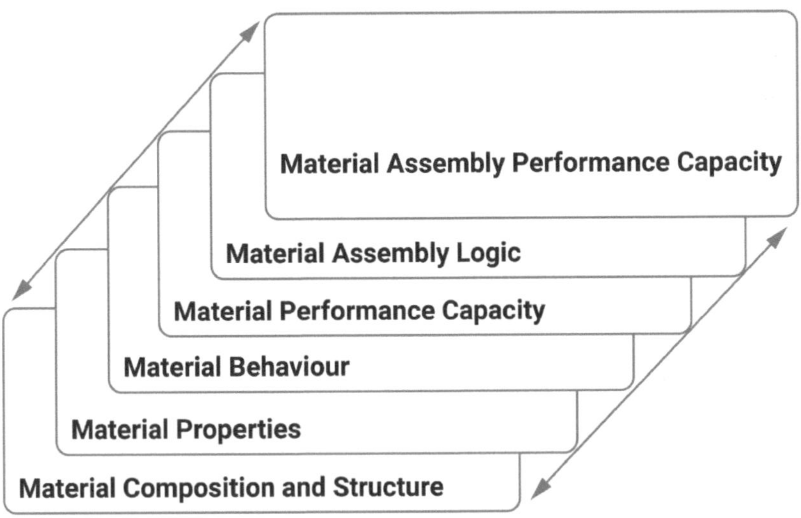

Fig. 30

Fig. 30
To instrumentalize material behavior one must first understand the relationship between material properties and the interaction of materials with their surroundings leading to material behavior, thereby making it possible to design material performance across scales of hierarchies from single materials to material systems and assemblies. Adapted from Hensel, 2013.

Therefore, when design based on *material performance* is desired, data and data-driven methods can play a key role. This includes existing and observational data, as well as data generated by simulations, etc. Moreover, an increasing number of experiments and works in architectural research explore material performance, generating data that were not readily available until now.

Fig. 31 Standardized testing procedures produce a vast amount of data, providing detailed insights into the properties and behavior of materials.

2.2 PROPERTIES

Material agency or *material performance* for design commences with an understanding of material *properties* that determine and delimit *material behavior.* Physical material properties include acoustical, electrical, mechanical, optical, and thermal properties. Chemical material properties include corrosion resistance, hygroscopy, pH, and reactivity. Isotropic materials display identical values of properties in all directions. Such materials include glass, metals, and plastic. Anisotropic materials do not display identical values of properties in all directions. Such materials include fiber-reinforced natural materials such as wood or manufactured composites.

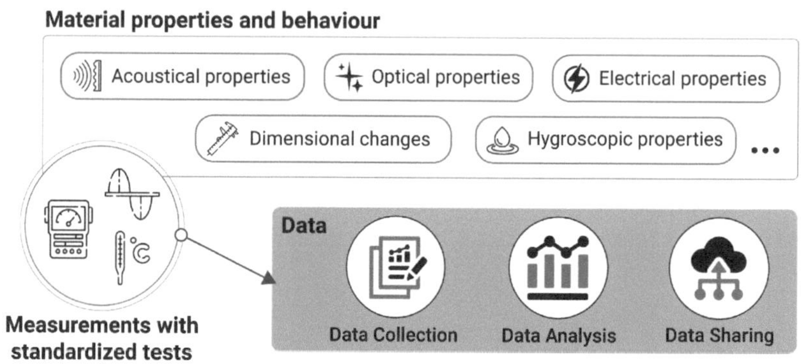

Fig. 31

To obtain reliable data, material properties and material behavior are measured by standardized tests, leading to data resources that are available in print, Web-based resources, etc. (Fig. 31). Physical testing of material samples that are assumed to be equivalent typically serves to define statistically derived properties that provide the basis for empirical specifications (Furrer et al., 2024). Industrially produced materials invariably need to comply with tight regulations regarding property profiles and related material behavior. Often the aim of designers and engineers is to minimize and neutralize material behavior such as, for instance, dimensional changes due to changes in ambient temperature, ambient humidity, etc. This is done for the purposes of compliance with existing regulations, risk mitigation, and related liability issues. Therefore, preference is typically given to full predictability of material properties and material behavior and the minimization or neutralization of material behavior. However, the assumption of equivalency of a material as the basis for statistically derived properties and related data is in some way flawed as "for a given material, the variations in chemistry [...], phase content [...], and structure [...] will lead to variations in mechanical properties" (Furrer et al., 2024, p. 475). This is of fundamental consequence for the understanding of materials, whether natural or engineered in that there exist degrees of variation in the structure and properties of materials that are deemed homogenous. This can then be addressed either through some measure of tolerance in the description of material properties and regulation of material behavior along the existing paradigm or, alternatively, through an approach that reframes variability from a material agency perspective.

The second issue concerns the fact that materials display *hierarchical organization* across scales, ranging from the nanoscale to the full scale of a material system and the correlation between material characteristics, properties, and behavior for the purpose of harnessing material performance (Fig. 32). For example, plant-based composite materials have at least five hierarchical levels:

/ Integral level: a plant consists of different tissues with different mechanical properties and functions.
/ Macroscopic level: the different tissues consist of different cell types with different properties and functions.
/ Microscopic level: the mechanically relevant structure of the cell wall can vary.
/ Ultrastructural level: the fine articulation of the cell wall can vary.
/ Biochemical level: the chemical composition of the cell wall can vary.
(Wagenführ, 2008)

Wagenführ described the macro-, micro-, and ultrastructure characteristics and variation of wood, as well as the impact of anisotropy on the physical properties and mechanical behavior of wood, indicating structural anisotropy of wood as a chance for technical innovation (Wagenführ, 2008). In the case of wood, this implies that tacit knowledge and new knowledge gained through experimentation needs to be transferred to a scientific mode of knowledge production based on scientific data on materials properties and material behavior, thereby fostering new materials research fields and novel material applications.

Fig. 32
Relational material property chart for the *Nested Catenaries* shell system developed by Defne Sunguroğlu Hensel, showing the correlation between structural and material properties and resulting performance from the nanoscale to the full-scale material system (Sunguroğlu Hensel and Baraut Bover, 2013, 2015).

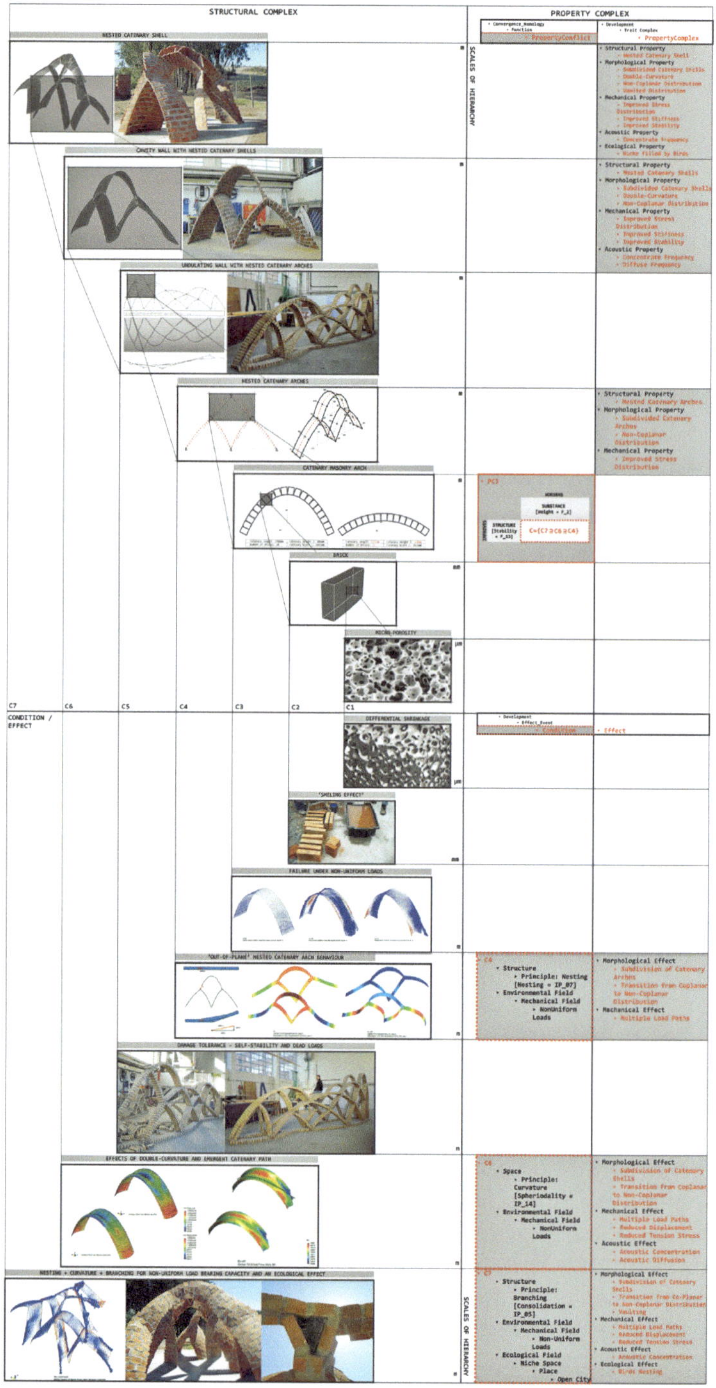

Fig. 32

The third issue concerns the correlation of material properties that need to be well understood to support the paradigm shift towards material agency. Here, it is useful to note some of the ways material properties and their combination and linkages are approached and instrumentalized. For instance, as described in Chapter 1, the *Ashby Material Property Charts* (Figs. 33–37) constitute an advanced data-based resource that provides a visual representation of material properties and their correlations (Ashby, 1989, 2011). They provide material data in the format of graphs that enable designers to compare and select materials based on specific property requirements and property relations. In so doing, the *Ashby Material Property Charts* offer a structured and accessible framework for exploring material properties, thereby facilitating informed decision-making in material selection. This can form a basis for considering trade-offs between different properties and property profiles and support the informed selection of materials. As the correlation between properties will affect material behavior it is necessary to visualize and instrumentalize these correlations in a data-integrated manner.

Ashby Material Property Charts focus "on data modeling aspects [...] where data is presented in charts [...]. Ashby's material selection charts are valuable for preliminary screening of materials [...]. The most thoughtful limitation of the chart method is that the chart limits the material selection decision to only solving two or three criteria. So, to solve this problem, multi-criteria decision making is established. The performance of a component depends on a combination of properties instead of a single property [...]. From this idea, one can build a plot of one property versus another." (AL-Oqla and Salit, 2017)

Ashby Material Property Charts are incorporated in ANSYS Granta software package: "each material has a range of values for each property, depending on the exact composition, grade, heat treatment, supplier etc. The materials are represented on the chart as ellipses or 'bubbles', whose width and height are determined by the range of the value of the properties. These charts can be used in many different ways [...;] they are interactive and (make it possible) to find out more about a property or material [...] to identify gaps where new materials would be useful [... and] to perform materials selection for new designs or to substitute a material in an [existing] product. They can be used for comparing and estimating data. They can also be used to identify trends in properties, including how processing affects properties, and the relationships between them." (ANSYS Granta, 2024)

Fig. 33
Example of an Ashby material property chart, showing the correlation between Young's modulus and density of a variety of materials. Image taken from the Ansys Education Resource "Material Property Chart Collection". Chart created using Ansys Granta Edupack™ software. Copyright ANSYS, Inc.

Fig. 34
Example of an Ashby material property chart, showing the correlation between Young's modulus and the tensile strength of a variety of materials. Image taken from the Ansys Education Resource "Material Property Chart Collection". Chart created using Ansys Granta Edupack™ software. Copyright ANSYS, Inc.

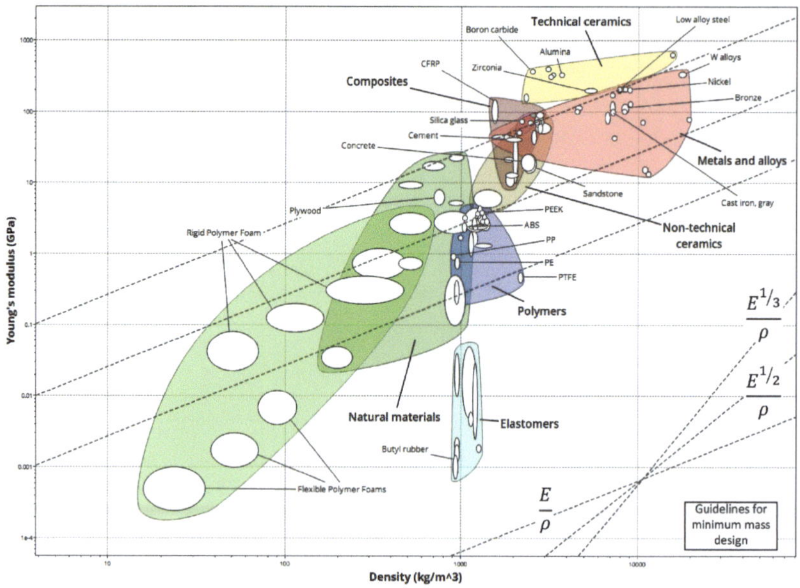

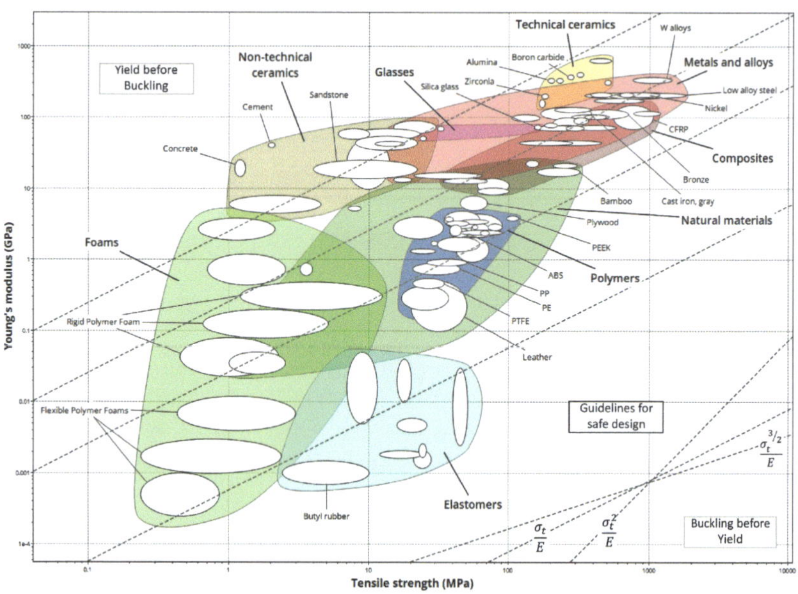

Figs. 33, 34

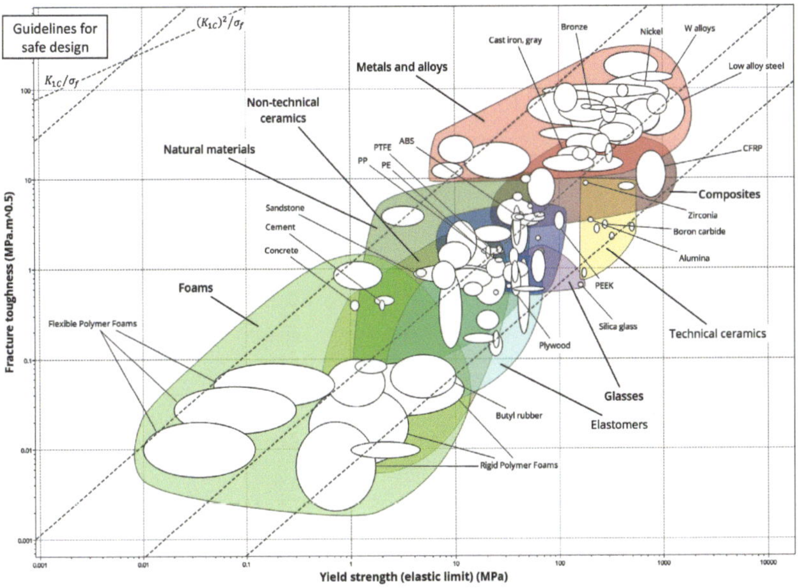

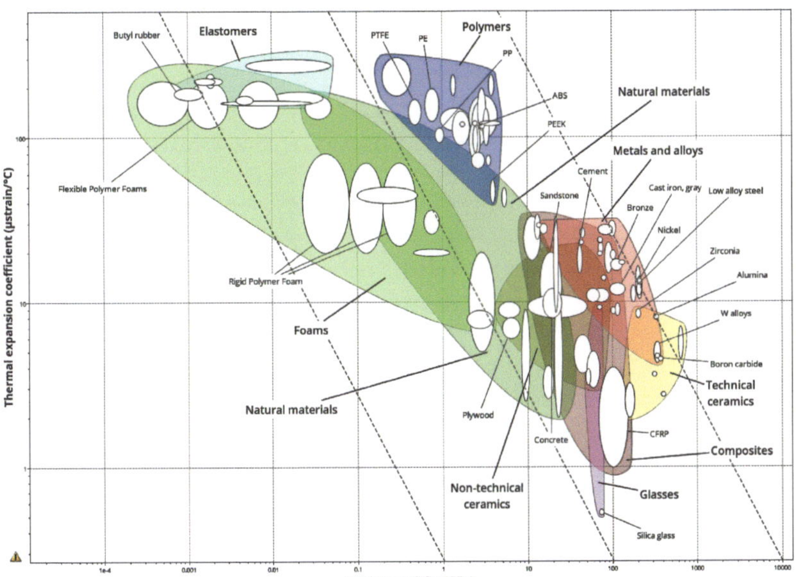

Figs. 35, 36

Fig. 35
Example of an Ashby material property chart, showing the correlation between fracture toughness and yield strength of a variety of materials. Image taken from the Ansys Education Resource "Material Property Chart Collection". Chart created using Ansys Granta Edupack™ software. Copyright ANSYS, Inc.

Fig. 36
Example of an Ashby material property chart, showing the correlation between thermal expansion and Young's modulus of a variety of materials. Image taken from the Ansys Education Resource "Material Property Chart Collection". Chart created using Ansys Granta Edupack™ software. Copyright ANSYS, Inc.

Fig. 37
Example of an Ashby material property chart, showing the correlation between thermal expansion and thermal conductivity of a variety of materials. Image taken from the Ansys Education Resource "Material Property Chart Collection". Chart created using Ansys Granta Edupack™ software. Copyright ANSYS, Inc.

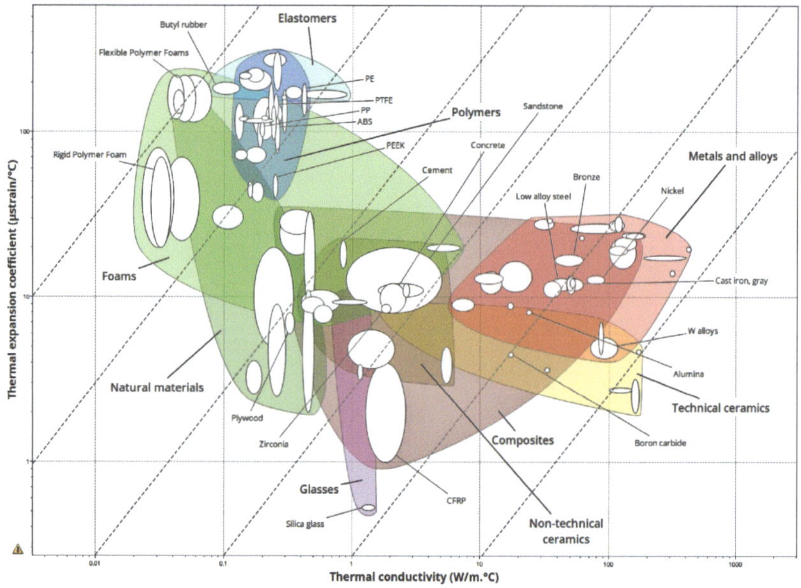

Fig. 37

The shift in perspective from minimizing and neutralizing material behavior based on predictable material characteristics towards utilizing material behavior based on material structure and properties across scales is momentous. It necessitates a different perspective on existing data on material properties and behavior, as well as different datasets that may not yet be available. In summary, to support the *material agency* approach it is necessary to instrumentalize (1) *material variation*, (2) the *hierarchical organization* of materials across scales, and (3) the *correlation of material properties*. Both existing and new data need to be structured accordingly in relational databases that correlate data in terms of material variation, hierarchical organization, and material properties.

2.3 BEHAVIOR

Material behavior is a two-way affair. Frequently, the discussion of material behavior focuses on the response of materials to extrinsic stimuli from the surroundings. However, materials in turn also affect their surroundings. One example of multi-scale negative impact of materials on the surroundings is the *urban heat island* effect. Deilami et al. explained that the urban heat island "is a phenomenon when urban areas experience a higher temperature than their surrounding non-urban areas and is considered as a critical factor contributing to global warming, heat related mortalities, and unpredictable climatic changes" (Deilami et al., 2018, p. 1). Among other factors material properties and material behavior play a key role in the urban heat island effect; less reflective materials absorb more short-wave radiation from the sun, building materials store heat, and impermeable materials reduce evaporation thereby increasing the felt heat (Oke, 1987; Santamouris, 2001). Therefore, a first critical insight is that an instrumental approach to *material behavior* needs to operate on correlational datasets that consist of material properties, environmental conditions, intrinsic and extrinsic stimuli, and related responses, in which both changes can occur both in the material and the environment. For example, various materials undergo dimensional changes due to variations in temperature or moisture content. Regarding the latter, timber, for instance, engages in a two-way material-environment interaction known as *hygroscopy*. Dinwoodie explained that "Timber is hygroscopic, that is it will absorb moisture from the atmosphere if it is dry and correspondingly yield moisture to the atmosphere when wet, thereby attaining a moisture content which is in equilibrium with the water vapor pressure of the surrounding atmosphere" (Dinwoodie, 2000, p. 49; Fig. 38). Since moisture content and dimensional changes, ambient humidity and felt temperature are directly linked, it is possible to utilize hygroscopic behavior as a way of modulating these relations.

Fig. 38 Photographic time-sequence showing wood releasing moisture to the environment as part of the two-way material-environment interaction called *hygroscopy*. To attain equilibrium, wood absorbs moisture from the atmosphere if it is dryer than the surroundings and releases moisture to the atmosphere when it is wetter (Dinwoodie, 2000). Photography: Michael Hensel, 2011.

Fig. 38

Considerable attention is directed towards a narrow definition of smart engineered materials, yet not enough attention is paid to understanding and deploying existing materials in a smart manner (Hensel and Menges, 2006; Hensel and Sunguroğlu Hensel, 2006; Hensel, 2009). Abdelmohsen et al. stated that "the adoption

Fig. 39
Material agency is the capacity of materials to sense, adapt, and act upon their environment as active agents rather than inert matter in architectural contexts.

of hygroscopic materials, particularly wood, is compelling as a basis for low-tech smart materials and systems with interchanging functionalities in the construction industry" (Abdelmohsen et al., 2019, p. 43). This approach is not new and is often found in traditional vernacular architectures as shown in chapters 2.4 and 2.5. In addition to a great wealth of historical precedents, recent research efforts have foregrounded material behavior as a focus of design experiments, thereby gaining experience with and data on material behavior. For instance, the hygroscopic behavior of wood was explored across numerous applications, including full-scale prototypical architectures (Hensel and Menges, 2006), culminating in installations like Hygroscope: Meteorosensitive Morphology (ICD, 2012a) and full-scale prototypical projects such as the Oslo Architecture Triennale Pavilion 2010 (Hensel and Sunguroğlu Hensel, 2011; Hensel, 2013) and *Hygroskin: Meteorosensitive Pavilion* (ICD, 2012b).

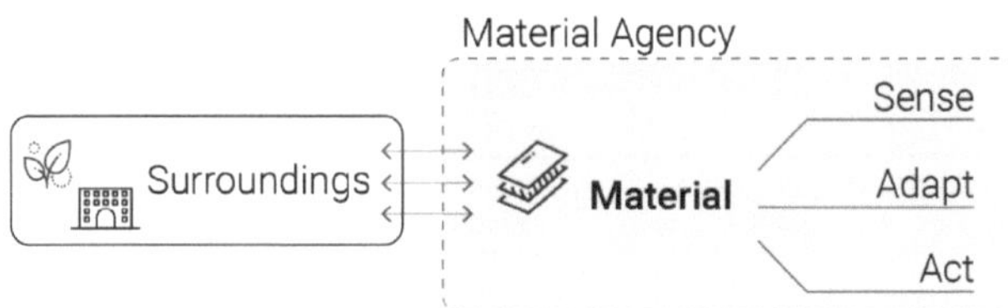

Fig. 39

Generally, the interaction between materials and surroundings becomes more complex with materials that are more differentiated and heterogenous. Differentiated material properties respond to their surroundings and in turn affect them differently. Likewise, different environmental conditions individually and collectively affect materials differently, depending on the material properties and behavior of a given material. With this realization questions arise as to how to address data, data analysis and modeling when *multivariate data are* involved.

Esbensen explained that "nature is *multivariate*, as are most (if not all) technological and other data-generating systems from the sciences, in the sense that any *one* particular phenomenon we would like to study in detail usually/most often depends on *several* factors [...]. It is thus often necessary to sample, observe, study or measure more than one variable *simultaneously* [...]. The basic assumption underlying the use of multivariate analysis is that your measured data carries *information* about the desired properties and experimental objectives[...]. But not even multivariate methods can help in cases where the data do not contain relevant information about the property that is being sought. The implied information in the data will depend on how well the problem to be solved has been defined, and whether one has performed the observations appropriately." (Esbensen, 2002, pp. 1–2) Therefore, adequate problem definition is required for the purpose of acquiring relevant data for *multivariate data analysis*. Moreover, since material behavior unfolds in time it is necessary to utilize data related to both space and time, thereby requiring *spatio-temporal data*.

Fig. 40
Computational intelligence used in knowledge-driven and data-driven methods enhances modeling, simulation, and design of material performance and behavior.

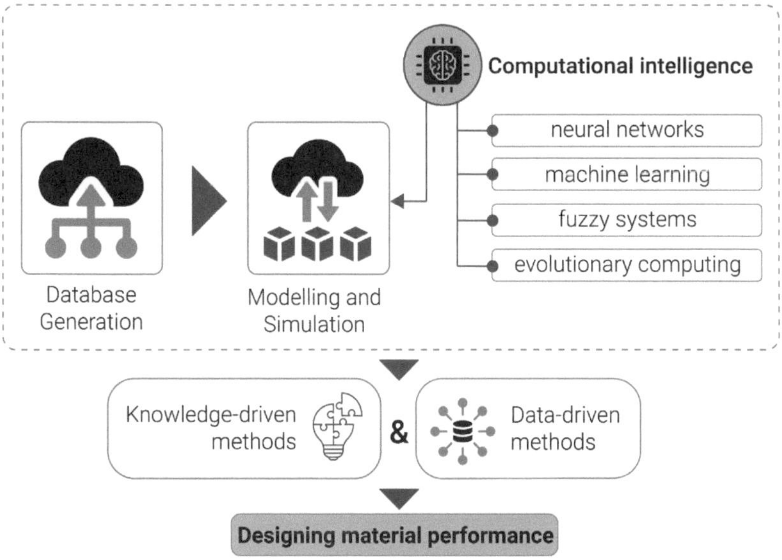

Fig. 40

Van der Giessen et al. discussed the transformative impact of computational modeling and simulation on *materials science*, especially with a focus on "gaining insight into the processes that govern materials behavior, and […] quantitative predictions that can be used as part of a design tool in full partnership with experimental synthesis and characterization. Modeling and simulation are the essential bridge from good science to good engineering, spanning from fundamental understanding of materials behavior to deliberate design of new materials technologies leveraging new properties and processes." (van der Giessen et al., 2020, p. 2)

Multivariate analysis in conjunction with data-driven modeling (DDD) and simulation offers a useful instrumental approach to instrumentalizing material behavior. Solomatine and Ostfeld explained that "data-driven modeling (DDM) is based on the analysis of the data characterizing the system under study. A model can then be defined based on connections between the system state variables (input, internal and output variables) with only a limited number of assumptions about the 'physical' behavior of the system. The contemporary methods can go much further than the ones used in conventional empirical modeling [... and] allow for solving numerical prediction problems, reconstructing highly nonlinear functions, performing classification, grouping of data, and building rule-based systems." (Solomatine and Ostfeld, 2008, p. 2) Solomatine and Ostfeld distinguished between two different modeling approaches:

/ "(1) *physically based (process)* model based on the description of the behavior, typically based on the first-order principles from physics, of a phenomenon or system (also called knowledge-driven or simulation models).

/ (2) *empirical*, or *data-driven* (DD) model involving mathematical equations assessed not from the physical process [...] but from analysis of concurrent input and output time series. Typical examples here are [...] various statistical models (linear regression, multi-linear, ARIMA) and methods of machine learning." (Solomatine and Ostfeld, 2008, p. 4)

As Solomatine and Ostfeld and others pointed out, data-driven modeling frequently involves data mining and knowledge discovery in databases, computational intelligence (neural networks, machine learning, fuzzy systems, and evolutionary computing), intelligent data analysis, soft computing, and pattern recognition, etc. Solomatine and Ostfeld explained that "data mining (DM) and knowledge discovery in databases (KDD) used ML methods and are focused typically on very large databases [...]. Data-driven modeling can [...] be considered as an approach to modeling that focuses on using the CI (particularly ML) methods in building models that would complement or replace the 'knowledge-driven' models describing physical behavior." (Solomatine and Ostfeld, 2008, p. 5) In the case of material knowledge, it would not be useful to replace knowledge-driven models since their contribution is evident, instead linking knowledge-driven and data-driven methods. This is specifically the case since a fast-increasing number of experimental prototypes play an important role in the understanding and exploration of material behavior with a view to designing material performances.

In summary, in order to work with material behavior as a key aspect of material agency, it is necessary to (1) instrumentalize the correlation between material properties and their interactions with the surrounding environment that lead to material behavior, (2) combine knowledge-driven and data-driven modeling to use all available resources for understanding and instrumentalizing material behavior, (3) and employ multivariate data and spatio-temporal data and related methods.

2.4 THERMODYNAMICS

In the context of architecture and design, Addington and Schodek stated that the thermodynamic conceptualization of materials necessitates comprehension of "the concept of the boundary as behavior [...]. Thermodynamic boundaries are [...] zones of activity [...]. This is where energy transfers and exchanges from, and where work acts upon the environment [...]. All change takes place at the boundary." (Addington and Schodek, 2005, pp. 51–52)

The field of thermodynamics focuses on the conversion of energy from one form of energy to another. The study of thermodynamics focuses on systems and their surroundings, as well as interactions between systems and their surroundings. A system is an "object, quantity of matter, or region of space that has been selected for study" (Klein and Nellis, 2012, p. 3). Fixed or moveable system boundaries separate systems from their surroundings. Different types of interactions exist between systems and surroundings. An *isolated system* does not interact with its surroundings. In a *closed system*, mass does not cross the system boundary, while in an *open system* mass does cross the system boundary. In *steady-state systems* the system properties do not change over time, whereas in dynamic state systems properties change over time. System properties are divided into *extensive* and *intensive* properties, whereby the former depend on the quantity of matter in the system, while the latter do not (Atkins, 2010). Gaskel and Laughlin explained that "thermodynamics concerns the relationship between energy and work, and the equilibrium states and variables of systems [...]. A central aim of applied thermodynamics is the determination of the effect of the surroundings on the equilibrium state of a given system." (Gaskell and Laughlin, 2017, p. 1) There are four equilibrium states: unstable, stable, metastable, and neutral, depending on the response of a system to a perturbation (Tschoegel, 2000).

The four laws of thermodynamics are as follows:

- The zeroth law, which provides a definition of temperature. (Atkins, 2010)
- The first law, which describes the conservation of energy and defines the internal energy of a system. (Atkins, 2010)
- The second law, which defines the concept of entropy as a property of thermodynamic systems, thereby accounting for the irreversibility of natural processes. (Atkins, 2010)
- The third law, which states that entropy entails "the unattainability principle, states that any process cannot reach absolute zero temperature in a finite number of steps and within a finite time." (Masanes and Oppenheim, 2017, p. 1)

Thermodynamics of materials concerns the interaction of matter and energy, and the way thermodynamic processes affect material properties across macro-, meso-, and micro- scales (Qing and Zi, 2011). Phase change of materials concerns the transitions from solid to liquid, liquid to gas, and solid to gas. The phase transitions of matter from solid to liquid, liquid to gas, and solid to gas are depicted in two- or three-dimensional diagrams known as phase diagrams. Figure 41, for instance, shows a phase diagram of water with the phase boundaries between solid, liquid, and gaseous states. In this figure, roman numerals indicated the different phases of ice.

Phase diagrams are a key to understanding the "processes governing [...] materials properties and development" (Kroupa, 2013, p. 3). Furthermore, computer simulations and machine-learning methods can serve to derive quantitative data on thermodynamic phase behavior for phase diagrams (Chew and Reinhardt, 2023).

In general, thermodynamic data are of central importance since they help predict the behavior of materials thereby enabling decision-making in materials science and engineering. Giffaut et al. explained that "thermodynamic modeling constitutes a critical tool for evaluating the nature and extent of chemical processes likely to affect the migration of polluting elements in complex, evolving geochemical environments. The accuracy and credibility of thermodynamic modeling output depends heavily on the quality and completeness of the thermodynamic database (TDB) which is used. A universally applicable TDB containing quality-assured mass action laws and thermodynamic constants for all possible equilibria involving the complete periodic table of elements does not exist. TDB do however exist, and are continually being

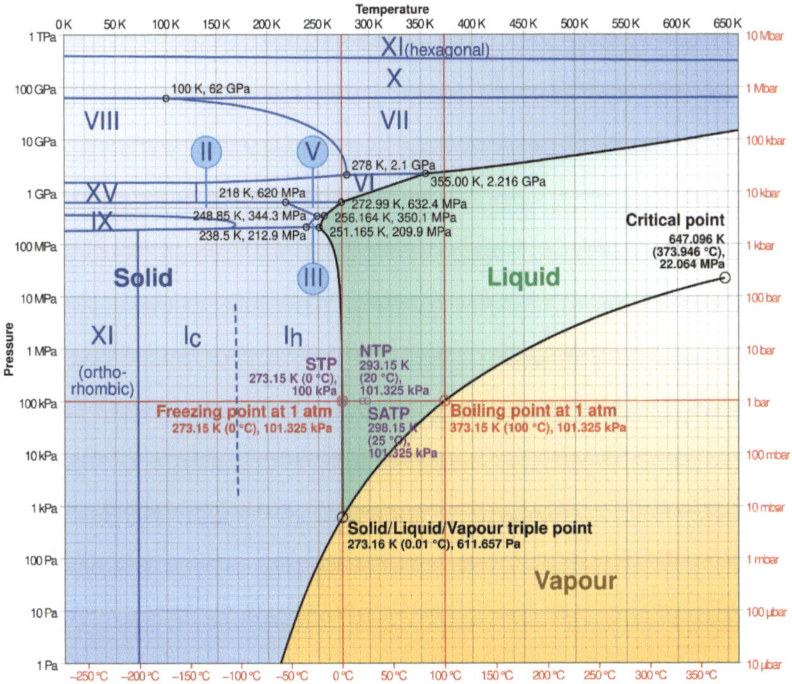

Fig. 41

Fig. 41
Phase diagram of water showing the phase boundaries between the solid, liquid, and gaseous states across which phase transitions occur. Source: Wikimedia Commons. Creative Commons Attribution Share Alike 3.0 Unported license. Cmglee, 2023.

developed and improved, with the objective of supporting the thermodynamic modeling requirements for broad-ranging environmental and/or industrial situations." (Giffaut et al., 2014, p. 225) Sector- or purpose-specific TDBs include the *Thermodynamic Reference Database* (HZDR, 2024) and the *Thermochemical Database* (TDB) Project (Nuclear Energy Agency, 2024).

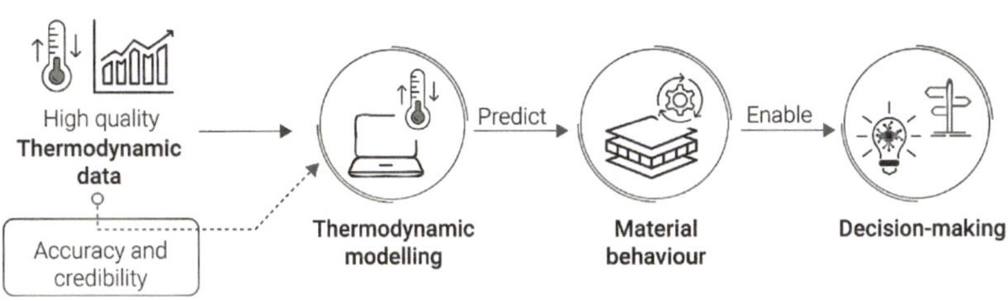

Fig. 42

Fig. 42
High-quality thermodynamic data enhances thermodynamic modeling, leading to more accurate predictions of material behavior.

Thermodynamic material properties and the interaction of matter and energy are not new topics in the planning and design of the built environment. As climate change unfolds, the thermal performance of materials, constructions, buildings, and cities will be under investigation, especially in relation to thermal insulation of buildings and the urban heat island effect. Thermal infrared imaging (IR) is a technology that detects electromagnetic radiation of constructions, buildings, etc. for the purpose of non-destructive analysis and diagnostics (Balaras and Argiriou, 2002; Figs. 43 and 44).

Fig. 43
Photograph of a portion of a terraced vineyard in Lamole, Tuscany, Italy. Department for Digital Architecture and Planning at TU Wien and LamoLab, 2019.

Fig. 44
Thermal infrared imaging (IR) of a portion of a terraced vineyard in Lamole, Tuscany. Thermography conducted by the Department for Digital Architecture and Planning at TU Wien and LamoLab, 2019.

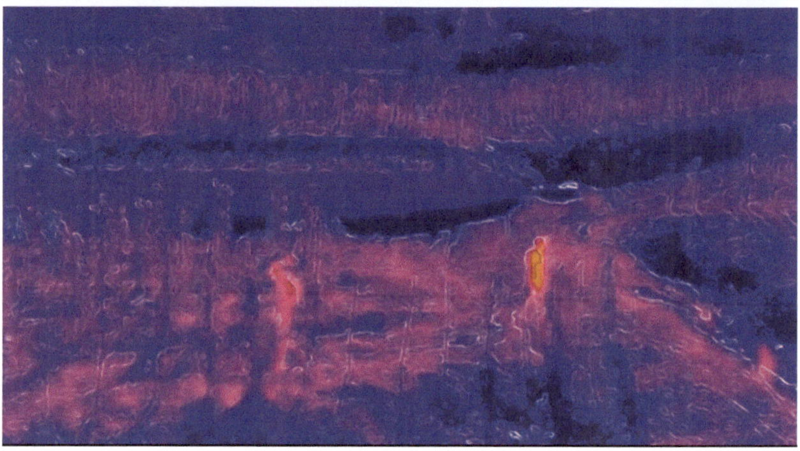

Figs. 43, 44

Instrumental and more integrative approaches to thermodynamic performance above and beyond the thermal performance of constructions and build environments are less frequent. However, throughout architectural history thermodynamics have played a key role, not only in relation to thermal performance, but also in terms of utilizing the phase change of water. In many hot and dry areas the active stimulation of condensation was the primary means of gaining water for irrigation in agriculture and horticulture (Laureano, 1999; Sunguroğlu Hensel, 2020). Another striking example of utilizing phase changes are Persian ice houses *(yakhchal)*. Located on arid desert plains, the purpose of the *yakhchal* was to produce ice from water and to store the ice. East-to-west-oriented shallow water pools that were up to 100 meters long and 10 to 20 meters wide were protected by an adobe wall on their southern, eastern, and western sides (Fig. 45).

Fig. 45
Scaled model of a Persian icehouse, with an east-west-oriented shallow water pool which is protected on its southern, eastern, and western sides by an adobe wall. The conical dome behind the wall contained the storage space for the ice. Photography: Michael Hensel, 2014.

Fig. 45

The pools were filled with a shallow layer of water that freezes during the cold desert nights due to heat loss by radiation to the night sky (Hensel et al., 2012; Fordham, 2024). Analysis has shown that daily harvesting of the ice yields the largest amount of ice compared to harvesting after several days (Figs. 46–48; Hensel et al., 2012).

Contemporary materials science and materials engineering includes the development of phase change materials. Raoux explained that “phase change materials (PCMs) can exist in at least two different phases (an amorphous and one or more crystalline phases), and they can be switched repeatedly between these phases. The different phases have distinctly different physical properties such as electrical conductivity, optical reflectivity, mass density, or thermal conductivity.” (Raoux, 2009, p. 25) While phase change materials are used in the AEC sector in buildings, “there is scarcely any study, experimental or numerical, that verifies the evaluation of PCM in real outdoor conditions. Therefore, more studies focusing on real full-scale buildings and real operation conditions should be carried out to prove the [...] reliability

Fig. 46
Hourly rate of ice build-up in the shallow pool of a Persian icehouse (*Yakhchal*). Copyright: Sustainable Environment Association (Michael Hensel, Defne Sunguroğlu Hensel, Mehran Gharleghi, Salmaan Craig), 2011.

Fig. 47
Daily rate of ice build-up in the shallow pool of a Persian icehouse (*Yakhchal*). Copyright: Sustainable Environment Association (Michael Hensel, Defne Sunguroğlu Hensel, Mehran Gharleghi, Salmaan Craig), 2011.

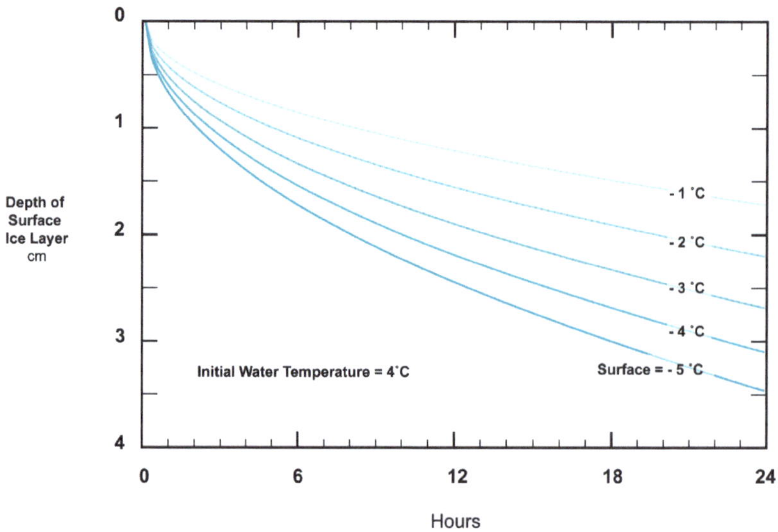

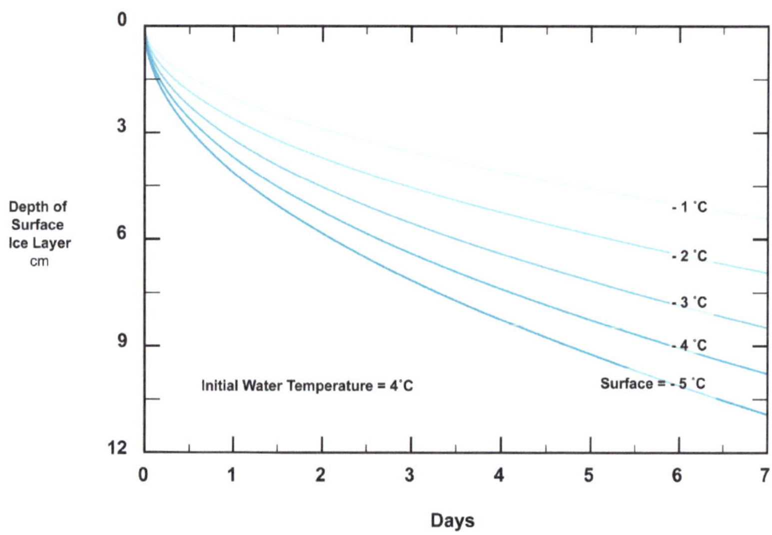

Figs. 46, 47

of current research." (Cui et al., 2017) As further development and utilization of phase change materials takes place, this will set out interesting potentials for applications in smart and IoT-enhanced environments.

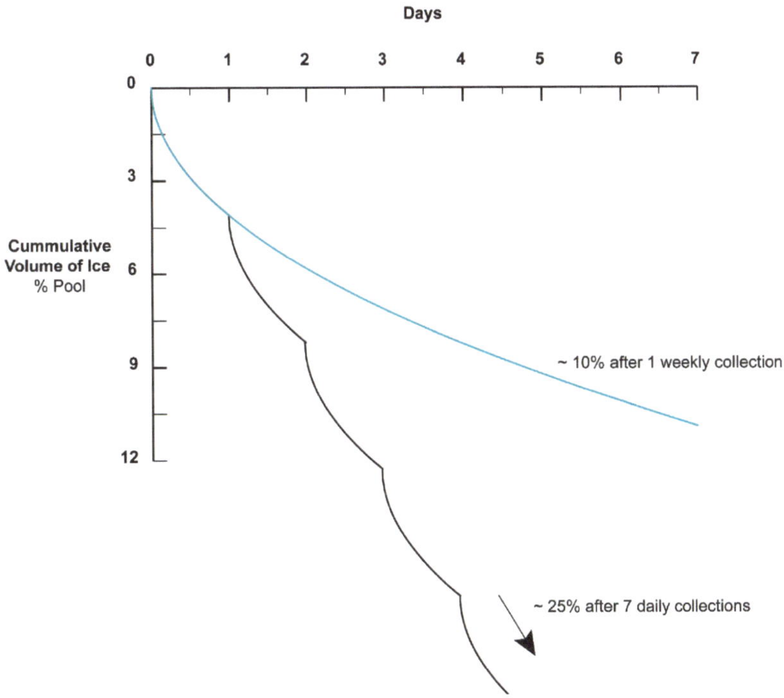

Fig. 48

Fig. 48
A comparison between daily and weekly ice build-up in a shallow pool of a Persian icehouse (*Yakhchal*) shows that daily collection yields a larger quantity of ice. Copyright: Sustainable Environment Association (Michael Hensel, Defne Sunguroğlu Hensel, Mehran Gharleghi, Salmaan Craig), 2011.

In summary, as performance requirements for materials become more complex, thermodynamic properties are rapidly taking a prominent role in planning and design. Therefore, it is necessary to study further and integrated developments, including the provision of thermodynamics databases, data generation and data mining to support thermodynamic computational modeling and decision support. Various efforts of interest are currently underway to integrate efforts. In this context, the CALPHAD journal, for instance, focuses on "computational thermodynamics through development of models to represent thermodynamic properties for various phases which permit prediction of properties of multicomponent systems [...], critical assessment of data and their incorporation into self-consistent databases, development of software to optimize and derive thermodynamic parameters and the development and use of databanks for calculations to improve understanding of various industrial and technological processes." (Elsevier, 2024)

Fig. 49
This painting from 1873 by John Frederick Lewis entitled "A Lady receiving Visitors (The Reception)" shows a room with Islamic wooden latticework screen walls, so-called *mashrabīyas*. The painting is based on drawings of Lewis's house in Cairo, Egypt. Yale Center for British Art. Public domain image. Source: Wikimedia Commons.

Designing targeted material performance from a performance-oriented design perspective is a complex task. To illustrate the notion of material performance that is pursued here, it is useful to examine a frequently referenced example of a vernacular architectural element: the Islamic wooden latticework screen walls or *mashrabīyas*, which are often used as a projecting oriel window on the upper floors of buildings in North Africa and the Middle East. *Mashrabīyas* consist of carved wooden lattices with open interstices (Figs. 49 and 50).

Fig. 49

Hassan Fathy explained that *mashrabīyas* regulate light, air flow, temperature, humidity, and visual access and control from the inside to the outside and vice versa (Fathy, 1986). This is accomplished by the articulation of the sizes of the balusters that make up the latticework and the interstices between them, as well as various compensatory devices. For instance, if interstices need to be smaller at seating or standing height to reduce glare, the resultant reduction in airflow can be compensated for by larger interstices higher up in the latticework where glare is not a problem or can be controlled by other elements, such as added horizontal timber elements. Fathy also explained that the hygroscopic behavior of the wood may have been used to take up and give off moisture to support evaporative cooling (Fathy, 1986), supported by vessels filled with water near the screen wall. While modulating various environmental and other conditions, the pattern of the balusters can be articulated in accordance with different formal preferences. Choices frequently ranged from floral ornamentation to abstract geometric patterns. The *mashrabīya* therefore demonstrates how formal and multi-functional needs and preferences can be jointly solved instead of being disentangled into separate single-function elements (Hensel, 2008). Moreover, this vernacular architectural element is typically finely tuned to the overall spatial and material articulation of the building envelope, the interior spatial organization of the building, and the range of environmental conditions in the given context (Hensel, 2020).

Fig. 50
View of a part of the façade of the Gayer Anderson Museum in Cairo, Egypt, Islamic wooden latticework screen walls, so-called *mashrabīyas*. Public domain image. Photography: Berthold Werner, CC-BY-3.0, Wikimedia Commons, 2010.

Fig. 50

A further striking example is the vaulted ceiling and surfaces of the music chamber in Ali Qapu palace in Isfahan, Iran. These surfaces contain cavities made from stuccowork placed on a timber lattice, which invoke the look of musical instruments embedded in the surfaces (Figs. 51 and 52). These cavities have the purpose of improving the acoustic performance of the music chamber, by reducing reverberation and by audibly extending upper and lower tones (Hensel, 2008).

Fig. 51
The walls and ceilings of the music chamber of Ali Qapu Palace in Isfahan, Iran feature cavities that improve the acoustic performance of the chamber by reducing reverberation and by extending upper and lower tones. Photography: Michael Hensel, 2006.

Fig. 52
The cavities in the walls and ceilings of the music chamber of Ali Qapu Palace in Isfahan, Iran display a high level of craftmanship. The cavities are made from stucco on a timber lattice that taper to a thinness of 5 to 8 millimeters at the edges. Photography: Michael Hensel, 2006.

Figs. 51, 52

Examples such as the *mashrabīyas* or the music chamber of the Ali Qapu palace demonstrate sophisticated responses to complex design problems in which formal preferences and performance requirements are tackled in an integrative manner. Such historical examples are based on a high level of craftmanship. They would scarcely be affordable today on a broad scale unless through affordable and sustainable computer-aided machine fabrication. In recent decades, numerous performance-oriented design experiments and built prototypes and projects have demonstrated this possibility, evidenced by a large body of publications. This also includes designs for contemporary multi-performance screen walls that typically serve as demonstrators and prototypes for performance-oriented design outcomes, such as the screen wall designed by Daniel Coll I Capdevila in 2005 (Fig. 53).

Fig. 53
Example of a contemporary 3D-printed screen wall designed by Daniel Coll I Capdevila, 2005. Photography: Michael Hensel and Achim Menges, 2005.

Fig. 53

In general, a key characteristic of performance-oriented design is its overcoming the perceived division between form and function (Hensel 2010, 2011, 2012, 2013) Targeted design for material performance commences with a detailed definition of the desired performance. It can then be determined whether existing materials can deliver the desired performance profile or specific materials need to be designed. In the latter case, Panchal et al. explained that "designing materials for targeted performance requirements [...] demands a combined strategy of bottom-up and top-down modeling and simulation which treats various levels of hierarchical material structure as a mathematical representation, with infusion of systems engineering and informatics to deal with differing model degrees of freedom and uncertainty [...]. Computational materials science and multiscale mechanics models play key roles in evaluating performance metrics necessary to support materials design. The interplay of systems-based design of materials with multiscale modeling methodologies is at the core of materials design." (Panshal et al., 2013, p. 4)

However, the key question in designing for performance is whether to understand this in the first instance as an engineering problem or a design problem. How would an engineering approach to a *mashrabīya* defer from a design approach? Rittel and Weber coined the term *wicked problem*, which implies whereas *tame* problems have a clear mission and a clear and often one best-possible answer, *wicked* ones do not: "the one-best answer is possible with tame problems, but not with wicked ones" (Rittel and Weber, 1973, p. 155). Nigel Cross elaborated further on this as follows: "it is now widely recognized that design problems are ill-defined, ill-structured, or 'wicked' (Rittel and Webber, 1973) [...]. They are not problems for which all the necessary information is, or ever can be, available to the problem-solver. They are therefore not susceptible to exhaustive analysis, and there can never be a guarantee the 'correct' solutions can be found for them [...]. To cope with ill-defined problems, designers have to learn to have the self-confidence to define, refine and change the problem-as-given in the light of the solution that emerges from their minds and hands." (Cross, 2006, p. 7) Cross and Dorst further elaborated that designers manipulate both the problem definition and possible solutions, thereby iteratively modifying problem and solution space to define matching problem-solution pairs (Cross and Dorst, 1998). This statement can be seen to imply both an iterative process and a dynamic approach to both design problems and design solutions. Horst Rittel suggested that complex planning problems (and by extension design problems) can be addressed by an iterative process that generates design variety, that is many alternative outcomes, and by evaluating and reducing design variety by way of set criteria (Rittel, 1970).

Designing along a performance-oriented design approach can thus iteratively produce possible design outputs that can be evaluated and ranked. If this is accomplished through a generative computational design process the question arises as to what kind of data-driven algorithmic process to employ. This choice can be guided by preferences as to how narrow or wide the solution space is set, and thereby what type and range of output is desired. These considerations will lead to a choice of algorithms that will drive the process of generating design variety. Likewise, evaluating- and ranking design outputs requires different algorithmic processes that evaluate in accordance with selected performance criteria.

Data play an important role both as an input derived from expert databases, as well as an output of the algorithmic processes that is fed back into design generation and that contains data for each design solution regarding its specific performance range. Collecting data on design outputs is key to future developments related to performance-oriented design in that they can be used for information modeling and design decision support through computational ontologies (see Chapter 1.3).

In summary, instrumentalizing material performance along a performance-oriented design approach requires: (1) an integrative approach to form and function, (2) a *data-driven design* approach to *design variety generation* in which each design output can be analyzed and ranked, (3) sharing data on design variations in a dedicated database for material performance to enable knowledge dissemination and design decision support.

2.6 MATERIAL SYSTEMS

Hensel and Menges proposed a definition of *material systems* as the interrelationship of form, material and structure, and their effect (performance) through interactions with the surrounding environment. A material system is a complex material assembly consisting of numerous elements that operates on a meso-scale, located between the micro-scale of the composition of materials and the macroscale of a building (Hensel and Menges, 2008). The performance of material systems is based on material inherent properties and behavior, and the organization of the system. Buildings can then be understood as assemblages of interrelated material systems that deliver performances on micro-, meso-, and macro-levels.

Based on this definition, the Islamic wooden latticework screen walls *(mashrabīyas)* are a relevant example of a material system that can be characterized by its multiple performance capacities. It would be useful to build a database that contains data on performance types, combinations, and ranges of different material

Fig. 54
Material systems capture how materials interact and behave when combined and conditioned to respond to environmental changes and user needs.

systems. For instance, *mashrabīyas* could be analyzed and compared based on physical measurements, as well as computational simulations, while extending this investigation to different types of screen walls. This effort would focus on accumulating a growing and open catalog of material systems together with their performance profiles, indicating critical design parameters and critical limits of performance ranges at which the performance of a material system under investigation fundamentally changes or fails. This would establish an important research trajectory for design for adaptation with focus on material performance, for example in a fast-changing climate.

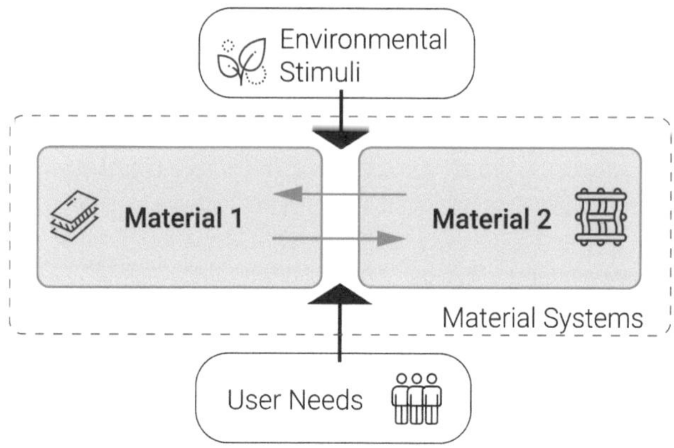

Fig. 54

Data-integrated computational form-finding and simulation methods play a central role in designing material systems along desired performance profiles. Computational form-finding plays a twofold role, first in establishing the specific form to be built and considering the conditions under which the system will be made and assembled; and second, the responses of the system to the surrounding environment that can affect the geometry of the system. Over the last two decades significant amounts of research have been conducted and published on the design of material systems (Hensel and Menges 2006, 2008a, 2008b; Hensel et al., 2010). However, as pointed out above, an open-source expert database for material systems and their performance capacities does not yet exist.

Finally, organization plays a key role in determining the state and performances of a material system. Ganti explained that "life is a function of material systems which are organized in a particular way [...]. It is therefore incorrect to speak about living matter; it would perhaps more appropriate to speak about living material systems [...]. A system is living if, and only if, certain characteristically composed processes [life process] occur in it." (Ganti, 2003, p. 75) Organization and performance are thus inseparably linked and need to be instrumentalized accordingly when analyzing or designing material systems, especially when living matter is involved.

2.7 SYSTEMS THINKING

Instrumentalizing *material performance* ranging from individual material to materials systems requires a non-reductionist holistic perspective. An approach to performance-oriented design needs to be capable of addressing complexity in an adequate manner that requires systems theoretical and systems thinking perspectives (Hensel, 2013). Particularly systems thinking and systems-oriented design can provide a suitable approach to tackle complexity in design (Sevaldson, 2022). Monat and Gannon explained that systems thinking "can be used to solve complex problems that are not solvable using conventional reductionist [...] thinking, because it focuses on the relationships among system components, as well as on the components themselves; those relationships often dominate system performance. It focuses on the properties of the whole that are neither attributable to nor predictable from the properties of the components. [Therefore, it] can be used to explain and understand dynamic nonlinear behaviors; it can be used to understand complex [...] problems, predict behaviors, and identify leverage points." (Monat and Gannon, 2015, pp. 24–25)

To employ a systems approach it is necessary to determine what is or is not part of the system under examination. Ulrich proposed the notions of *boundary* criterion and *boundary judgment* for this purpose: "everything within the boundary can then be said to belong to the system, while everything outside the boundary belongs to the system's 'environment' [...]. Determining the system in question [...] is not a matter of arbitrary definition; apart from value judgements, it takes empirical knowledge to draw the boundary in a meaningful way. Such a boundary judgment amounts to both a theoretical and a practical [normative] proposition about the real-world context in question." (Ulrich,

1983, p. 191) In general, boundary judgements mean that professional propositions require choices regarding which facts (observations) and norms (valuation standards) are considered relevant and are included, and which are less relevant and can be left out. For complex systems subjected to changing dynamics this constitutes a considerable challenge and methods that can help tackle complexity or wicked problems. In the context of the discussion of *material performance* ranging from individual material to materials systems multi-domain knowledge is frequently required, as well as determinations about conditions that are actually or potentially trans-scalar. The latter implies that effects of material and environment interactions are frequently not stratifiable into discrete scales, but instead can range across and cascade upwards in scale such as, for instance, the urban heat island effect.

To support designers in understanding and tackling complex relations and interactions, Birger Sevaldson developed an approach entitled *Systems Oriented Design* (SOD), which he describes "as a skill, rather than a theory [...] mainly a mindset with a few tools" (Sevaldson, 2022, p. 28). A key process tool of SOD is what Sevaldson has termed *giga-maps*. These involve "visualizing complex systems. They are process tools [...] for visual thinking" (Sevaldson, 2022). Giga-maps contain and visualize an extensive number of items and relations (not unlike an ontology), for the purpose of questioning and redrawing system boundaries and, as envisioned by Sevaldson, identifying new ways of intervening with design based on a significantly expanded view of a given sys-

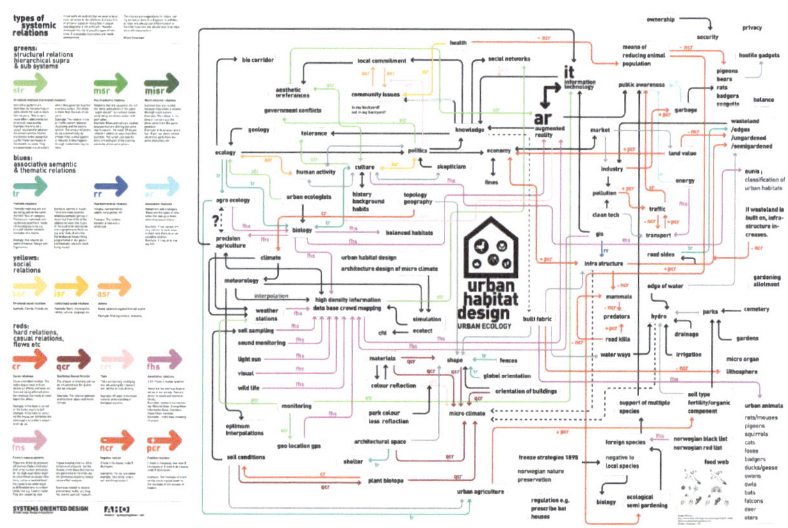

Fig. 55

Fig. 55
Relational map of urban habitats involving urban ecology. Courtesy of Young Eun Choi, Oslo School of Architecture and Design, 2013.

tem. Sevaldson explained that "a central aspect of working with very complex tasks is to keep as many aspects of a problem field in play for as long as possible throughout the process" (Sevaldson, 2022, p. 227). Figure 55 shows an example of a giga-map designed by Young Eun Choi, which visualizes relations of urban habitats involving urban ecology. Color-coded arrows define different types of systemic relations among various aspects of urban habitat.

The challenge in *performance-oriented design* is not to reduce complexity at any point in the process, with boundary judgment necessarily a perpetual process. Capturing and instrumentalizing extensive systems is a prerequisite higher-level activity to enable tapping into *material agency* and *material performance*. Approaches like SOD can deliver key insights, approaches, and methods for the task at hand.

2.8 OUTLOOK

Data-driven approaches to designing material will, in future, utilize expert databases that will be increasingly expanded with data on *material behavior* and *material performance* and *material systems performance*. Data, and especially experimentally derived data, that are already available will need to be pooled in accessible expert databases and data that do not yet exist will need to be added over time.

It is likely that designers will soon have access to visual programming-based tools that facilitate both extensive system mapping, as well as computational ontologies for decision support with focus on material and material systems performance(s). Multivariate data and spatio-temporal data, data mining and data analytics, data-driven modeling, and simulations for the purpose of design and multi-criteria optimization will play a role.

Regarding *material properties*, it is necessary to instrumentalize (i) *material variation*, (ii) the *hierarchical organization* of materials across scales, and (iii) the *correlation of material properties*. However, it is also important to note that there are extensive data on technical materials, yet comparatively few on biological materials. As Vincent et al. pointed out, the available data on "biological materials is due almost entirely to the efforts of Wegst (Wegst and Ashby, 2004) and is as yet unavailable generally" (Vincent et al., 2006, p. 478). Regarding *material behavior*, it is necessary to (1) instrumentalize the *correlation between material properties and their interactions with the surrounding environment*, (2) combine *knowledge-driven* and *data-driven* modeling, and (3) employ *multivariate data and spatio-temporal data* methods and tools. Regarding *material performance* and *material systems performance,* it is necessary to: (1) link the listed aspects concerning the analysis of material properties and material behavior into a *data-driven design* approach to *design variety generation* in which each design output can be analyzed and ranked, and (2) share data on *material performance* and *material systems performance* in a dedicated open-source expert database. Overall, this development is moving towards an integrative approach, methods, and toolset, which can bring about a novel specialized knowledge domain: the material and environmental performance expert in architecture and planning.

CHAPTER

3

TIME

What can be measured and treasured in architecture, but never be seen? *Time* has got its hold on everything and everyone, everywhere in the built and unbuilt environments. While time cannot be seen, its consequences are perceptible. Kevin Lynch (1972) stated that people experience the passage of time in the urban environment through 'rhythmic repetition' and through 'progressive and irreversible change'. The former relates to, for example, heartbeat, breathing, sleeping, and waking, hunger, the cycles of the sun and moon, the seasons, waves, tides, and clocks, whereas the latter refers to growth and decay, "not recurrence, but alteration" (Lynch, 1972, p. 65).

Time can be categorized in multiple ways, such as *interval, diurnal, seasonal, generational, natural,* and *eventual.* Architecture and urban systems relate to these in various ways. *Interval* refers to the space between two points (from here to there). *Diurnal* indicates the circadian day/night cycle of 24 hours, and *seasonal* the cycle of various seasons throughout a year. *Generational* connects to the differences that occur between successive stages of life (usually 15–35 years). *Natural* time follows the laws of nature in longer and shorter cycles, while *eventual* deals with the inevitable and unpredictable future (Soh, 2019). All these temporal measures resonate in physical, infrastructural, and architectural fabric, albeit in very different ways. What they have in common are their *recurrence* and *alteration. Recurrence* is more predictable than alteration. *Alteration* – or change – manifests itself over time and space, potentially with low levels of probability regarding physical or mental consequences. *Contingency* requires all living things to master the art of *adaptation.* Essentially, architecture and urban systems exist as a function of change that occurs through the passing of time. Yet, observing the way in which many cities take shape, it seems that dynamic principles are often taken for granted in favor of static design approaches. As it turns out, *time* remains an imperceptible concept for many professionals in the building sector.

According to Jeremy Till, architecture greatly depends on uncertainty and contingency, and despite the claims of autonomy, purity, and control that architects might make about their practice, architecture is buffeted by uncertainty and contingency (Till, 2013). This may be due to architects' tendency to pursue perfection, as Till suggests, but such an attitude in itself is created,

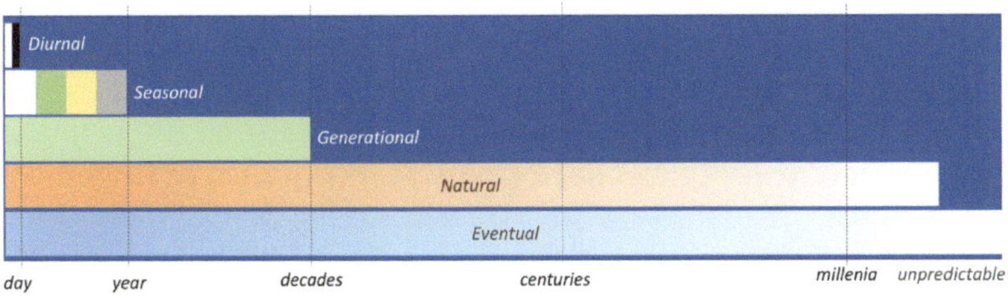

Fig. 56

Fig. 56
Diurnal, seasonal, generational, natural, and eventual time dimensions

Fig. 57
Adhesives in building materials may cause the accumulation of 'forever-chemicals' in products and the environment. Photography: Bob Geldermans, 2024.

supported, and maintained by a larger system of city-makers. It might be fairer to say that humankind has traded the ability to surf the waves of time for the desire to control frozen moments. Still, anticipating change in architecture is not unmanageable, as will be discussed in multiple sections of this chapter. Control can be better asserted through data than stones. Anticipation of alterations in the ways architecture and urban systems are used and perceived can indeed be lubricated by effective application of data and unlocked for stakeholders at suitable moments in time. Although many built examples showcase at least some of these criteria, they are often absent in contemporary approaches to city-making. Industrial tempos to produce housing in competitive markets, for example, have induced a general tendency to overlook natural rhythmic repetition, such as diurnal schemes of light/dark and warm/cool. Moreover, natural phenomena of decay are nowadays expelled by protective measures, often using potentially harmful chemicals that time has no hold on. In a generational and eventual sense, it is observed that building after building must be refurbished to meet prevalent needs or be demolished altogether. It must be admitted that humans in general, and the building sector in particular, has developed a rather ambivalent relationship with the notion of *time.*

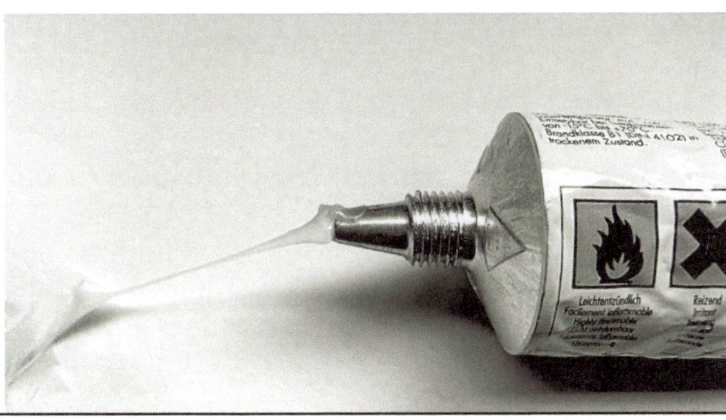

Fig. 57

Certain buildings and infrastructural works have been in existence for hundreds or thousands of years, in a quasi-permanent state, yet open to adaptations over time. For instance, several sanctuaries and observatories in ancient cultures still stand as "mute monuments of the sociopolitical, economic, and ideological systems of their creators" (Hansen, 1998, p. 49). Other (pre) classic architecture has managed to retain functional purpose over time, through conscientious abiding by ground rules that have not become obsolete in the given context. In that respect, the Vitruvian attributes of *firmitas, utilitas et venustas* (strength, utility, and beauty) are – quite literally – a solid foundation for architects who need to confirm that all is under control, that is, stable and static (Woods, 2009). Another example of ancient architecture is the Grand Shrine of Ise, Japan, which is essentially a new building – an exact replica – every 20 years so that it will be forever both new, ancient and original (Tange and Kawazoe, 1965). This benefits the transfer of data on material use and construction techniques. However, in cities dominated by secular change, environmental concerns, demographic shifts, or social and technological trends, architecture must follow swiftly (Cox, 1968). Dynamic urban and social systems are inherently complex, requiring appropriate material responses and associated data.

3.2 SPATIO-TEMPORALITY

Material performance and material flows unfold in space and time and play a pivotal role in sustainable design. To capture and instrumentalize material performance and flows it is necessary to expand datasets beyond static spatial or singular temporal representation towards spatio-temporal data, which combines data on both space and time (Figs. 58 and 59).

In the field of materials science, domain-level ontologies (DLOs) enable the description of material properties, as well as material processes and structures, thereby supporting data integration, interoperability, and knowledge discovery (Baas et al., 2023). In this context, the question arises as to how spatio-temporal data can be addressed in terms of representation, reasoning, and query?

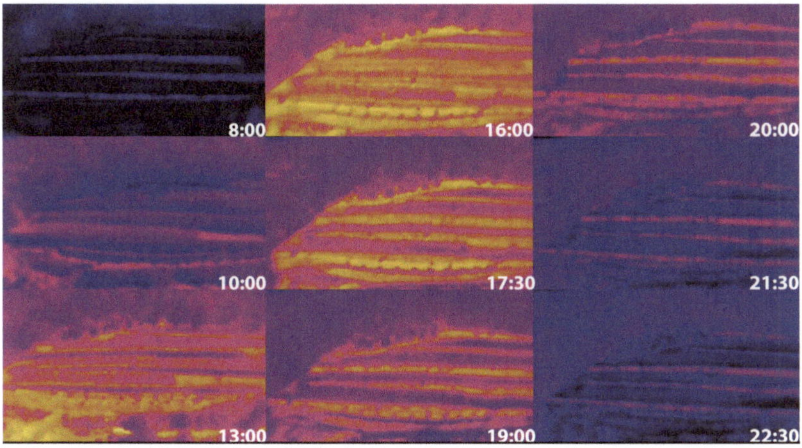

Fig. 58

Fig. 58
Example of a spatio-temporal dataset: time sequence of the thermal performance of dry-stone walls from 8:00 am to 22:30 pm in a high-altitude terraced vineyard in Lamole, Tuscany. Thermography conducted by the Department for Digital Architecture and Planning at TU Wien, 2019.

Pim Martins, Professor of Planetary Health at Maastricht University, called for a new paradigm – sustainability science – that can fully embrace the complexity and multidimensionality of sustainable development. For Martins this new paradigm needs to address spatial, temporal, and functional scales, as well as multiple dynamics and processes, actors, and failures (Martins, 2006). Clearly, all the required aspects rely on the time dimension, as processes, agency and systemic failures unfold in time. Data requirements for engendering this new paradigm are considerable. However, some useful approaches are available, such as spatio-temporal data. Wang *et al.* describe five different types of spatio-temporal data:

/ *Event data:* composed of discrete events occurring at specific locations and time points.
/ *Trajectory data:* usually obtained from the location sensors deployed on a moving object.
/ *Point reference data:* generated by a set of moving reference points in a particular space and time interval.
/ *Raster data:* collected at fixed locations of a given space and at regular or irregular time points.
/ *Video data:* consisting of a sequence of images. (Wang et al., 2022)

Spatio-temporal data and databases are used, for instance, for geographic information systems (GIS) and environmental information systems (EIS). Spatio-temporal data analysis is a research field in Big Data analysis (Heavy AI, 2024). Spatiotemporal data mining involves discovering patterns and knowledge from spatiotemporal data (Han et al., 2012) based on computational techniques for

Fig. 59
Example of a spatio-temporal dataset: Total sunlight hours on 22 March, 22 June, and 22 December at Val Lumnezia in Graubünden, Switzerland. Lumnezia Studio, Arne Leibnitz and Veselin Dzhedzhev. Courtesy of Department for Digital Architecture and Planning at TU Wien, 2020.

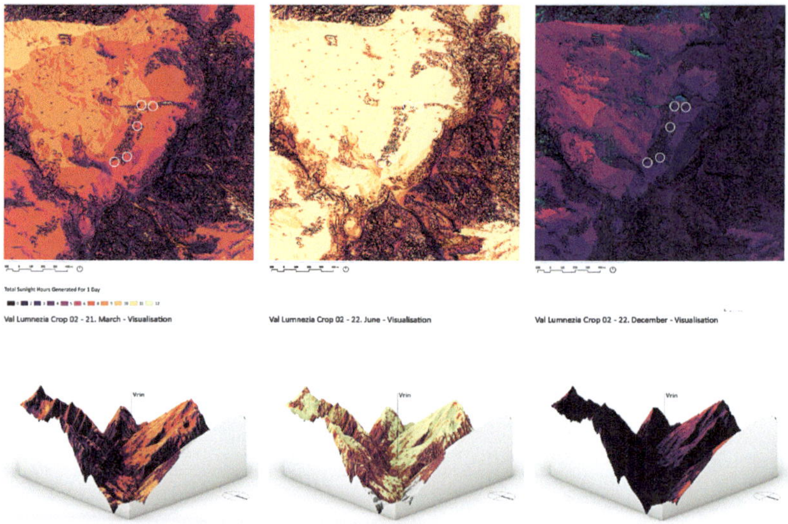

Fig. 59

analysis of large spatiotemporal databases (Venkateswara Rao et al., 2012). Deep learning (DL) models can be applied to different types of spatio-temporal data for spatio-temporal prediction (e.g., of environmental data) (Amato et al., 2020). DL models include supervised and unsupervised deep learning (e.g., stochastic, convolutional, and recurrent neural networks, sequence to sequence models, autoencoders, etc.; Wang et al., 2022). Amato et al. point out that DL models "have proved to be able to capture spatial, temporal, and spatio-temporal dependencies" (Amato et al., 2020).

Furthermore, computational ontologies can enable representation, reasoning and querying based on spatio-temporal data. Batsakis and Petrakis proposed that dynamic ontologies can represent "information evolving in time and space, [...] events with objects and properties changing in time and space" (Batsakis and Petrakis, 2010). This offers a powerful entry point to methods that tackle questions of materials in time, in terms of performances, flows and other dynamic aspects.

Fig. 60
Example of a multi-scale dataset showing thermal performance data related to viticulture on three different scales: the landscape scale (left), the vineyard scale (center), and the scale of selected areas within an individual vineyard (right). Department for Digital Architecture and Planning at TU Wien, Jakub Tyc, 2020 (Tyc *et al.*, 2021).

The use of multi-scalar data has become commonplace in data-driven design and planning in architecture, urban design, and landscape architecture. This involves different aspects of understanding and designing architectures (Sunguroğlu Hensel et al., 2022). Examples of multi-scale approaches and computational simulations include the analysis of traditional viticulture at high altitudes in Lamole, Italy (Tyc et al., 2021). Figure 60 showing thermal performance data related to viticulture on three different scales, the landscape scale, the vineyard scale, and the scale of selected areas within an individual vineyard. The combination of different analyses into a multi-scale dataset enables a better understanding of the correlation and mutual influence of thermal performance on different scales. This type of analysis and multi-scalar data can then be used for performance-oriented data-driven design and planning; in this case for data-driven design of terraced vineyards (Tyc et al., 2022).

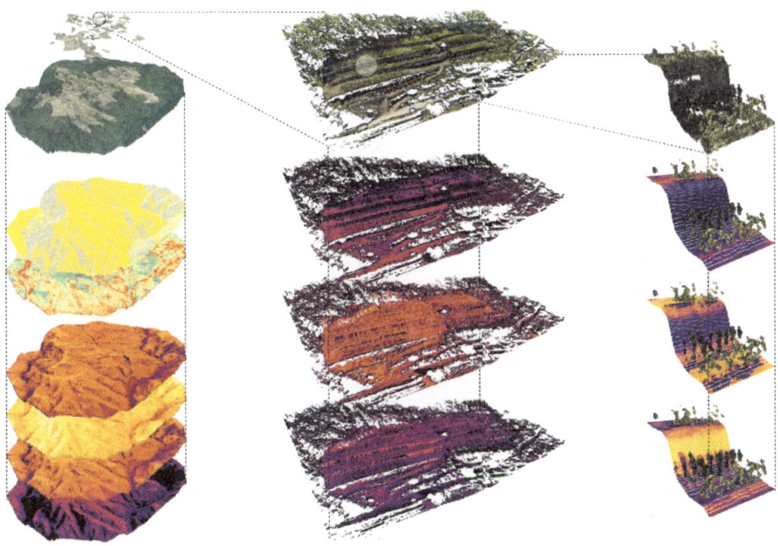

Fig. 60

A further example is multi-scalar and multi-domain data integration approach developed for the Horizon 2020 research project ECOLOPES – ECOlogical building enveLOPES (Ecolopes, 2024). The Department for Digital Architecture and Planning at TU Wien developed a relational database in conjunction with a voxel-based approach to spatializing data in the CAD environment of Rhinoceros 3D. The ECOLOPES voxel model approach is a key component of a data-driven and ontology-aided generative computational design process for multi-species building envelopes, catering for humans, animals, plants, and microbiota (Ludwig et al., 2021; Weisser et al., 2022). The functionality of the ECOLOPES voxel model rests on its ability to enable efficient storage and retrieval of data pertaining to different scales and domains, data-layering, correlation and analysis, and interoperability with computational ontologies to facilitate interdisciplinary queries and algorithmic processes for design generation (Figs. 61–63).

Multiscale modeling and simulations in materials science frequently involve both spatial and temporal scale ranges. Several decades ago, Malinov and Sha pointed out that "a computer modeling approach of different processes and correlation in the materials science is [...] becoming very popular [...]. The main aim of the software packages is to help for optimization of the processing parameters with minimum investment of time and money for experimental work." (Malinov and Sha, 2003, p. 179) This implies that useful insights can be derived from, and data

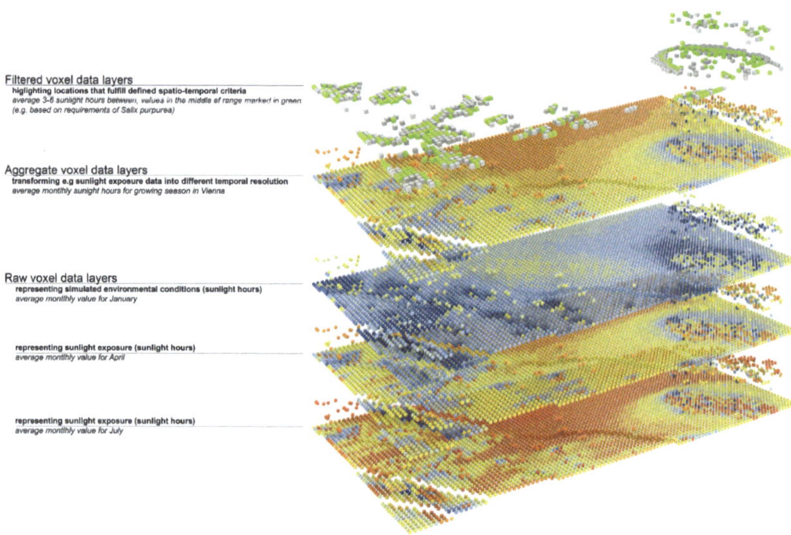

Fig. 61

Fig. 61
The ECOLOPES Voxel Model combines a relational database in conjunction with a voxel approach to spatializing data in the CAD environment of Rhinoceros 3D / Grasshopper, facilitating multi-scalar and multi-domain spatio-temporal data integration at a site in Vienna, Austria. Datasets contained in the voxel model include raw, aggregate, and filtered voxel data layers. Raw data layers represent dynamically generated spatial reprojections of datasets loaded into the voxel model. Aggregate data layers are composite datasets created through aggregation of raw data layers, for instance, to change the temporal dimension of the voxel data. Filtered data layers represent aggregate data layers that are processed, for instance, according to suitability criteria. Department for Digital Architecture and Planning at TU Wien, Jakub Tyc, 2020.

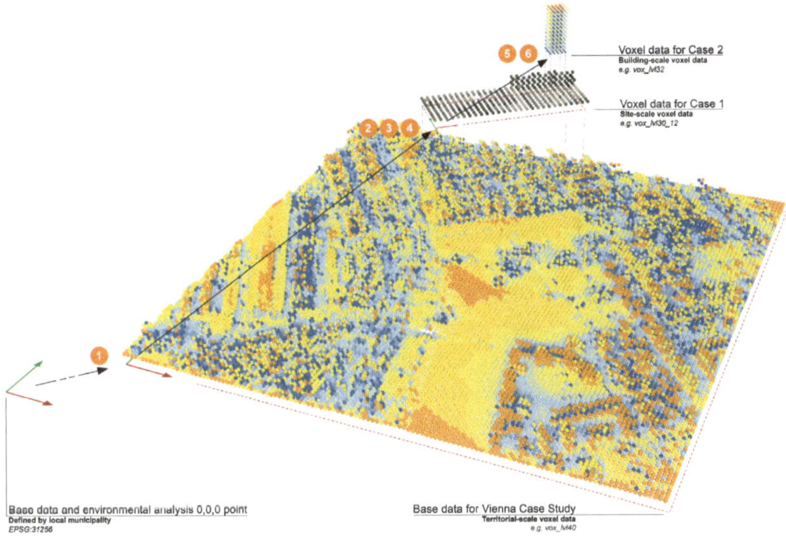

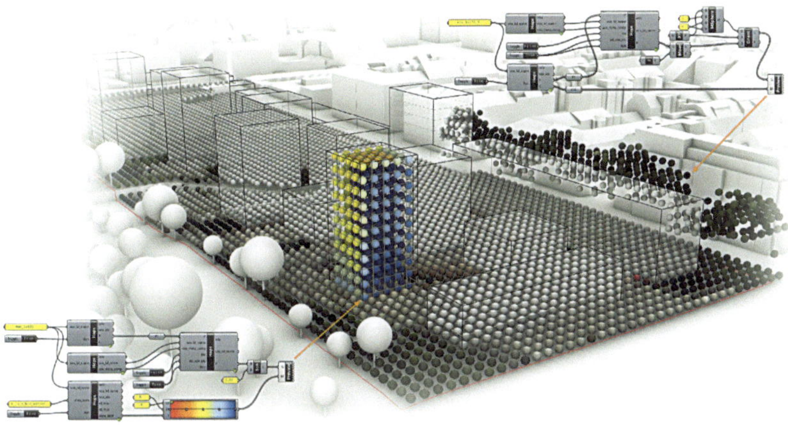

Figs. 62, 63

Fig. 62
Ecolopes Voxel Model contains spatio-temporal data layers at multiple spatial and temporal scales, including urban scale, plot scale, and building scale. The spatialized data are implemented and visualized in the CAD environment of Rhinoceros 3D / Grasshopper. Department for Digital Architecture and Planning at TU Wien, Jakub Tyc, 2020.

Fig. 63
Visualization showing the implementation of spatio-temporal data layers on a building scale. The spatialized data are implemented and visualized in the CAD environment of Rhinoceros 3D / Grasshopper. Department for Digital Architecture and Planning at TU Wien, Jakub Tyc, 2020.

can be generated through computational methods in addition to physical experimental work, especially when resources are not available for the latter.

Addressing various problems in a range of different sciences requires spatial and temporal scale ranges since properties and processes that take place on one scale affect the behavior of systems across other scales (Lu and Kaxiras, 2004). This also holds true for materials science where microscopic scales govern macroscopic material behavior. Since this is of importance for material design and engineering and hence for industrial applications, multiscale material simulations involving both spatial and temporal ranges have the potential to underpin and engender technological innovation (Lu and Kaxiras, 2004; Bishara et al., 2023).

Multiscale simulations are computationally expensive in terms of resources and time and are hence still not widely used by industry (Bishara et al., 2023). Nevertheless, the rapid development of Artificial Intelligence (AI), Machine Learning (ML), and computational resources, and the availability of relevant data begin to suggest a way forward, whereby ML methods display their "potential to provide an excellent innovative class of multi-scaling techniques. The application of these techniques is straightforward since ML can provide an alternative computational tool for the physical-based modeling, and thus, it enables a smooth transition between the scales [...]. The overlap of ML and multiscale modeling is promising for creating robust predictive models and exploring massive design parameter spaces more efficiently. Moreover, the ability of ML to fill the gap between the experimental data and the physical-based models enables rapid materials discovery. These features enable AI-based machine learning methods to lead a revolution in manufacturing paradigms, including modeling, design, and production." (Bishara et al., 2023, p. 216)

The use of machine learning for the purpose of multiscale material modeling and simulations is gaining traction as a focus of research (Bishara et al., 2023, Ingólfsson et al., 2023; Lee et al., 2024) and is frequently coupled with other computational methods. For instance, data-driven design methods have been proposed in the context of engineered metamaterials, which exhibit properties that differ from or exceed those of natural materials. Lee et al., elaborated that "data-driven metamaterials design typically includes three modules, 1) data acquisition: acquiring a precomputed dataset of unit cells; 2) machine learning (ML) based unit cell design: using ML to extract information from data and help unit cell designs; 3) multiscale design: utilizing unit-cell database and ML models for design synthesis at the system level [...]. The core idea underlying data-driven design [...] is to extract meaningful patterns from data that are unavailable or difficult to obtain with physical models and incorporate them into the design process to simplify the complexity in traditional design approaches. Although these capabilities come with the cost of data collection and model training, deploying the trained model has the benefit of negligible inference time, which can significantly speed up the design process." (Lee et al., 2024, pp. 1–2)

Kalina et al. developed a data-driven multiscale approach based on combining artificial neural networks and autonomous data mining: "the core feature of the approach is given by a completely autonomous mining of the required data set within an overall loop. In each iteration of the loop, new data are generated by gathering the macroscopic deformation states from the macroscopic finite element simulation and subsequently sorting by using the anisotropy class of the considered material. Finally, all unknown deformations are prescribed in the RVE simulation to get the corresponding stresses and thus to extend the data set." (Kalina et al., 2023, p. 827) This approach showcases the possibility of generating data from simulations, where they are not otherwise available, in a linked process that enables the number of simulations to be reduced (Kalina et al., 2023).

While frequently specific to material groups and material behavior, such approaches are rapidly growing in number and scope across various sectors. Moreover, data-driven design methods coupled with machine learning are already being used for various purposes in the planning and design of the built environment. However, data generated through multi-scalar simulations are not always available through open access databases. A sustained data sharing effort could help advance the field more rapidly.

3.4 DATA FOR NEW PARADIGMS

The field of material data is growing rapidly, driven by advancements in technology and data science, as well as increasing demands for sustainability and efficiency. Advancements in technology play a critical role. Traditional methods of material characterization and data collection were often time-consuming and resource-intensive. However, with advanced imaging techniques, such as electron microscopy and X-ray spectroscopy, researchers can now visualize and analyze materials at the atomic level (Van Tendeloo et al., 2012). These techniques provide unique insights into the structure and behavior of materials, enabling more accurate and detailed data collection. Additionally, the development of high-performance computing has empowered researchers to simulate and model material properties at various scales (Wilson, 2007). This capability enables predictive modeling, allowing scientists to predict how materials behave

Fig. 64
Data science is used to predict material properties and extract indicative patterns and insights.

under different conditions without exhaustive physical testing. Spatio-temporal data such as time series in Geographic Information Systems (GIS) simulations, enhance designers' ability to monitor and analyze material performance over time and across different locations (Peuquet, 1994).

Data science has revolutionized the handling and analysis of material data (O'Mara et al., 2016; Hill et al., 2016; Yuan et al., 2018; Lv et al., 2021; Rumor and Andrade-Campos, 2022; Hearley, et al., 2023). Data-driven approaches involve collecting and processing large datasets to extract indicative patterns and insights. This provides the ability to predict material behavior based on existing data (Fig. 64). Incorporating spatio-temporal data enhances predictive capabilities for material design and application by enabling detailed monitoring and examination of material performance over time and in different geographic areas (Muhammad et al., 2022). Machine learning algorithms, such as neural networks and regression models, can learn from extensive quantities of spatio-temporal data and make accurate predictions about material behavior and material flows. Moreover, data science techniques enable rapid identification of connections between material properties. These developments can support the discovery of new materials with tailored properties and behavior, as well as optimization of existing materials for specific applications.

Fig. 64

The increasing global focus on sustainability and efficiency has brought about a paradigm shift in material data. Historically, materials were often chosen primarily for their performance characteristics. However, current considerations include the environmental impact of materials throughout their lifecycle, which has led to the integration of sustainability metrics into material data paradigms (Fig. 65; Keoleian and Spitzley, 2006). Using time series in environmental simulations provides a dynamic perspective, allowing for assessing material performance and environmental impact over time, further enriching the decision-making process in sustainable material selection.

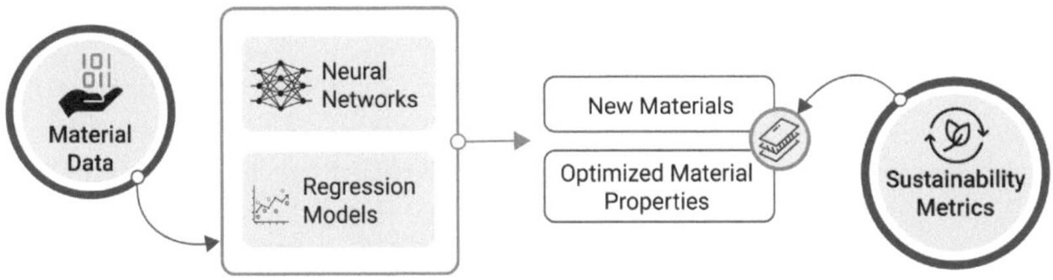

Fig. 65

Fig. 65
Integration of sustainability metrics in material data for assessing the environmental impact of materials throughout their lifecycle

Materials databases now include information about a material's carbon footprint, energy consumption during production, and potential for recycling or reuse (Bajpai et al., 2020). This holistic view allows decision-makers to select materials that match environmental goals over time. Hence, material data contain information on broader implications of material choices on ecosystems and resource utilization. The incorporation of time-series data in simulations facilitates dynamic analysis of material impacts, enabling predictions of long-term environmental effects and optimizing material use in response to changing conditions.

The combination of these factors – advancements in technology, the influence of data science, and the emphasis on sustainability – has given rise to several new paradigms in the field of material data. These include the following:

/ *Materials informatics and data science:* Integrating data science and informatics techniques with materials science led to the emergence of materials informatics. This paradigm uses computational tools and machine learning algorithms to analyze large datasets, predict material properties, and discover novel materials with specific characteristics (Butler et al., 2018).

/ *Open materials databases:* Open-access materials databases allow researchers, engineers, and innovators to access and contribute to a large amount of material data. These databases enable collaboration, accelerate research, and provide widely available information for diverse applications (Hill et al., 2016; Jain et al., 2020).

/ *Real-time sensor data integration:* Sensors embedded in materials provide real-time data about the material's condition, structural health, and performance. This paradigm encourages the development of intelligent materials with applications in infrastructure monitoring (Hao et al., 2022).

- *Sustainability and circular economy:* With a growing focus on sustainability and the circular economy, material data paradigms now concentrate on apprehending information about the environmental impact, recyclability, and life cycle of materials. This enables informed decision-making to support eco-friendly practices (Shehata et al., 2022).

These developments highlight the transformative nature of the material data field, where technology and innovation are changing the understanding, utilization, and designing of materials in both space and time to meet increasingly complex requirements.

3.5 DESIGN FOR CHANGE

According to the space-time theory of relativity (Einstein, 1905) space and time are inseparably linked. Rooted in the abstractions of physics, this theory may seem to have little direct relevance to the AEC sector, yet it is intrinsically linked to how our built environment is perceived and operated. For instance, materials and buildings could be understood through relationships between physical matter and events, relative to the observer. The time and space it requires to mine, grow, cultivate, apply, enjoy, reuse, and replenish resources can be considered as design criteria (Carpenter, 2002; Ashby, 2022) in addition to operations and interventions before, during, and after any building's service life. However, unlike space, time is perceived to have only one dimension and one direction, as "the continued sequence of existence and events that occurs in a linear succession from past, through the present, into the future" (Oxford Dictionaries, 2023). Although the AEC sector does not easily internalize non-3D temporal notions, designing and constructing for change is quite literally the only way forward, since buildings and infrastructures are essentially part of dynamic settlements. Regardless of their service lives, any building should anticipate change, however unpredictable this may be for designed and constructed intentions. Architected materials can be encoded with a temporal degree of freedom such that they evolve over time and respond to various stimuli, including mechanical actuation, changes in temperature and chemical environment, and variations in electromagnetic fields (Xia et al., 2022). Given the reduced cost and increased effectiveness of embedded computing and dynamic building components in recent years, it seems likely that ever more buildings will be designed with components that respond to change in terms of use and environment. Meagher (2015) describes this as the *poetic potential* of responsive elements (Meagher, 2015), reimagining architecture following so-called *Shearing Layers of Change*, as introduced by architect Frank Duffy and elaborated by Stewart Brand (Fig. 66; Duffy and Hannay, 1992; Brand, 1994).

Fig. 66
Pace-layers' or "shearing layers" with different rates of change (after Brand, 1994, and Duffy, 1992)

Initially related to capital costs, *Shearing Layers of Change* became a key concept in coupling socio-cultural user-centric dynamics to technical operationalization of material flows. According to Duffy, the changes within a building over fifty years cost three times more than the original building. Structure expenditure is overwhelmed by cumulative financial consequences of multiple generations making use of the interior and its building services (Brand, 1994). From this financial vantage point, Brand distinguished six layers with different rates of change of their components: the geographical setting (site); the foundation and load-bearing elements (structure); exterior surfaces (skin); the "working guts" of a building: wiring, plumbing, HVAC, etc. (services); the interior layout (space-plan); and the *mobilia* (stuff) (Brand, 1994).

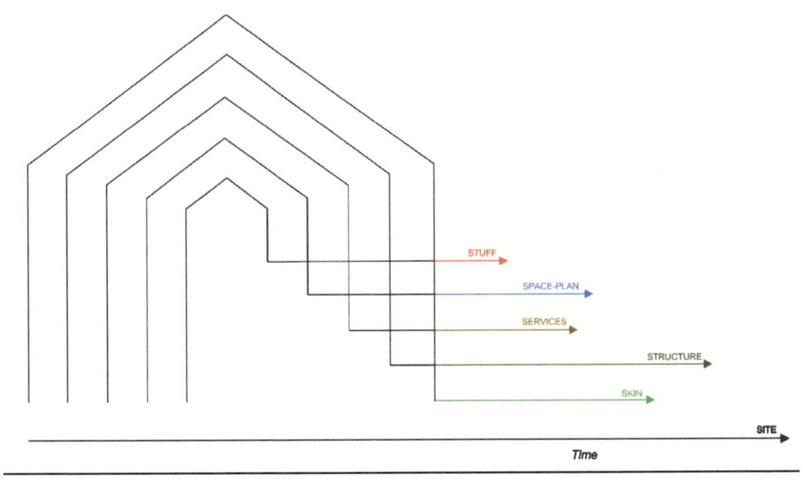

Fig. 66

Design for Change is associated with multiple targets that move through time. The circular economy responds to this by providing

Fig. 67
Circular Design & Impact Matrix for co-creative decision-making in building design (Geldermans, 2016).

concrete incentives from social, ecological, and economic viewpoints. The rationale behind this is that shifting the focus from *take-make-waste* to *take less, make better, use longer, remake and retake* has benefits for all aspects of sustainability. Naturally, this implies a systemic transition, which is inherently complex (Rotmans and Loorbach, 2009). However, for the AEC sector, the basic rule is straightforward: apply an integrated approach to design, production, construction, operation, maintenance, repair, discharge, and reuse.

The distributed control over materials, and their embedded impact, is hard to retain over time. Diversified datasets and data-management can help a great deal to guide this process (Pagoropoulos et al., 2017). Co-creation becomes paramount in integrated trajectories. The matrix displayed in Figure 67 connects the shearing layers of change with circular strategies, in analogy with the various stages of built elements through time. This streamlines the process of knowledge and know-how exchange between stakeholders in circular design for change trajectories. The method is fueled by collaboration between experts and sectors, underscoring the cross-disciplinary nature of circular value networks. It reveals differences in vocabulary and interpretation, as well as knowledge gaps that necessitate additional data or research. On the vertical axis of Figure 66, a building is divided into shearing layers with diverging material turnover rates (or 'service lifetimes'), with the longest intended lifespan below and the shortest on top. The horizontal axis displays circular strategies from *avoiding material use by design* to *most optimal reapplication route for materials* bridged by *appropriate management of materials in operation* (Cramer, 2014; Bocken et al., 2016; Potting et al., 2016). In other words, looping from one beginning to another. Every cell

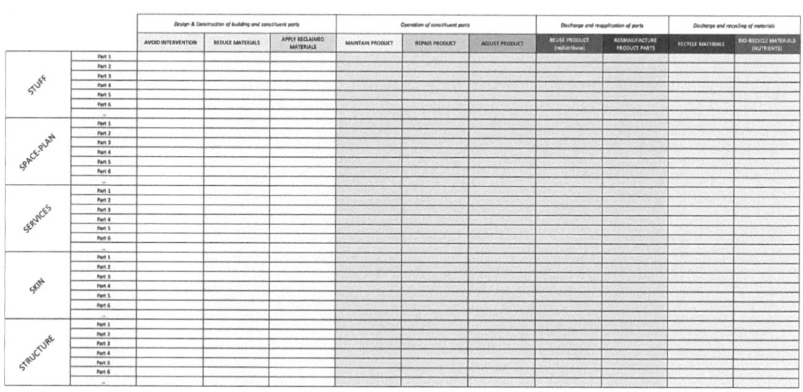

Fig. 67

can contain specific considerations, discussions, responsibilities, data, and third-party input.

The matrix of Figure 67 fits in a broader tradition of 'holistic management' toolboxes and frameworks, not least referring to the values-based and proactive decision-making approach to managing complexity first developed by Alan Savory in the 1960s (Gosnell et al., 2020; Savory and Butterfield, 1999). Circular as well as regenerative, built environments require human systems that co-evolve with natural systems in favor of local life and resilience (Mang and Reed, 2012). We may need new methods, but we can build on old notions to unravel the complexity associated with designing and building our living environments. In that respect, progress is multi-directional, looking backwards and forwards, as well as up, down, and around.

3.6 REGENERATION

Questions concerning the relationship between materials and time include material life cycles and the way materials are resourced, transformed, made, reused, recycled, re/distributed, and disposed of (see Chapter 4). As material resources begin to run short due to global overconsumption, the notion of *regeneration* has come into focus. Cole stated that the "notion of regeneration [...] has been variously applied in relation to the built environment and the communities it supports following major acts of devastation or when a prior condition had declined to an extent considered ripe for renewal – and, of course, where the commitment has been found to initiate rebuilding. The resulting transformed condition, while embodying traces from its prior condition, is infused with new aspirations and possibilities. Over the past years, however, regeneration has been garnering increasing interest as a means of reframing green building practices and, carrying with it, qualitatively different and broader connotations than that used previously." (Cole, 2011, p. 1) As Cole has pointed out, "regenerative design [...] relates to approaches that support the co-evolution of human and natural systems in a partnered relationship. It is not the building that is 'regenerated' in the same sense as the self-healing and self-organizing attributes of a living system, but by the ways that the act of building can be a catalyst for positive change within the unique 'place' in which it is situated. Within regenerative development, built projects, stakeholder processes and inhabitation are collectively focused on enhancing life in all its manifestations – human, other species, ecological systems – through an enduring responsibility of stewardship." (Cole, 2011, p. 1).

Chrisna du Plessis argues that "the dominant sustainability paradigms are reaching the limitations of their usefulness due to their conceptual foundation in an inappropriate mechanistic worldview and their tacit support of a modernization project that prevents effective engagement with a complex, dynamic and living world. The regenerative paradigm provides an alternative that is explicitly designed to engage with a living world through its emphasis on a co-creative partnership with nature based on strategies of adaptation, resilience, and regeneration. It provides a foundation for a sustainability paradigm that is relevant to an ecological worldview." (du Plessis, 2011, p. 7)

Regenerative materials tie in with regenerative building design and regenerative planning, thereby constituting a key aspect of regenerative sustainability. In this context, Gibbons points out that "regenerative development (as part of regenerative sustainability) provides the framework to identify life-giving patterns and actions in a living system, regenerative design is an integral part of the process of giving form to patterns and actions (Mang and Reed, 2011). [...]. Regenerative design in the built environment largely focuses on facilitating healthy processes and flows within one focal scale of a system without catalyzing change at larger scales (Gibbons et al., 2018). As part of regenerative development processes, however, regenerative design can develop the necessary capabilities for regeneration over time and across scales." (Gibbons, 2020, p. 7) This suggests that datasets for regenerative design must be spatio-temporal and trans-scalar.

In the AEC sector the notions of *reuse, recycling,* and *upcycling* are often conflated with that of *regeneration*. Since various aspects of *reuse, recycling,* and *upcycling,* especially in the context of material flows and circular economy, are addressed in Chapter 4, focus is placed here on the *regenerative*. The notion of regenerative material pursued in this chapter focuses on regenerative biological materials that "are 100 percent biobased, 100 percent biodegradable, and sourced from locally abundant biomass that is otherwise under-utilized and does not compete for land use or food security. When they can no longer be used, these materials have the potential to regenerate natural ecosystems in the form of compost and soil amendment." (Materiom, 2024)

Building materials composed of biomass can exhibit similar properties (i.e., mechanical, thermal, acoustic, etc.) to conventional building materials and exhibit improved environmental performance during their life cycle. However, as Mouton et al. have shown, this assessment is typically "drawn from cradle-to-gate LCA studies excluding impacts occurring after the product has left the factory" (Mouton et al., 2023, p. 2). This realization prompted Mouton et al. to extend evaluation criteria by adding the global warming potential (GWP) indicator, as this is the main reason bio-based construction materials are promoted. To identify potential environmental trade-offs, Mouton et al. carried out an environmental hotspot analysis based on a comprehensive set of environmental indicators for identifying the most important impact indicators, life cycle stages and most contributing processes (Mouton et al., 2023). Such studies are valuable in that clear indicators are selected and related data can be acquired and utilized.

A growing number of online resources on bio-based materials are emerging such as, for instance, *Materiom*, which is "an open access platform for creating sustainably sourced biomaterials, made from locally abundant natural ingredients. The *Materiom* community includes material scientists, designers, engineers, data scientists, and sustainability experts. The project supports companies, cities, and communities in creating and selecting materials sourced from locally abundant biomass that are part of a regenerative circular economy." (Materiom, 2024) The Federal Institute of Technology (ETH) Zurich provides the ReMat – Regenerative Material online platform "as an open-source knowledge center, aiming to support the understanding and diffusion of Regenerative Materials in the context of Sustainable Construction for all" (ReMat, 2024).

3.7 OUTLOOK

In architectural design, considerations of time in relation to materials frequently focus on questions of wear and weathering, limiting unwanted material behavior, and material life cycles. In data science, considerations of time frequently focus on the duration of computational processes or spatio-temporal data. Less appreciated is perhaps the fact that the increasing attention paid to the time dimension and spatio-temporal and multi-scalar material data in planning and design, as well as in materials science and materials informatics, has begun to challenge deeply entrenched architectural design and urban planning preconceptions at a fundamental level, while opening otherwise closed processes related to the built environment to larger anthropogenic and environmental processes and dynamics. Novel resource and waste management processes, including reuse, recycling, upcycling, circularity, and regeneration, have become central topics in urban planning and design as well as in architectural design (see Chapter 4). As this development fosters an advanced understanding and instrumentalizing of increasingly complex dynamics, the relationship between spatial, temporal, and functional scales comes to the fore as called for by Martins in the context of sustainability science. Martins posited the need for a new research paradigm that would need to incorporate "different magnitudes of scale (of time, space and function), multiple balances (dynamics), multiple actors (interests) and multiple failures (systemic faults)" (Martins, 2006, p. 36) In this context, data-driven computational simulations are increasingly taking center-stage in urban planning and architectural design. As computational resources steadily increase, geographic information systems applications are beginning to be coupled with architectural design software (Sunguroğlu Hensel, 2022), indicating a trend towards multi- and trans-scalar methods utilizing spatio-temporal data. It stands to reason that in the next development stages modeling and simulations related to earth and environmental science will be increasingly interoperable with urban planning and design and architectural design software packages. In the European research project *ECOLOPES – ECOlogical building enveLOPES* (Weisser et al., 2022) computational design workflows entail linking ecological models with computational form generation approaches to multi-species architectural design (ECOLOPES, 2024). This makes it possible to understand possible ecological ramifications of different designs over time. As described in Chapter 5, these types of research projects foreground the importance of water, soil, and biomass as key materials of the built environment along a critical zone research approach which focuses on "the heterogeneous, near-surface environment in which complex interactions involving, rock, soil, water, air and living organisms regulate the natural habitat and determine the availability of life-sustaining resources. Many science disciplines – hydrology, geomorphology, biology, ecology, soil science, sedimentology, materials research, and geochemistry – are bringing novel research tools to bear on the study of the Critical Zone as an integrated system of interacting components and processes." (National Research Council, 2001, p. 2) In general, these developments suggest that a major advancement of and through interdisciplinary work is impending, which can deliver the paradigm change Martins called for. They also suggest that architectural design has begun to embrace the time dimension in a new and more wholesome manner.

CHAPTER 4

FLOWS

In this chapter, materials and data are positioned in relation to spatial and geographical distribution. Particular attention is placed on questions of sustainability. Materials are an essential part of the resources that sustain human societies around the globe. Therefore, materializing the built environment is no longer solely a matter of applying nearby natural resources. Architecture and urban systems depend heavily on resources and more complex substances that come from far away. This has inspired new building paradigms and manufacturing processes, as well as anomalies in the global distribution of construction resources and its associated ecological and social impact. As part of this development, the amount of data needed to monitor, assess, and control material – flow – performance has grown exponentially, both in number and complexity.

This chapter examines material flows together with their spatial and geographical characteristics. The concept of *circularity* receives specific attention in this respect, due to its inherent potential for curbing wasteful side-effects of linear economic processes and approaches. Focus is placed on the geographical distribution of resources in general, followed by an exploration of resource flows associated with the AEC sector. This leads to a discussion of material stocks and material flows in the built environment, distinguishing fast flows, which are often human induced, from slow flows of natural progression, while outlining the role of Material Flow Analysis (MFA). MFA is further addressed in relation to recent developments and data requirements, looking at new ways of defining system boundaries and shifting towards higher resolutions of detail. Subsequently, the urban metabolism metaphor takes center stage, by way of examining macroeconomic data-processing. This is followed by an examination of the human scale, considering local conditions, vernacular architecture, and notions of 'genius loci'. Next, the non-linear movement of substances through human societies is addressed, unraveling aspects of sustainability and circularity through various concepts, notably the circular economy and circularity in the built environment. Both concepts gained significant traction in the last decades. The focus then shifts to spatial and territorial implications of global resource flows, which are often overlooked but become extremely relevant in relation to sustainable, circular economy propositions. The term *value* is crucial in this context, looking at (product) design with its associated business models and networks of decision-making. Geodesign-based methods come into view, aimed at close collaborations between stakeholders and decision-makers throughout entire processes, starting at problem identification and finishing at proposed interventions.

Furthermore, material tracking techniques and material passports are addressed, pinpointing multiple facets and criteria that are at stake in this domain. Material ID-systems, once enriched with high quality data, regarding material flows, environmental impact, Building Information Modeling (BIM) and Geographic Information Systems (GIS), among other factors, are becoming indispensable and meaningful tools in architecture and (urban) design. Consequently, such methods are also becoming increasingly intricate and complex. The outlook highlights a few developments and innovations revolving around the topic of material flows, space, and data, specifically considering ways to better measure, monitor, and understand the associated systemic complexities.

4.2 GEOGRAPHICAL DISTRIBUTION OF RESOURCES

Natural resources – clean water and air, materials, energy, and arable soil – are the basis of human society. When poorly managed, they can also be the basis of social upheaval or collapse. This was convincingly addressed in the first Limits to Growth report (Club of Rome, 1972), based on computerized datasets for systemic impact, and confirmed in later updates with alarming conclusions (Meadows et al., 1972; Meadows et al., 2004). Throughout the twentieth century, the world increased its fossil fuel use by a factor of 12, while extracting 34 times more material resources (Tukker et al., 2013; Moreno and Garcia-Alvarez, 2018). Although relative decoupling of population growth and resource use intensity has occurred over the last decades, this effect is overshadowed by an ongoing absolute rise in global resource extraction. Despite a slowing growth rate, the global population continues to grow, and will exceed 9 billion by 2050 and 10 billion by 2100 according to studies by the United Nations (UN, 2022). Most of this growth is expected to take place in emerging economies, particularly in cities (UN, 2022; UNEP, 2011). The growing demand for natural resources is not backed by evenly growing supplies. On the contrary, despite slight fluctuations (temporary lower demand associated with global crises followed by quick recovery) significant constraints can be discerned on energy resources, water, land, biotic and abiotic resources (Tukker et al., 2013; IEA, 2008; Haberl et al., 2004). However, not all constraints are equally alarming and, more importantly for this chapter, constraints are strongly context-dependent, not least geographically. Concerning construction minerals, for example, limits on extraction are especially felt in small, densely populated countries (Tukker et al., 2013). Most countries are exporters of some and importers of other resources, but the center of gravity regarding massive international trade flows has shifted to the BRIICS countries (Brazil, Russia, India, Indonesia, China, South Africa). Global trade is back at – and above – pre-pandemic levels, hitting a record level of 28.5 trillion US dollar in 2021 (UNCTAD, 2022). Transboundary trade has helped alleviate some of the disparities in the distribution of resources (OECD, 2021). But if prosperity for all without exceeding planetary boundaries is a global goal, then resource use can no longer be approached with existing measures of efficiency and trade alone (Rockstrom et al., 2009). According to a recent report by the Intergovernmental Panel on Climate Change, overall resource management and efficiency are still not well understood and addressed from a policy perspective, leading to severe, irreversible ecological impacts (IPCC, 2022). Although multiple sustainable options can be discerned for demand management, materials efficiency, and circular material flows to curb or reduce negative effects, how those options are best applied varies strongly across regions and material types (IPCC, 2022). Alongside the spatial distribution of resources, there is a spatial differentiation of measures. This implies a need for interconnected generic, as well as contextualized intelligence.

The AEC industry depends on resources. Physical substances are required as processed goods that materialize ideas into subsets of our built surroundings. To process and transport these goods, other resources are required, such as energy, water, and land. Furthermore, architecture is essentially a manifestation of interactions between man-made and natural phenomena. When interpreted as a synergistic bond, this could be part of 'design for human ecosystems' (Lyle, 1985). This holistic perspective on resource use, differentiated in both time and space, is inextricably linked to the act of design and construction. However, developments in this direction have accelerated and become complex in ways virtually impossible to oversee and comprehend (Ioannou et al., 2022). Instead of relatively straightforward vernacular architecture and construction activities, which depend largely on local skills, labor, and resources (materials, energy, water, land), contemporary urban environments are often dependent on faraway resources and associated supply-chains, which are obscured from view. The construction sector is hugely important for overall global resource use, and its associated negative environmental impact. It accounts for an estimated 40 percent share of global energy use (of which 80 percent is fossil-fuel based), 39 percent of all greenhouse gas (GHG) emissions, up to 40 percent of waste generation, and 50 percent of all the extracted materials (GABC, 2019; UNEP 2022). Thus far, sustainable building initiatives have not had a substantial effect on the global footprint of the construction industry. The UN reported a trend of incremental improvements in energy efficiency in recent years, but with a persistent discrepancy between relative and absolute decoupling, and concluded that solutions must go beyond technology and carbon efficiency gains alone (UNEP, 2022):

/ The sector's emissions intensity in kilograms of CO_2 per square meter dropped from 43 in 2015 to 40 in 2021.

/ Energy intensity in kilowatts per hour per square meter slightly decreased, from 153 in 2015 to 152 in 2021.

/ Investments in building energy efficiency rose by 16 per cent in 2021 compared to 2020 levels, reaching USD 237 billion.

/ The sector's growth is outpacing all efforts on energy efficiency and reduced energy intensity.

Fig. 68
The concept of 'relative' and 'absolute' decoupling between economic growth and resource use with associated environmental pressure.

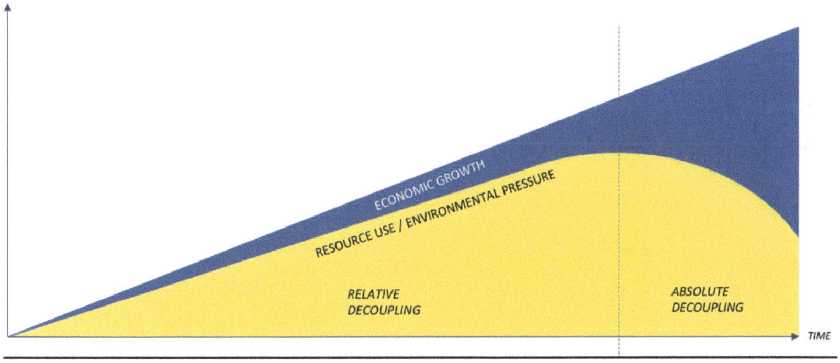

Fig. 68

4.3 SLOW FLOWS AND FAST FLOWS

Flows in the built environment are often faster and less complete than those in nature. It can be said that these anthropogenic flows comprise short-cyclic subsets of larger ecological systems. However, this suggests a false pretense of synergism. The tragic paradox is that many man-made systems depend greatly on the movement of energy, materials and water at volumes and speeds that compromise the very functioning of ecological foundations for human comfort. This underscores the key field of interest for this section; namely to understand material stocks and material flows from the vantage point of sustainable resource management. In this section, we address common stocks and flows in the built environment, as well as insights and innovations to align stocks and flows with environmental and social quality.

Fig. 69

Fig. 69 Fast flows of single-use plastics can leak into slow biogeochemical cycles (Photo: B. Geldermans, 2024)

Analyzing material stocks can be rather simple and straightforward but also extremely elaborate and complex, depending on the purpose. Basically, stocks are inventories of materials multiplied by a certain factor of use-intensity (Arora et al., 2019). Looking at the built environment, rudimentary data of applied, *embodied* materials can already generate useful statistics and guide urban development strategies in the face of environmental or social challenges. Based on averages regarding material use and lifespan per built typology, for example, large contributors to carbon-footprints can be identified. Policymakers could then decide to avoid premature demolition of buildings or limit the use of energy-intensive and scarce materials. On a macro-economic level such analyses provide data concerning resources and emissions attributed to domestic or foreign activities. Stocks are thus never static but rather comprise 'stagnant flows', representing the throughput resulting from input minus output. This connects to the first law of thermodynamics: matter can be neither created nor destroyed in any physical transformation process (mass balance principle). Material inputs into a system must therefore always equal material outputs plus net accumulation of materials in the system (Fischer-Kowalski et al., 2011). Such accounting methods are data-heavy and require well-defined system boundaries. In recent decades, the toolbox in this realm has expanded and become more refined. The method of Material Flow Analysis (MFA) takes center stage in this development. Data on material stocks and material flows greatly helps to reveal the associated complexity and reduces the challenges of managing them sustainably.

Stocks and flows of materials in a chosen geographical boundary and temporally defined system can be studied and assessed by means of Material Flow Analyses (Brunner and Rechberger, 2004; Broto et al., 2012). Such systems need to be well-defined to work within the emerging boundaries, and could take the shape of countries, companies, or any other administrative configuration. The purpose of an MFA study, and the associated system boundary, determine the data requirements and data availability. MFA integrates specific sequences of material processes within the given system: from extraction, production, and manufacturing, to storage, use, and discharge. Notions of material movement, accumulation, scarcity and availability come to the surface, as well as those of emissions and waste. This has made MFA the go-to method for identifying and quantifying material flow patterns in the face of resource-related concerns at different scale-levels. However, the downside is that conventional MFA applies a 'black box' approach (Furlan et al., 2020). This means that only the *inputs* and *outputs* of main processes are studied and balanced, leaving the inner workings – i.e., those processes between input and output of (sub)systems – largely unexplored. It is believed that hidden within these intricate inner networks of material processing lies one of the keys to more sustainable societies, certainly relating to products and services in envisioned circular economies (Geldermans, 2016). Thus, knowledge and data associated with these inner workings need to be unlocked and applied in ways that serve the greater good, without violating regulations of consent. Research and practice must go beyond the physical study of material flows and study socioeconomic consequences at a deeper level (Bruel et al., 2019). Informed by contemporary demands, MFA is further developing, tapping into other tools

Fig. 70
Basic concept of MFA within a system boundary

and methods, such as Input-Output Analyses (I-O), Life Cycle Assessment (LCA) and Geographic Information Systems (GIS), and datasets concerning economic activities or waste patterns on a local level, for example. To this end, Meglin et al. (2022), developed a model aimed at critical hotspots for decision-makers to move from linear to circular resource strategies for construction and demolition waste in the Swiss context (Meglin et al., 2022). This model showed, among other things, that associated legislation needs to focus on actors on the *demand side*, purchasing secondary resources, rather than – or as well as – the *supply* sector. A similar approach of linking CDW flows to policy making was deployed within the project *Resource management in Peri-urban Areas* (REPAiR) for several European regions (Varju et al., 2020).

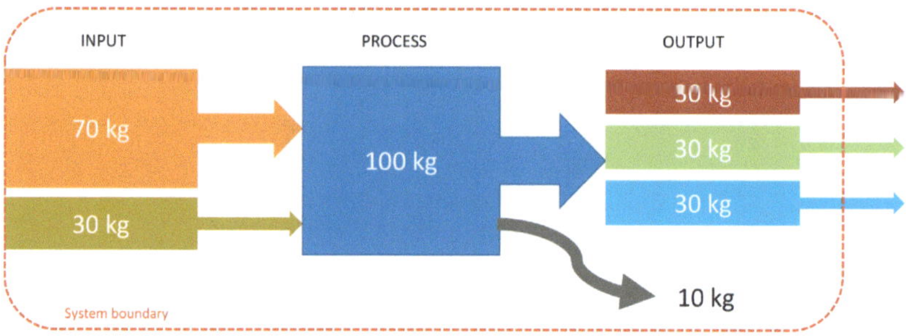

Fig. 70

4.4 MATERIALS, FLOWS, AND DATA

New Material Flow Analysis developments, based on the integration of critical flow-features, aim to tap into specific 'tailored' data such as the material composition of products, volumes, geographical coordinates, and temporal patterns. This usually involves multi-layered sets of information which are not easy to understand and generally defined as Big Data, in which 'big' refers to complexity, not necessarily size (Ward and Barker, 2013; Xu et al., 2015). Complexity, in this context, relates to factors such as heterogeneity in data types and sources, differences in terminology, and lack of structure (Furlan et al., 2021; Sileryte et al., 2022). At a macroeconomic level, material flow data associated with construction are gradually becoming more abundant and sophisticated. In 2023, the Circular Building Coalition, a collaboration between consultancies and non-profit organizations, published a report to support the 'circular transition' while examining challenges related to market, finance, and ownership. An MFA was generated for construction material use in Europe, distinguishing 12 material input categories, four Euro-zones, and nine building typologies (Fig. 71). It also analyzed and mapped which process methods are applied to construction waste from Europe (Fig. 72).

Multiple MFA studies operating at lower – city or metropolitan – scale levels were scrutinized in the EU funded CityLoops project, while aiming to elaborate further on the potential of coupling MFA with the concept of circular material use in cities (Bellstedt et al., 2022). Table 2 shows the indicators that were identified as key to measuring the level of circularity of urban metabolism regarding total material use. The associated data are quantifiable in terms of mass or ratios. The notion of urban metabolisms' is further explored in Section 4.4.

Fig. 71
MFA of construction material use in Europe per building typology in kilotons. Courtesy of: Circular Building Coalition, 2023.

Fig. 72
MFA of construction waste from Europe in relation to process methods in kilotons. Courtesy of: Circular Building Coalition, 2023.

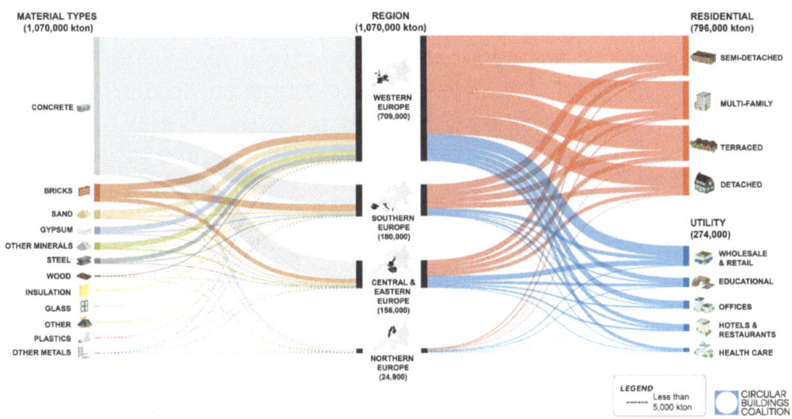

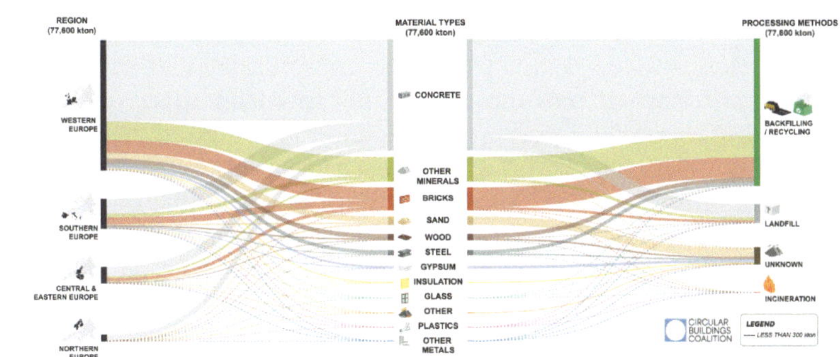

Figs. 71, 72

	scale indicators						
	input/output		*city correction*	*interim flows*	*material loop closing*	*balance*	
INPUT-SIDE INDICATOR	direct material input	domestic material consump-tion	domestic material consump-tion corrected	processed materials	secondary materials	net addi-tion to stock	
OUTPUT-SIDE INDICATOR	domestic processed output	x	local and exported processed output	interim outputs	secondary materials	net addi-tion to stock	

Table 2

For the Amsterdam Metropolitan Area (AMA), Delft University of Technology developed a method to gain grip on construction and demolition waste originating and departing from commercial activities in the region, to respond to circular economy strategies of the AMA administration (City of Amsterdam, 2020). This method, termed the Activity-based Spatial Material Flow Analysis method (AS-MFA), links waste activities to actors, providing spatial significance through a Geographic Information System and material significance through a waste classification system. Various existing datasets are joined in the AS-MFA, together with additional information for obtaining a high level of representativeness regarding the material flow simulation. Existing databases include the *Nomenclature d'Activités économiques dans la Communauté Européenne* (NACE) to classify economic activities; the European Waste Catalog (EWC) to classify waste; and the ORBIS database for a list of private companies. Additional information concerns, among others, mass, energy, emissions, monetary units, and social standards. The AS-MFA aims at the output side and does not prioritize the inclusion of input and throughput. Rather than enabling a full-blown yet crude mass balance, it builds on data points that are later aggregated in different ways to better understand the associated complexity (Furlan et al., 2021). As such, AS-MFA explicitly works with bottom-up data. Furthermore, the AS-MFA includes data points *outside* of the chosen system boundary, based on their flow relation to data points *within* the geographic delineation. These flows are represented on a map with the same level of detail (Fig. 73).

	circularity indicators				
	rates			*efficiency*	*intensity*
physical trade balance	input socio-economic cycling rate	input ecological cycling rate potential	input non-circularity rate	material productivi-ty	material intensity
physical trade balance	output socio-economic cycling rate	output ecological cycling rate potential	output non-circularity rate	material productivi-ty	material intensity

Table 2
City loops circularity indicators (based on Bellstedt et al., 2022)

Fig. 73
Outward flows from the Amsterdam Metropolitan Area colored according to European Waste Catalog codes, relative to 2016. Courtesy of: Delft University of Technology.

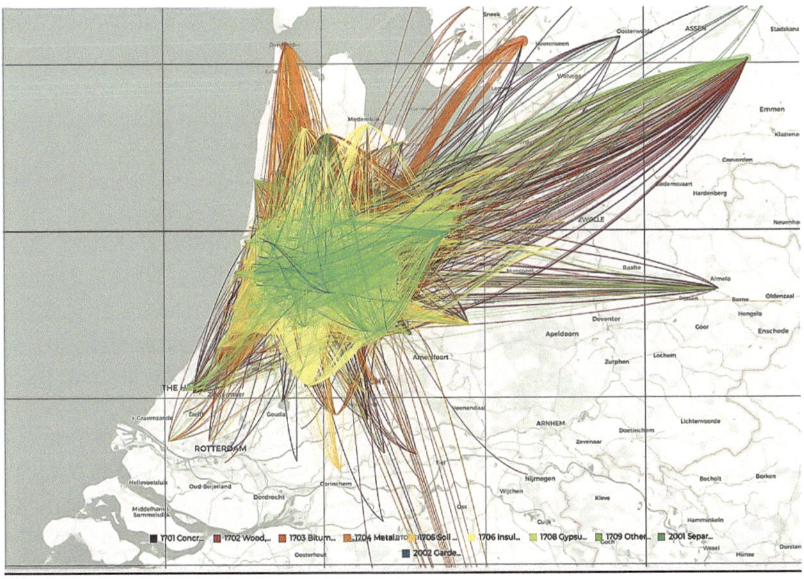

Fig. 73

Closely connected to MFA, the concept of *urban metabolism* describes the flows of resources *in* (e.g., energy, materials, water), resources *out* (e.g., waste, heat, pollutants, residual materials), and resources *within* (stocks) a given – urbanized – system boundary. Urban metabolism (UM) is a metaphor, conceptualizing cities as living organisms (Lucertini and Musco, 2020). In the 1960s, Wolman (1965) coined the UM concept, aiming to understand resource processes of a hypothetical town (Wolman, 1965). Kennedy et al. broadened the UM definition to "the sum total of the technical and socioeconomic processes that occur in cities, resulting in growth, production of energy, and elimination of waste" (Kennedy et al., 2007, p. 44). Metabolism-thinking, per definition, binds resource-use to temporal factors. Time is an essential factor in the distance (space) between origin and destination. This is true for the natural world as much as it is applicable to the built environment, while facilitating human needs and identities.

UM has emerged as a prime methodology for quantifying patterns of use and consumption in urban environments, but it has older roots (Pincetl et al., 2012). Key principles of UM can be traced back to Marx's approach to analyze "dynamic internal relationships between humans and nature" (Heynen et al., 2006, p. 7). According to Foster (2000), Marx applied the concept of metabolism to express the human relationship to nature as one that encompassed both nature-imposed conditions and the capacity of human beings to affect this process (Foster, 2000; Pincetl et al., 2012). In the last century, the UM metaphor has increasingly been applied to model metabolic processes and resource management in cities. One of the oldest known studies with a comprehensive urban metabolism perspective was conducted by ecologists Duvigneaud and Denaeyer-De Smet in the city of Brussels, Belgium (Duvigneaud and Denaeyer-De Smet, 1977). UM studies provide insights based on highly aggregated data, which are usually too rudimentary to be of any significant use in the face of flow pattern complexities that modern urban societies deal with. However, expanded urban metabolism frameworks have been developed, based on combined tools and disaggregated data. For example, Pincetl et al. suggested analyzing biophysical material and energy parameters of cities in relation to the organizational – social, cultural, political, financial – (sub-)systems that structure and govern these parameters (Pincetl et al., 2012). Furthermore, in their 2023 report on market, finance, and ownership challenges, the Circular Building Coalition analyzed the current import of construction materials for the built stock of Europe, as well as the output. Their findings underscored the fact that, since the start of the industrial age and throughout the twentieth century, global material trade has gradually taken over the material identities of many buildings and cities (Fig. 74).

Figures 75 and 76 use a framework and data developed by *The Growth Lab* at Harvard University. They contain detailed macro-economic info on the resource use of nations and continents. This example shows the bulk category 'ores, slag and ash' (prime raw materials for contemporary construction products) imported to and exported from Europe between 1995 and 2020, with distributed percentages. The data-processing is based on 'harmonized systems' as part of the Structural Analysis Database (STAN). STAN is a tool for analyzing industrial performance at a relatively detailed level of activity across countries, including annual measures of output, value added and its components, labor input, investment, and capital stock, from 1970 onwards. This allows users to construct a wide range of indicators and to focus on areas such as productivity growth, competitiveness, and general structural change. STAN uses standard industry lists compatible with those presented in OECD databases, while enabling international comparisons. STAN is primarily based on member countries' annual national accounts by activity tables and any missing detail is estimated using other sources of data, such as national business surveys/censuses, which are maintained by OECD, Eurostat or compiled directly from national sources. Many of the data points in STAN are estimated and flagged for the attention of users. in other words, they do not represent official member country submissions (OECD, 2023). Multiple factors determine the nature of these trade details, including geopolitical forces and resource availability, but the common denominator in such – international trade – accounting systems is usually the monetary unit (European Central Bank, 2003).

Fig. 74
Import and export of construction materials to and from the EU in kilotons. Courtesy of: Circular Building Coalition, 2023.

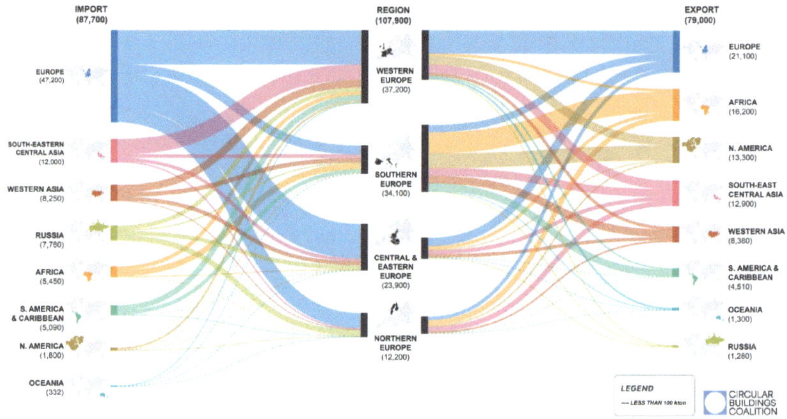

Fig. 75
Gross import of ores, slag and ash to Europe, 1995–2020 (Data from The Atlas of Economic Complexity/The Growth Lab at Harvard University. http://www.atlas.cid.harvard.edu.).

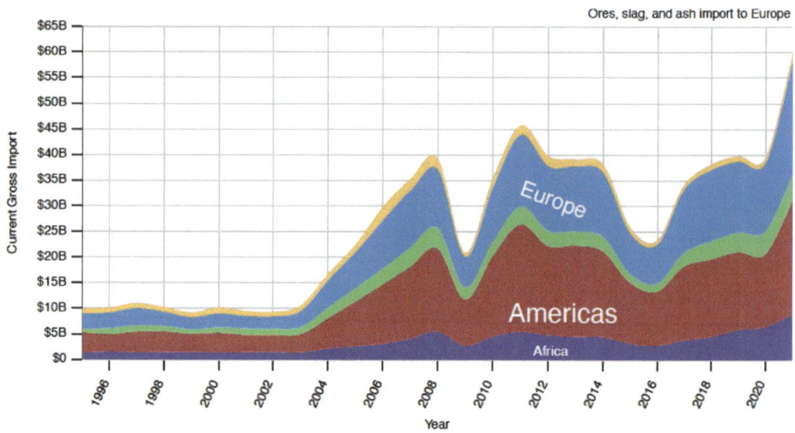

Fig. 76
Gross export of ores, slag and ash from Europe, 1995–2020 (Data from The Atlas of Economic Complexity/The Growth Lab at Harvard University. http://www.atlas.cid.harvard.edu.).

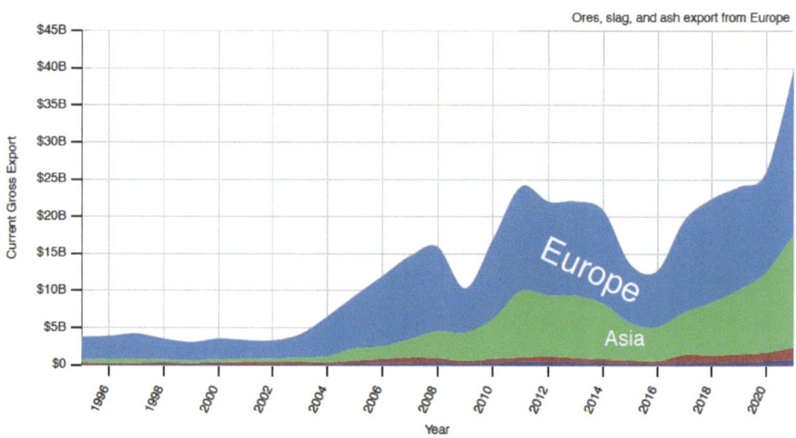

Figs. 74–76

Buildings are dynamic and heterogeneous entities, not static and homogenous ones. They are human-made configurations comprising a myriad of materials temporarily assembled in a functional order on a given geographic location. Aside from those examples that serve an intended long term, for religious or spiritual purposes, for example, many vernacular buildings and building techniques inherently carry notions of temporality and ease of assembly and disassembly, not only in anticipation of changing circumstances but also in awareness of material behavior over time and in specific local conditions. Twentieth-century urban regions, certainly those that rapidly developed after WWII, followed different patterns, informed by housing needs, industrialized production, international trade, shifts in societal priorities, and other forces that left little attention for "deep currents of form, place, and understanding flow" of our environments (Habraken, 2000). Knowledge and know-how of construction practices became more fragmented, in tandem with the distributed control of building parts (Kendall, 1990). This new complexity around architecture demanded a systemic organization that came much later, through the development of computer science. By the late 1950s and early 1960s, several practitioners and scholars had critiqued the modernist urban planning and architecture of that time, arguing that it oversimplified the complexity of human lives (Jacobs, 1961; Habraken, 1961; Alexander, 1977; Brand, 1994). To an important extent, these critiques are all related to the neglect of 'genii loci' and the obliteration of human connections with the 'flows' of their environments. This is important, in the context of this book, as it can be identified as one of the key drivers for establishing new means to exchange data for thriving buildings, neighborhoods, and cities. From the vantage point of materials and architectural data, the work of Stewart Brand is particularly compelling, especially his *The Whole Earth Catalog* ("access to tools") in the 1970s and the *How Buildings Learn* ("what happens after they're built") book and TV series in the 1990s. The latter has been at the core of renewed approaches to analyzing architecture and engineering in accordance with sustainability concerns.

Human needs and identities are at the heart of vernacular architecture. In 'Genius Loci – Towards a phenomenology of architecture', Christian Norberg Schulz starts from the premise that architecture provides existential grip for humanity. Not the func-

Fig. 77
Vernacular architecture built with local materials in Fukushima, Japan, late 18th/early 19th century (Photo: B. Geldermans, 2009)

tional aspect of building, living – and working – marks the difference, but the deeper *meaning* of architecture, in sync with daily life (Norberg-Schulz, 1979). From that perspective, architecture is thus intrinsically intertwined with local conditions, such as climate and biotic and abiotic factors. This leads to a range of constructed typologies, including cities built from local 'mud', such as the high-rise architectures at Shibam, Wadi Hadhramout in Yemen. Salman (2019) distinguishes five definitions of 'vernacular architecture', pinpointing the relevance of geography for material use in construction (Salman, 2019):

/ Vernacular architecture is unpretentious, simple, indigenous, traditional structures made of local materials, and following well-tried forms and types (Curl, 2006).
/ Vernacular architecture is an architecture style that develops from the climate and social conditions of a place (Kennedy, 2004).
/ In vernacular architecture, each tradition is intimately related to the social and economic imperatives it has developed to meet specific needs within each cultural milieu (Oliver, 1998).
/ Vernacular architecture offers dramatic metaphors for regional forms of shelter, as well as rational responses to the local climate (Abel, 2000).
/ Vernacular architecture is the built environment (city, architecture, and interior spaces) created based on the society's needs. It is built in accordance with the natural environment (geography, topography, site, climate, local materials, labor experience, and building techniques) fulfilling people's physical, economic, social, and cultural norms (Hmood, 2019).

Fig. 77

Fig. 78

Fig. 78
Air-conditioning equipment depends on global material flows and local air (Photo: B. Geldermans, 2023)

Next to materials that comprise buildings or building interiors, for longer periods of time (years, decades, centuries), multiple resources flow 'through' buildings in faster cycling rates (hours, days, weeks), to sustain the lives of the building users. Notable transient flows are related to air, heat, electricity, water, food, and beverages, as well as associated packaging materials (glass, plastics, cardboard, paper), and waste. Although such flows are not part of 'built hardware', they determine physical architectural and urban outcomes/manifestations to a large extent. Although this relationship has lost its relevance somewhat in contemporary construction developments, its existence has always been self-evident. This includes, for example, settlements near essential resources and architectural designs to increase daylight penetration or avoid

Fig. 79

Fig. 79
As this example shows, air-conditioning has also been added to traditional buildings, resulting in redundancy of traditional methods of interior climate modulation and often in building maintenance problems. This photo shows an air-conditioning unit in the courtyard of a traditional residence in Yazd, Iran. Buildings like this are characterized by a well calibrated relationship between the use of local materials, spatial dimensions, consideration of size and number of openings in exterior walls, and airflow as a key element of interior environment modulation, facilitated by traditional wind towers. Photography: Michael Hensel, 2006.

overheating. Driven by a renewed awareness of sustainability issues, transient flows are increasingly anticipated in building and urban development plans. For example, solutions for water and space heating are more often sought locally, rather than being dependent on energy carriers from faraway places. Apart from the associated transport miles (notably of fossil fuels, such as coal, oil, and gas) and the unsustainable profile of these raw materials, geopolitical forces are a huge factor here. However, nowadays, the global transboundary shipments of fossil fuels for the built environment far outstrip the share of local – and renewable – sources (IEA, 2023). With respect to materials, particular attention should be given to the materials that are required to produce the technological equipment and infrastructure, for instance, HVAC and photovoltaics, many of which come with serious concerns due to critical metal content (Schrijvers et al., 2020).

4.7 CIRCULARITY

Circularity, in the context of this book, refers to the non-linear movement of substances through human societies. These include natural resources, such as biotic or abiotic materials, but could also refer to 'human-made' materials. Natural resources concern all naturally occurring living and nonliving elements of the earth system on which humans depend to survive and thrive (Bansard and Schroder, 2021). Human-made materials (substances and goods), on the other hand, do not naturally occur, but are produced by humans – or human-made machinery – and are aimed at satisfying our needs and wants. The nonlinearity aspect of circularity stands in opposition to the 'Take, Make, Waste' paradigm, based on one-directional movements from raw materials to waste, which are central to most contemporary economic systems (EMF, 2013). Circularity is thus essentially a dynamic concept, focused on cyclic flows of materials through temporal and spatial scales. As a concept with metaphorical qualities, it is open to multiple readings and schools of thought, but some academic consensus has emerged in the last decade as to what circularity entails for the built environment. This chapter examines that consensus, describing the basics and associated data requirements. The following definition of circularity is adhered to: Circularity is the movement of parts – substances, materials, products, components – through a system and constituent sub-systems in shorter or longer loops, either avoiding premature degradation of comprised materials and substances or promoting biodegradation by design.

Basic principles of circularity, as defined above, can be traced back to pre-industrial times, but gained renewed relevance through environmental awareness as of the 1960s, and the notion of sustainable economic development in the 1980s (Boulding, 1966; Stahel, 1981; Brundtland et al., 1982; Hynes, 1989). The first explicit mention of associated terminology can be attributed to Stahel and Reday in their report on substituting manpower for energy for the Commission of European Communities (1977), in which economic efficiencies of labor and resources were examined. Their basic rationale was that for any stock or capital it takes fewer resources to refurbish than to make new ones, forming the fundamentals of the 'performance economy' (Stahel and Reday, 1981). In the 1990s, chemist Michael Braungart and architect William McDonough developed the design concept Cradle to Cradle® (C2C), challenging the emphasis on economic efficiencies in sustainability concepts, while shifting the focus to effective, positive impact through biological and technological loops of resources (Braungart and McDonough, 2002). C2C explicitly internalized ethical aspects along supply chains as well as health and wellbeing concerns. The concept of circular economy got a boost in 2012 with the first publication from the Ellen MacArthur Foundation: 'Towards the Circular Economy: Economic and Business Rationale for an Accelerated Transition'. Based on these – academic and practical – grounds, in conjunction with systems approaches such as *regenerative design*, *industrial ecology*, and *urban metabolism*, the core and enabling elements of circularity for the built environment were formed (Table 3).

Klein et al. (CBE Hub, TU Delft) developed a 'scales to aspects' model for circularity in the built environment, highlighting interrelations across scales and between six key aspects that influence the circularity potential in construction value chains (CBE Hub, 2023). This model shows that a circular material flow perspective usually comprises multiple viewpoints in a systemic affair. Figure 80 represents that 'scales to aspects' model. The outer ring displays six aspects that condition the scale interdependencies, from materials to regions (Ioannou et al., 2020). A virtually limitless list of agents may thus be involved in building projects, from initiation (pre-use) through operation (in-use) and discharge (post-use/re-use). Physical materials, knowledge, and data flow between these agents.

Table 3
Key elements of the circular economy (Based on: Circle Economy, 2021)

Fig. 80
Interconnected scales and conditioning aspects. Courtesy of: Circularity in the Built Environment Hub, 2023.

CORE ELEMENTS	ENABLING ELEMENTS
Prioritize regenerative resources: Ensure renewable, reusable, non-toxic resources are utilized as materials and energy in an efficient way.	Rethink the business model: Consider opportunities to create greater value and align incentives through business models that build on the interaction between products and services.
Stretch the lifetime: While resources are in use, maintain, repair, and upgrade them to maximize their lifetime and support subsequent use iterations through adaptive design and take back strategies.	Team up to create joined value: Work together throughout the supply chain, internally within organizations and with the public sector to increase transparency and create joint value.
Use residual flows as an input: Utilize residual streams – such as waste and emissions – as a source of secondary resources and recover them for reuse and recycling.	Design for the future: Account for a systems perspective during the design process, by using the right materials, designing for an appropriate lifetime, and for extended future use.
	Incorporate digital technologies: Track and optimize resource use and strengthen connections between supply chain actors through digital, online platforms and technologies that provide insights.
	Strengthen and advance knowledge: Develop research, structure knowledge, encourage innovation networks, and disseminate findings with integrity.

Table 3

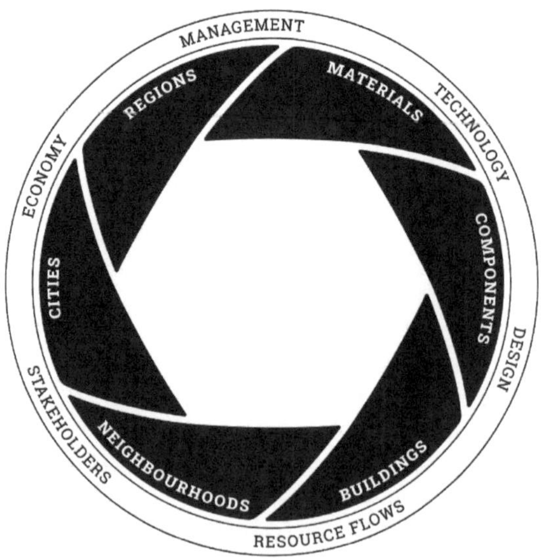

Fig. 80

Fig. 81
Loops to support optimal material use in a circular economy. One or more of the loops are part of designed circular intentions with an integrated scope: from shorter 'inner' loops for extending the service life of materials and products (maintenance, repair, internal reuse) to strategies for external 'life-extension' (reuse, remanufacturing and refurbishing), and recycling as the designated strategy to close loops on a raw-material level, avoiding material destruction through incineration (with or without energy recovery).

Key elements of the circular economy (CE) have spatial and territorial implications that follow different 'rules' than flows and stocks in the – linear – economy as we know it, but are often neglected or overlooked (Tapia et al., 2021). Our prevailing global market economy, based on the production and exchange of goods and services according to supply and demand, allows for the integration of mechanisms that support sustainability goals, as is demonstrated around the world, not least in China, Europe, and the United States of America (Neves and Marques, 2022; Ranta et al., 2018). However, many barriers obstruct the shift towards a circular, more regenerative, paradigm in material use. Path-dependent socio-industrial systems, related to (transnational) trade agreements and waste management go hand-in-hand with infrastructural implementations that are not easily circumvented. This weighs heavily on global material dispersion. Operations that are becoming more local are often dependent on global material markets as well, particularly those relating to renewable energy technologies (Tsui et al., 2020; Hagelükken et al., 2016). Moreover, the 'inner loops' of a circular economy – designed for local collection, maintenance/repair, and reuse (Fig. 81) – have the most effect; that is, the least costs and resources, and the most direct value retention. This implies that in a circular economy multiple operations take place nearby. These two juxtaposed perspectives of material flows and stocks in a circular configuration – local and global – are further addressed below.

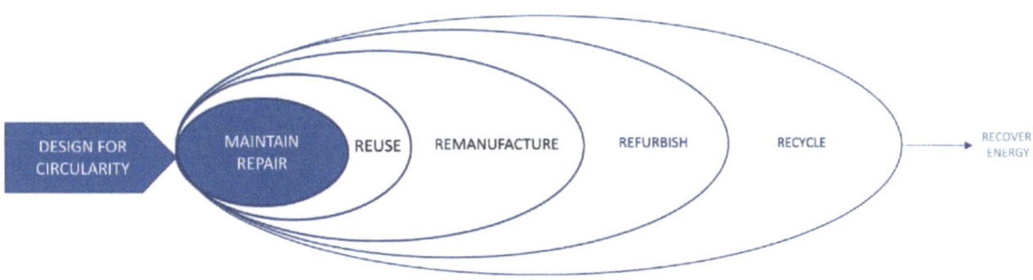

Fig. 81

Because cyclic, regenerative, and adaptive actions are central to circular development, it is imperative to designate space and infrastructure supportive of these circular actions in city-regions (Williams, 2020). Consequently, an important role is attributed to urban planning, to facilitate symbiotic relationships between industries, and allow for optimal storage and handling of temporarily 'homeless' construction materials, for example. Moreover, urban planning based on property speculation – which is common practice in many cities around the world, especially those that are space-scarce – needs to be reconsidered, since it has resulted in the loss of industrial land to luxury commercial and residential development (Jessica and Jones, 2016; Williams, 2020). A circular economy has the power to integrate both sustainable and inclusive objectives, if based on democratic principles of urban development. The role and position of urban manufacturing is an interesting one in that respect, because it holds a two-directional promise. On the one hand, urban manufacturing assumes the empowerment of the 'maker movement', enabling local communities to share resources, while securing optimal operations of maintenance and repair. On the other hand, there is no evidence that urban manufacturers are embedded locally, making use of local suppliers, produce for a local consumer base, and contribute to local economic development (Tsui et al., 2020). Moreover, 'micro-impacts' taking place in the direct surroundings of circular urban activities may be perceived as negative effects, such as nuisances of noise and smell coming from certain manufacturing processes, or increased transport movements associated with local material handling (Tsui et al., 2020). In essence, an envisioned circular built environment would develop in close interaction between multiple actors, such as citizens, planners, architects, financial institutes, real estate developers, public authorities, material producers, suppliers, knowledge centers, and other (inter-) national organizations. Based on that notion, circular built environments include 'unbuilt environments' and can be regarded as a complex adaptive multi-level network of local to non-local material and immaterial resources, assets, institutions, and entities (Bucci Ancapi et al., 2022). Such systemic affairs require additional guidance on spatially aware material-circularity:

- Training urban planners and designers to include material-flow thinking.
- Understanding the land and soil impact of the – linear and circular – economy.
- Establishing co-creation processes across scales and value chains.
- Differentiating governance approaches to engage stakeholders and diffuse knowledge.
- Learning between cities and regions.
- Developing integrated spatial decision environments.

Alongside causes and effects of local activities, the spatial impact of a circular material economy is felt globally. Looking at several important metals, Graedel et al. concluded that it is virtually impossible to achieve a circular economy at the level of a single country (Graedel et al., 2019). Observing that many architectural designs and interventions nowadays involve technological solutions to deal with questions of energy provision and climate control, concerns over critical raw materials are increasing. Although architectural materialization has become an international affair *tout court*, specific minerals and metals, such as aluminum, copper, lithium, nickel, cobalt, and indium, are at the heart of strategic reports (Vogtlander et al., 2019; EC, 2018; IEA, 2022). Ironically, many reports and strategies (for industries or governments alike) are informed by financial and geopolitical concerns, rather than ecological awareness (IPCC, 2022; Van der Voet, 2022). Focusing on global spatial impact, however, an ever-increasing amount of evidence is unlocked, and – if it had ever been – is no longer sensible to ignore the real impact hidden behind abiotic depletion, marine aquatic ecotoxicity, global warming, or any other form of environmental and social damage. Those terms comprise very tangible effects, often elsewhere or later in time. In that respect, every global impact is local.

Most of the major supplier countries of critical raw materials (CRM) to the European Union are in other continents, notably Asia, Africa, and North and South America (European Commission, 2023). Zooming into these locations reveals the spatial impact caused by some of these extraction operations. And something similar is happening further downstream, where the impacts continue in distributed ways, associated with manufacturing, transport, construction, demolition, and discharging activities. A poignant example is the use of extruded polystyrene foam in packaging and insulation materials, grains of which are found on land and in water bodies around the globe, containing so-called 'forever chemicals' that bioaccumulate in organisms (Hale et al., 2020). Quantifying the environmental persistence and spatial distribution of such materials is still in its infancy (Ward and Reddy, 2020). This underscores the importance of geospatial reference data, combining high-quality datasets to enhance the evidence base of spatial ecological and social impact.

Against the backdrop of ecological awakening and sustainable development goals, the license to operate for design and architecture seems to be in circular material models rather than linear ones. Even if the ins and outs of a circular economy are not yet fully understood, let alone set in stone, it provides a model that is more in sync with the notion of slow and fast material flows, as addressed in former subchapters. Circularity leads to inherently richer datasets, since it implies that materials circulate between multiple actors, all of which assign potentially different meanings and purpose to the material in question. Meaning attributed to materials may once have been in tacit agreement with what nature offered us, but that has largely faded. Circular and regenerative models dictate that materials can no longer be without value. A material may lose value for the actor who wishes to dispose of it, but there is always a next application, maybe ultimately as a nutrient for the soil from which we source our food or building materials. Value is a relative term, but it relates to a positive quality, not a negative, wasteful, or damaging, one. There is more at stake than monetary value. Retaining the multifaceted value of materials and products requires a closer look at how associated actors are united in networks around values, interests, and decision-making (EMF, 2013).

Materials flow through our society in products and buildings. They have their origin in nature, to which they will ultimately return, while tapping into the Earth's metabolism. This inextricably binds our built environment to the natural one. To comply with this sustainably, we need to rethink materialization, not least from the perspective of interconnected networks of actors who claim some level of control over the materials. Achterberg et al. (2019) proposed the metaphor of a *value hill*, which works well to illustrate the flows of materials throughout design and business models. The value hill (VH) applies to strategies that either *add value* (uphill) or *retain value* (downhill), while avoiding the linear destruction of value (Achterberg et al., 2019). The VH highlights 'circular design', 'optimal use', and 'value recovery', adhering to circular and frameworks (Stahel, 1981; Bocken et al., 2016). Every step of the way comes with specific data requirements to safeguard an appropriate continuation of the intended – material-centric – business/value model (EMF, 2013; Cramer, 2014; Potting et al., 2016; Reike et al., 2018; Rood and Hanemaaijer, 2016). All product designs, and associated business models, have a material implication, and subsequently a material-*flow* implication. In orchestration it has the power to provide a comprehensive value system for any product that flows through society. To avoid material input in the first place, the starting point is to *rethink* the product or business rationale. Once materials are applied in a design that facilitates circularity, notions of maintenance and *repair* come into the picture, followed by value recovery through *reuse*, *refurbish*, *remanufacture*, and *recycle strategies* (Fig. 81). The objective is to keep products in the system without premature value destruction, while attributing intended circular pathways based on the nature of the products in question: from long lasting structural steel (service lives of centuries) to short cyclic insulation materials (service lives of decades).

Fig. 82
Lack of differentiated material value retention in conventional waste management. Photography: Bob Geldermans, 2022.

Fig. 82

To manage such intricate value networks optimally, appropriate governance and decision making is required on all relevant levels. Collaborative initiatives on the 'meso' (industry & community) levels have the potential to act as a bridge between 'micro' and 'macro', allowing integration from a material and product level to an urban planning level, while reflecting a combined top-down, bottom-up approach (Meath et al., 2022). This implies long and complex decision-making trajectories. To make this more manageable in concrete territorial settings, Arciniegas et al. developed an open-source tool based on a geo-design approach and co-creation relating to urban waste management and CE strategies (Arciniegas et al., 2019). This tool, the Geo-design Decision Support Environment (GDSE), is an example of what might be termed 'holistic decision-making', aimed at consensus that is reached between multiple actors or organizations with diverging interests or vantage points. *Geo-design* is a leading methodology to couple design proposals with impact simulations (Steinitz, 2012). It is based

Fig. 83
Bi-directional supply chain between materials and buildings in multiple process steps and with actor involvement. In circular economy configurations the complexity of such value networks increases.

on close collaboration between stakeholders and decision-makers throughout the entire process, starting at problem identification and finishing at proposed interventions. Specifically, the GDSE offers a framework for iterative decision processes, linking co-creation and design proposals to geographically referenced impact-simulations, systems thinking, and digital technology. Thus far, the tool has been applied for strategic planning in the Amsterdam Metropolitan Area, drawing on empirical evidence from the pioneering application of the tool to promote spatially explicit circular economy strategies.

4.10 MATERIAL TRACKING

Materials that make up buildings are usually transported from external locations, nearby or faraway, depending on the type of material and the building context. These materials 'flow' from somewhere, are then 'stored' and operate in a building context for a certain amount of time and are taken out of that context again, at predicted or unpredicted moments in time, to 'flow' to another location, either nearby or farther away. Flow-stock-flow pathways occur and reoccur at different frequencies but are in essence the fate of all building materials. Knowing the challenges regarding resource use, it is imperative to apply materials in the most efficient and effective way. Some control over these pathways or patterns is thus required.

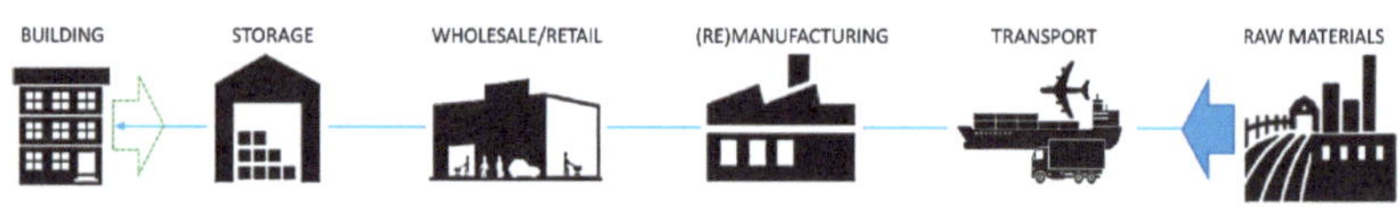

Fig. 83

This section focuses on material tracking techniques, pinpointing multiple aspects and criteria that are at stake. To take account of spatial and temporal distribution of materials, a lot of data are involved. These data are seldom homogeneous or in any other way harmonized to the needs of all stakeholders. Key is to keep track of the origin of materials (when from where, and via which routes), the composition of materials (what parts are distinguished and how is the material composed), the connection of the materials to the construction context (how is it assembled), its operation (how is the material used), and future (what happens after discharge). Additional to these five aspects (*origin, composition, connection, operation, future*) is the question of control (who takes decisions regarding the material throughout the whole cycle). If all information is available, optimal material flows can be facilitated. However, in most cases, practice is fractious. Parts change from rudimentary states to complex artifacts such as building components and buildings, they are deformed, have elements removed or added, and are assembled and disassembled (Kendall, 1990). The associated processes and operations, located in space and time, are of great interest, defining the level in which quality is lost, gained, or retained. Kendall (1990) referred to this phenomenon as 'the ecology of production' (and the significance of 'distributed control'). Until now, fragments of this concept have been integrated in tools such as environmental product declarations (EPD), life cycle analysis (LCA), material flow analyses (MFA), building information modeling (BIM), and multi-year maintenance planning frameworks (MMPF). However, the integration of whole – *origin, composition, connection, operation, future* – iterations, enhanced with notions of control and responsibility, is quite another matter. Even if modern computer software allows for mapping complex systems, attributes of daily life obstruct appropriate overarching management structures, relating to the highly diverse array of – partly unpredictable – relationships (Sargut and McGrath, 2011). Nonetheless, new insights and solutions emerged in recent years, not least driven by ecological awareness and sustainability realism. Notably the concept of *material passports* is important in this respect. Material passports are sets of data that describe defined characteristics of materials in products and buildings, providing them with an identity and giving them value for recovery and reuse (Heinrich and Lang, 2019). There is reason to believe that material passports can significantly support sustainable material flows, but practical evidence is still building up.

Material tracking is enhanced with geospatial reference data. Capturing, storing, checking, and displaying data related to positions on Earth's surface through Geographic Information Systems (GIS) helps to connect data, while providing individuals and organizations a better understanding of spatial patterns and relationships in material matters. The use of Geographic Information Systems and mapping software architectural contexts has been growing since the 1970s and becomes even more relevant in light of material flows in a circular economy context. Datasets include information on settlements and displacement, industrial facilities, water features, infrastructure, territorial characteristics, species distribution, land covering, population statistics, and transport movements. Geographic Information Systems are also integrated into construction monitoring and Building Information Modeling (BIM), linking design engineering to precise 'on-the-ground' layout of construction facilities for better data management, project management, and quality control (Parkinson, 2017).

In addition, the interactions between building parts and people (as 'agents of control') constitute a relevant field for further data enhancement (Kendall, 1990; Geldermans, 2019). To an important extent, this is compatible with recent material tracking methods, involving the effective exchange of meaningful data from one stakeholder to another, constantly moving the center of control to wherever is most relevant and useful. The body of knowledge and practical experience in this direction is ever expanding. For example, enriched with Geographic Information Systems and Life Cycle Assessment datasets, BIM can be a powerful tool to create digital twins for building projects that support circularity, from design to discharge (Caceres et al., 2023; Su et al., 2013; Xue et al., 2021; Zhang et al., 2019).

4.11 OUTLOOK

This chapter commenced with the statements that (1) natural resources, providing clean water and air, materials, energy, and soil, are the basis of human society, while (2) the dependence of design and architecture on faraway resources often obscures associated supply chains. Several frameworks, methods and tools were highlighted throughout the chapter that could help in mapping material flows over spatial and temporal distances, supporting a circular rather than a linear society.

One of the main advantages of the circular economy concept is its broad applicability at variable scales, from global economy-wide to single firm assessment, in different contexts, and for numerous materials and products. That broad applicability also has a flipside which is less advantageous, since it has allowed for a broad bandwidth of definitions, terms, and indicators that blurs the evaluation process to measure benefits (Tanzer et al., 2019). This myriad of interpretations leads to a lack of clarity concerning the type and timing requirements of data. Circular material flows, being dynamic, require data that consider variable circumstances in terms of spatial locations and stakeholder needs. On one hand, this necessitates geo-referenced data, as was addressed in former sections. On the other hand, specific collated product-related data are essential to provide materials, products – including buildings – with an identity. As with all data applications, the extent to which any claim of *retaining circularity potential* is justified depends on the quality and accessibility of the data. If the right people have the wrong data, or the right data are with the wrong people, the opposite may be the case. This is fundamental in relation to geographically dispersed flows of materials in a circular value network, specifically regarding control over these materials. Toolboxes of sustainability and industrial ecology offer several invaluable tools and methods for quantifying and qualifying the sustainability impact of interventions on various scale levels, in particular relating to lifecycle performances. However, these tools have their limitations and drawbacks. Various experts have addressed divergent modeling approaches to measure environmental impact related to mineral resource use, revealing ongoing debates on scientific accounting methods (Sonderegger et al., 2019; Berger et al., 2020). Moreover, the sheer complexity inherent in rigorous analytical Life Cycle Asessment studies has ushered in the development of simplified methods and fast tracks, thereby cutting off specific aspects that may be crucial to assessing geographically distributed environmental impacts of a circular economy (Raugei and Ulgiati, 2009).

Two primary perspectives come into view. First, scientific methods to measure and monitor geographically distributed environmental and social impacts of material use are limited and constantly developing. Second, arguably all levels of governance are important to appropriately address the systemic impact of materials, which increases the complexity to wicked proportions. To help solve these issues, several initiatives have recently emerged. Within the European project 'Buildings as Material Banks' (BAMB), for example, a material passport was developed, underscoring that information technology has become a central aspect for implementing the circular economy in building practice (Heinrich and Lang, 2019; Walden et al., 2021). Multiple material passport propositions have been marketed in recent years, with variable scopes but usually adhering to aspects such as material composition, life cycle assessment, traceability, due diligence efforts, and associated circular economy services/scenarios (e.g., repair, redistribution, remanufacturing). A recent example is the Product Circularity Data Sheet (PCDS) standardization scheme. This

Fig. 84
Digital tools for enhanced material-data exchange. Left: Material Passports; right: 360-degree photography outsourced to robots (depicting 'SpotWalk' by HoloBuilder)

initiative of the Ministry of the Economy of Luxembourg aims to create a digital circularity fingerprint for products. It was developed to provide a data basis for high-quality material loops effectuating the circular economy. PCDS involves the circulation of physical resources and information to establish transparency and trustworthiness along supply chains, in close anticipation of circular strategies and health concerns. The underlying hypothesis was that a decentralized, open-source template containing basic circular economy criteria, and supported by standardized circular economy definitions and data protocols for products, could facilitate the exchange of circular economy metrics globally in a more accurate and complete way (Mulhall et al., 2022; ISO, 2023). The PCDS connects material health and safety to design, engineering, and geographic distribution through global trade, integrating information on product and company identification (GGDL, 2023).

The innovation of creating passports for buildings and building materials has been coupled with the potential of digital technologies. Simulations in 2D and 3D, such as georeferenced building information modeling, 360-degree photography, and enriched – virtual or augmented – digital surroundings, can become powerful drivers for advanced data-exchange and communication between partners. Such technologies can help improve the accuracy of building orientations, enhance material orders and associated transport miles, reduce waste, and cut costs. Better quality control and inspection processes are thus facilitated. However, a lot of the impact boils down to more down-to-earth organizational aspects, such as awareness, skills, behavior, planning, and advanced incentivizing schemes. Establishing circular material flows over time and spatial constructs thus requires concerted efforts in multiple domains, with an equal amount of attention for low-tech and high-tech aspects.

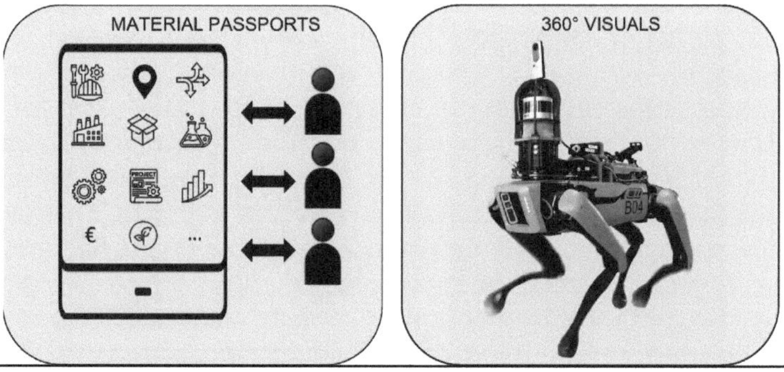

Fig. 84

CHAPTER

5

UBIQUITY

At a time of apparently fast-diminishing material resources, it may seem counterintuitive to consider material ubiquity. However, there are always materials available. The question is whether they are recognized and used as a resource. Historically, this recognition existed, especially in situations of scarceness. In a report to the United Nations on traditional knowledge, Pietro Laureano stated that the "principle [...] where each residue of a system is used by other systems, where the idea of waste or the possibility to resort to external resources do not exist, has allowed the survival of people throughout history. Multipurpose techniques have been successful even in hard times. The collaboration and the symbiosis by reusing what is produced within a system enabled the autopoiesis, the self-reproduction, the self-propulsive development, which does not depend on exogenous or occasional factors." (Laureano, 1999, p. 5)

This is a valuable insight at a time when rapid urbanization consumes vast amounts of material resources. As discussed in Chapter 4, the concept of urban metabolism describes the flows of *resources in* (energy, materials, water, etcetera), *resources out* (e.g., waste, heat, pollutants, residual materials), and *resources within* (stocks) a given urbanized system boundary. Moreover, metabolism-thinking links *resource use* with *temporal factors*. Verhagen et al. have shown that "a substantial percentage of the built environment is demolished each year, especially in already developed urban regions, which generates large volumes of waste that could be reused as secondary construction material" (Verhagen et al., 2021, p. 1). This implies that material resources need not originate from outside of cities, but instead can be derived from constructions that have reached the end of their service lifecycle. This approach is known as *urban mining* and relates to contemporary thinking in waste management.

In addition to materials that can be regained through urban mining, there is another type of ubiquitous 'material' in urban environments which is beginning to be recognized as a key material resource in urban planning and architectural design for advancing green city and green architecture approaches. One promising approach is critical zone research and its potential linkage to planning, design, and management of cities and architectures. Critical zone research focuses on the Earth's complex near-surface environment where the interaction between climate, water, soil, rock,

Figs. 85, 86

Fig. 85
Urban mined glass materials in the shop of Rotor Deconstruction & Consulting, Brussels, Belgium. Photography: Bob Geldermans, 2023.

Fig. 86
Urban mined wooden materials in the shop of Rotor Deconstruction & Consulting, Brussels, Belgium. Photography: Bob Geldermans, 2023.

and organisms regulates the natural environment and provides the necessary resources for life (National Research Council, 2001). While it is understood that rock, soil, water, air, and biomass are important resources for natural environments, sustaining life including that of humans, such 'materials' in their natural form are commonly not directly associated with the built environment. This is in large part due to the persistent human-nature dichotomy that insistently separates the natural from the human-made. However, it stands to reason that the human-nature dichotomy stands in the way of advancing nature-integrated planning and design of considerably greener cities. For this reason, water, soil, and biomass are addressed in this chapter. Discussing water in a chapter entitled *Ubiquity* may at first seem counter-intuitive, since there exist in principle three conditions: (1) balanced water regime; (2) overabundance of water due to heavy precipitation or flooding; or (3) drought and lack of water – of which at least two present a situation that seems inadequately addressed by the notion of ubiquity. However, water is required in all locations where life as well as food production and construction take place. The question is how to relate to local water regimes, as well as how to gather and distribute it to tackle local problems. It is from the perspective of required ubiquity that water is addressed in this chapter.

5.2 URBAN MINING

Urban metabolism, a concept developed by Wolman (1965), focuses on the socio-economic and technical processes in urban environments (Kennedy et al., 2007). In principle, urban metabolism is key concern of the State of the Environment (SOE) reporting that seeks to evaluate the sustainability of a given city, by way of providing relevant, representative, and scientifically valid data and assessment on questions of energy consumption, cycling of materials, waste management and infrastructural aspects of the urban environment, such that citizens and urban planners can understand and compare data and developments over time (Kennedy et al., 2011). In the context of transitioning from a linear to a circular economy this has shifted attention in various expert domains, including waste management and urban planning, away from an exclusive focus on limited raw material resources and towards anthropogenic stocks of materials, such as those used for construction (Baccini and Brunner, 2012), thereby providing the basis for urban mining (Stallone, 2011). It involves "actions and technologies designed for the recovery of materials and energy from products of the urban catabolism. Therefore, Urban Mining provides a systematic management of anthropogenic resources stocks and waste (products and buildings), in the view of long-term environmental protection, resource conservation, and economic benefits." (Cossu, 2013, p. 497) Computational methods for visualization of urban stocks of materials are currently being researched across various sectors, including AEC (Richthofen et al., 2017; Bindreiter et al., 2013; Wurzer et al., 2023). Geographic Information Systems (GIS), for instance, can play a critical role in characterizing and visualizing the distribution of recyclable materials, as well as collection systems, in urban environments (Zhu, 2014).

However, Geographic Information Systems data have so far not been applied to national building stocks or prospective models. Doing so would have the advantage a more accurate quantification of material stocks and spatio-temporal dynamics associated with building stocks dynamics and material flows (Heeren and Hellweg, 2019). For this reason, Heeren and Hellweg discussed “a component-based, prospective, and probabilistic modeling approach to quantify the material composition of Swiss residential buildings, which can then be aggregated geographically to model building material stocks and flows of regions. Furthermore, we use scenarios, based on probability sets, to study model sensitivity and policy scenarios. Finally, the material flows are evaluated for their environmental impact by using Life Cycle Assessment (LCA) and considering different environmental impact categories.” (Heeren and Hellweg, 2019, p. 254) Furthermore, the integration of Building Material Stocks (BMS) analysis with Life Cycle Assessment (LCA) can serve to evaluate aspects such as energy use, material stocks and material flows, and environmental performance related to the life cycle of building stocks (Pei et al., 2024, p. 254).

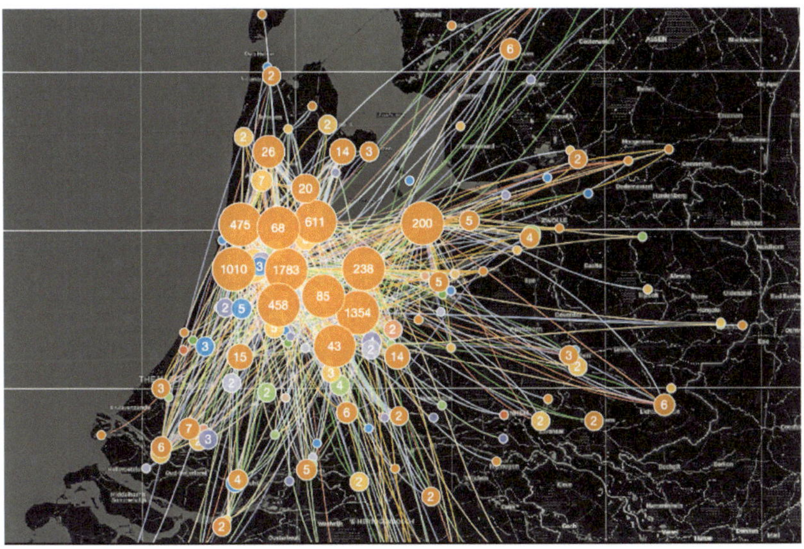

Fig. 87

Fig. 87
Visualization of numbered and specified CDW flows with activity-based GIS data of departure and destination relating to the Amsterdam Metropolitan Area in 2016 (Image made with open source GDSE software, developed within the REPAiR project, Delft University of Technology, 2016–2020)

Fig. 88
GIS is used to map recyclable resources and materials distributed throughout the urban environment, utilizing various logistics strategies to optimize the location, distribution, and accessibility of these materials.

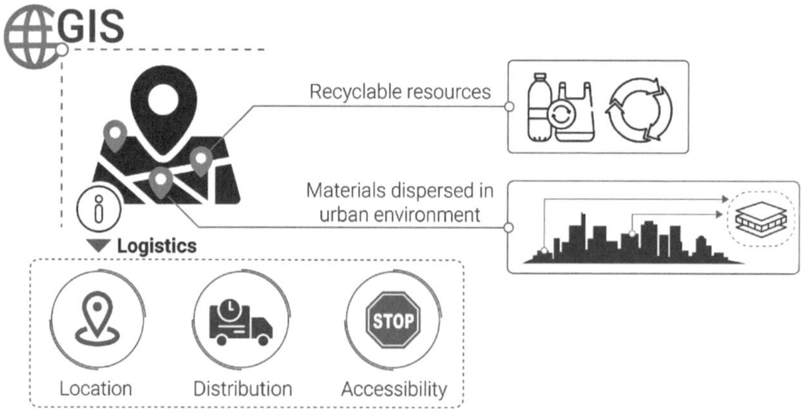

Fig. 88

Other related developments are currently being discussed and developed that can further improve utilization of material stocks and material flows in urban environments and their location-specific planning over specified time periods. Pehlken and Baumann identified, for instance, the need to transmit production information to the recycler, for example in the form of a bill of materials, and the use of digital twins for the purpose of providing this information to end-of-life (EoL) stakeholders to support the circular economy (Pehlken and Baumann, 2020). Köhler and Schnitzer explained that data and a cadaster of secondary resources relevant to different types of buildings is lacking and that efforts are needed to provide such data in an accessible and interoperable manner (Köhler and Schnitzer, 2014). An important preview of what the circular economy in the digital age promises to become was provided by de Wolf et al. (2024), who examined how data, BIM and digital twins, Geographic Information Systems, AI, ML, Extended Reality, advanced manufacturing, robotic fabrication, material passports, etc., can provide significant digital innovation for circularity. Furthermore, they examined in which way these digital tools can be combined into useful workflows to support the shift from a linear to a circular economy, thereby highlighting opportunities for further research and development.

In summary, the picture that emerges is that a broad set of digital technologies can and in part already are being used in the context of urban circularity, advanced waste management, and urban mining. Regionally or locally specific dedicated databases are in the making in various places and ubiquitous anthropogenic material stocks in cities will dramatically change the way materials are viewed and sourced. Questions of material adaptation

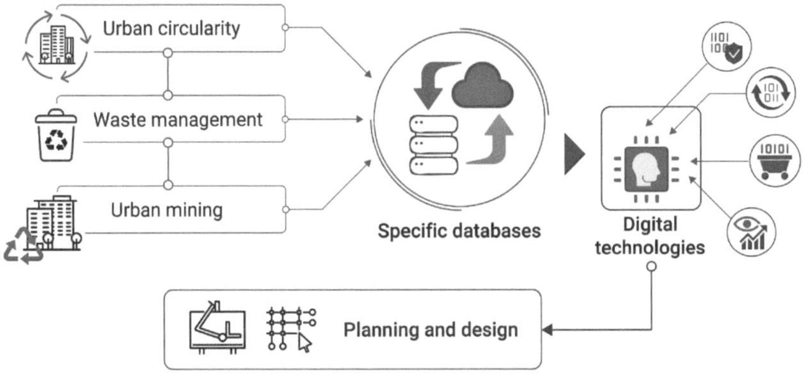

Fig. 89

Fig. 89 Data on urban circularity, waste management, and urban mining can enhance planning and design with novel material properties by utilizing a broad range of digital technologies.

and material processes and the type of data that is required will play a central role in this approach, asserting considerable transformative impact on planning and design.

5.3 CRITICAL ZONE

As part of its 2030 Agenda for Sustainable Development (United Nations, 2024a) the United Nations developed 17 Sustainable Development Goals (SDGs) which constitute "an urgent call for action by all countries – developed and developing – in a global partnership. They recognize that ending poverty and other deprivations must go together with strategies that improve health and education, reduce inequality, and spur economic growth – all while tackling climate change and working to preserve our oceans and forests." (United Nations, 2024b) In principle, this indicates an understanding of the complex entanglement of SDGs, which are inadequately addressed in isolation.

The key SDG for urban planners and architects is SDG 11 *Sustainable Cities and Communities*. The connection of SDG 11 to human health and well-being, enshrined in SDG 3 *Good Health and Wellbeing*, and to climate change, enshrined in SDG 13 *Climate Action*, is well established and the focus of sustained research and action. However, the links to SDG 6 *Clean Water and Sanitation* and to SDG 14 *Life on Land* have been explored less, even though there exist numerous programs and projects that focus on greening cities and green architectures, as well as so-called blue-green infrastructure. A recent report by the statistical office of the European Union, which shows the EU's progress on the Sustainable Development Goals over a period of five years, identifies only medium progress on SDG 11, moderate progress on SDG 6, and negative development on SDG 13 and SDG 14. And while there has been moderate progress on SDG 3 *Good Health and Wellbeing* it stands to reason that regress in issues related to urban climate and urban nature hampers a more successful implementation of related measures to ensure human health and well-being (European Commission, 2023). Therefore, a different approach is needed that can serve to address the linkage between and co-development of the SDGs en route to *Sustainable Cities and Communities* via city and nature integration. An alternative approach needs to focus on the interaction between technical and natural systems based on the systems and processes that sustain life on Earth.

Critical zone research can offer a suitable paradigm. In a report entitled *Basic Research Opportunities in Earth Science*, the National Research Council (2001) described critical zone research as focusing on "the heterogeneous, near-surface environment in which complex interactions involving, rock, soil, water, air and living organisms regulate the natural habitat and determine the availability of life-sustaining resources. Many science disciplines – hydrology, geomorphology, biology, ecology, soil science, sedimentology, materials research, and geochemistry – are bringing novel research tools to bear on the study of the critical zone as an integrated system of interacting components and processes." (National Research Council, 2001, p. 2) The Critical Zone Exploration Network was set up in 2006 as a network for researching critical zone processes. The sharing and integration of spatio-temporal data across disciplines and the network of observatories facilitates a better understanding of environmental variables and effects of geomorphological and biological processes, anthropogenic disturbances of environments, etc. (CZEN, 2024). In 2007 the next major step was the start of establishing critical zone observatories (CZOs), first in the US and subsequently in other countries. These serve to advance understanding of the terrestrial life support system on a local basis and across the network. CZOs integrate geological and ecological sciences, thereby representing "a unique opportunity to transform (the) understanding of coupled surface Earth processes and to address quantitatively the impacts of climate and land use change and the value of Critical Zone functions and services [...] a fundamental concept applied from ecological economics is that the Critical Zone embodies natural capital as a means of production to support flows of materials, energy, genetic information, and human population over time." (White et al., 2015, p. 18) Various data-driven computational methods and tools can play in critical zone research. For instance, Big Data on different aspects on landscape evolution can be utilized in conjunction with machine learning and rule-based methods to pinpoint and compare emergent patterns with established domain knowledge, leading to new insights in critical zone research by utilizing data-driven methods in conjunction with hypothesis-driven scientific inquiry (Bui, 2016).

Currently, the processes and materials of the critical zone climate, water, soil, rock, and biomass are not considered to be part of the resources that make up the built environment. As such, these materials are barely accounted for unless their removal or processing incurs costs, or they are implicated in pollution that must be prevented. However, advancing an agenda for green cities beyond the current status quo arguably needs to consider these materials in various ways. Some research is beginning to examine the relationship between cities and the critical zone (Bagheri, 2015) and the integration of architecture and landscape architecture hybrid designs that address and incorporate materials and processes of the critical zone (Hensel and Sunguroğlu Hensel, 2023, 2024). Tapping into critical zone systems and processes and related data and linking them with planning and design data and data-driven planning and design methods is a current research gap that needs to be addressed in the effort to advance sustainable green cities and architectures. This involves specifically water, soil, and biomass.

5.4 WATER

Water is essential for sustaining life, but also for cities and construction. Cities and buildings tap into the water cycle and consume a vast amount of water. However, while this has been known for a long time, research into water consumption in the AEC sector is not as advanced as might be expected. The same applies to state-of-the-art research into how to better understand the relationship between the natural and technical water cycles and how to link them to ensure a more advanced and holistic management of water.

Water plays a key role in the UN's Sustainable Development Goals. It is the topic of SDG 6 *Clean Water and Sanitation*, as well as SDG 14 *Life Below Water*, albeit in this case as habitat. It is also a key impact factor for numerous other SDGs. Furthermore, the critical role of water is stated in critical zone research which concerns "the heterogeneous, near-surface environment in which complex interactions involving, rock, soil, water, air and living organisms regulate the natural habitat and determine the availability of life-sustaining resources" (National Research Council, 2001, p. 2). Therefore, as environmental degradation, climate change, population growth, industry, and industrial agriculture, as well as urbanization and construction accelerate the shortage and pollution of freshwater, its consumption and use must be accounted for at a more advanced level.

A useful starting point is to account for water through water footprint, which serves as an indicator for "direct (domestic water use) and indirect (water required to produce industrial and agricultural products) water use of a consumer or producer" (Vanham and Bidoglio, 2013, p. 61). There are generally two ways of assessing the water footprint for a given location: the Water Footprint Network (WFN) and the Life Cycle Assessment. Nallaperuma et al. pointed out that "the WFN considers water footprinting as a volumetric approach (total volume of freshwater used by an individual/community/business activity) focusing on water productivity. It views freshwater as a limited global resource, and the environmental relevance of both consumptive (green and blue waters) and degradative (gray water) freshwater uses are accounted (for,) referring to the sustainability limits, environmental needs, efficiency of use and equitability of global freshwater resources [...]. The Life Cycle Assessment quantifies potential environmental impacts related to a particular freshwater appropriation [...] and extends the freshwater use assessment to the consequences resulting from water consumption (impact-based water footprinting) through weighting and characterization pertinent to the case of interest. Moving beyond the volumetric water use accounting (inventory level/LCI – life cycle inventorying), the Life Cycle Assessment approach works on life cycle impact assessment (LCIA) [...]. This integration of freshwater use into life cycle assessments by the Life Cycle Assessment community has formulated the international standard on water footprinting in ISO 14046." (Nallaperuma et al., 2023, p. 801) Nallaperuma *et al.* further recommended that the WFN and LCA approaches should be seen as complementary methods.

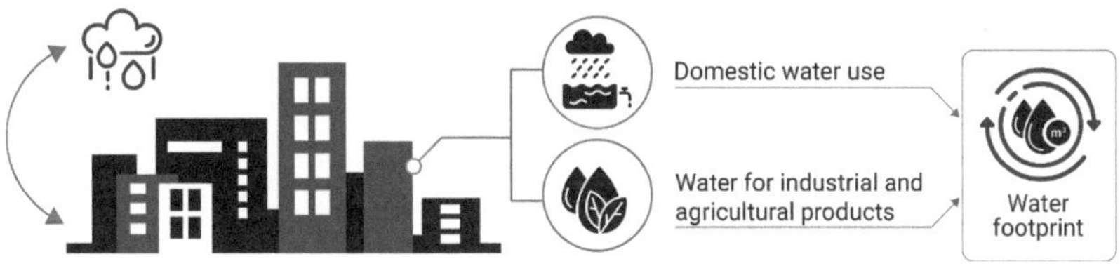

Fig. 90

Fig. 90
Water footprint indicates domestic water consumption, and the water needed to produce industrial and agricultural goods by a consumer or producer.

Data play a key role in quantifying freshwater use in the AEC sector. However national and other legislative borders can present obstacles for assembling required datasets. As Nallaperuma et al. showed, there are various obstacles to deriving reliable quantification of water use in the construction industry, including AEC sector disaggregation and lack of shared fine resolution data along the supply chain (Nallaperuma et al., 2023). For this reason, it will be necessary to apply a multi-scalar approach to data collection and integration that is not constrained by legislative, national, or other borders. Additionally, it is necessary to account for water consumption in and of different building typologies during their lifespan of use, as this accounts for a large amount of global freshwater consumption. Moreover, there are no adequate knowledge and data regarding water consumption of the built environment in highly water-stressed countries where water consumption is even more consequential (Mannan and Al-Ghamdi, 2022). Currently only limited region-specific studies on building types, especially residential buildings, exist (Mannan and Al-Ghamdi, 2022).

Recently, *AquaBIM*, a methodology that integrates BIM, IoT, and FM has been proposed to analyze and automatize water consumption in commercial buildings (Batista et al., 2022). Furthermore, smart water metering has been proposed as a way of collecting valuable data on human water consumption (Boyle et al., 2013). Still, advanced databases are not yet broadly available and data collection will need to be undertaken in many regions for a broad range of building typologies. Nevertheless, water is one of the materials that is required not only to sustain life, but also for construction and building operation. Water must therefore be rigorously accounted for, and related research needs to focus on rapidly addressing related pressing questions to help maintain this essential resource.

The key process regarding water is the natural *hydrological cycle*. Inglezakis et al. explained that the hydrological cycle is the natural process by which water gets recycled. This process entails that “water evaporates, generally from the sea, lakes, etc. (and)

Fig. 91
Water consumption data in construction must encompass both the construction phase and the water usage of different building types over their operational lifespan.

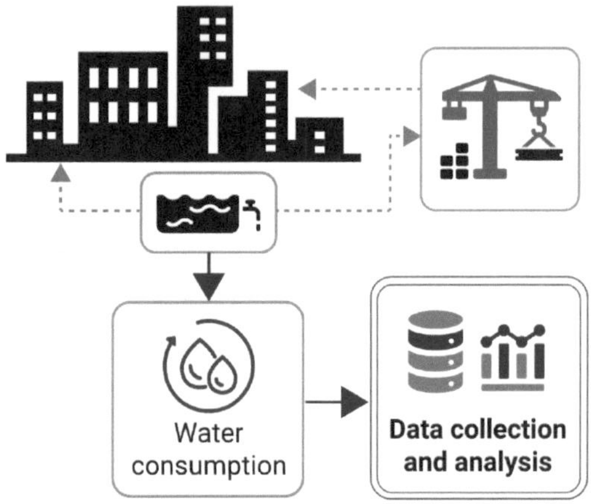

Fig. 91

from plant leaves through the mechanism of *transpiration*. As the steam rises in the atmosphere, it is being cooled, condensed, and returned to the land and the sea as precipitation. Precipitation falls on the earth as surface water and shapes the surface, creating [...] streams of water [...] lakes and rivers. A part of the water precipitating penetrates the ground and moves downward through the incisions, forming aquifers. Finally, a part of the surface and underground water leads to (the) sea. During this (cycle) water is converted in all phases: gas, liquid, and solid." (Inglezakis et al., 2016, p. 146–147)

As can be seen from critical zone research, the hydrological cycle involves interactions between atmosphere, lithosphere, and biosphere, as well as the environment transformed by humans, the anthroposphere. In this context, research needs to focus on the way human activities and transformation of the environment, as well as climate change collectively interact with water resources and the hydrological cycle across spatial and temporal scales. For this purpose, multi-scalar data and models are required (Yang et al., 2021). Anthropogenic transformations, such as the urban water cycle assert significant negative impact on the natural hydrological cycle, such as water shortage, pollution, droughts, floods, and ecosystem service degradation (Wu et al., 2013). Data collection on the hydrological cycle for the purpose of analysis, for instance in the context of climate change, is a major undertaking. Hagemann et al. pointed out that "the European Centre for Medium-Range Weather Forecasts (ECMWF) has prepared a new 40-year reanalysis dataset (ERA40). Based on the observational data that were used, the whole ERA40 time-period 1958–2001 can be divided into three parts: the satellite period 1989–2001 when a large amount of satellite data was assimilated into the ERA40 system, the pre-satellite period 1958–1972 when no satellite data were available, and the transition period 1973–1988 when the amount of satellite data that were assimilated increases with time. These three periods correspond also to the three streams which were produced separately during the ERA40 production time frame. The ERA40 dataset is expected to be a major dataset for climate research. Within the ERA40 project, the MPI (Max Planck Institute for Meteorology) had the task to perform a validation of the hydrological cycle." (Hagemann et al., 2005)

Rast et al. stated that at present, existing Earth system models do not provide the data-richness and spatial resolution for complex tasks such as accounting for non-linear anthropogenic impact on the terrestrial hydrological cycle and do not realistically represent it in terms of its equally non-linear responses to various scenarios (Hibbard et al., 2010). To overcome this problem various experts proposed the development of "new hyper-resolution hydrological land surface models, which can be fully coupled to regional and global climate models to combine global with regional hydrology. These models should be based on first-order principles, close the terrestrial energy, water and carbon balance at all scales, should be able to overcome these scale issues by coupling the very small with the very large processes and should be able to tap the rich global data archives available through remote sensing (Hibbard et al., 2010; Wood et al., 2011; Mauser and Bach 2009; Su et al., 2010)." (Rast et al., 2014, p. 494) While this level of data-based modeling will not be attainable for planners and architects in the short run, it will nevertheless be necessary to follow up on these developments in the Earth sciences. This also includes utilization of available data on local scales, and incorporation of hydrological cycle related parameters, into resource management, planning and design of the built environment.

One major anthropogenic factor that asserts negative impact upon the natural hydrological cycle is the so-called *urban hydrological cycle*. Urban water management helps secure compliance with local and global standards concerning water quality and quantity of consumption. This also involves various models to support the tasks related to urban water management and to model the various parts of Urban Water Cycle (UWC) and their interactions (Peña-Guzmán et al., 2017). Data play an important role in water management and various data-driven methods for urban water management purposes have been proposed. Some of these methods serve, for instance, the purpose of reducing surface water pollution due to rapid urbanization and climate change. To accomplish this task effective data sharing is necessary across organizational, municipal, and other boundaries, to involve all stakeholders related to the Urban Water Cycle (UWC) (Manny, 2023). Some useful resources already exist. The *Urban Water Blueprint*, for instance, contains analytical data on the condition of water in numerous places and cities across the world, and provides science-based guidelines for different natural solutions that can be integrated with existing infrastructure to improve the state of water (The Nature Conservancy, 2024). Data sharing and integrating multi-scalar data and spatio-temporal data is a first step in data-driven modeling of the urban water cycle. Further steps need to include linking urban hydrological cycle models to data-driven planning and design methods. Some aspects of the hydrological cycle have already been integrated into simulation and analysis software. *Evapotranspiration* of plants, for instance, is integrated in the ENVI-met environmental simulation software package.

There are, however, important aspects that remain still largely under-researched and under-utilized, such as *condensation*. The latter can play a significant role in tackling water shortage. In a report to the United Nations Laureano stated that "it is useful to understand how humans have dealt with water shortage during droughts and desertification throughout history as valuable insights and strategies can be gained from this understanding [...] urban areas contribute to the desertification process either in a direct or in an indirect way. In the former case the massive urbanization process itself is desertification because of the presence of constructions on very large natural areas; it is indirect because it occurs through the absorption and the destruction of natural resources in high-demographic areas." (Laureano, 1999) Various experts have pointed towards historical examples and methods of gathering water through condensation to support agriculture in areas suffering from lack of water and desertification (Georgiadis et al., 2014; Manea et al., 2016; Sunguroğlu Hensel, 2020; Zhang et al., 2023).

Overall, the scale-spanning character, ranging from individual households to urban quarters and larger urban water regimes) and multi-domain requirements for modeling the linked natural and urban hydrological cycles is a complex undertaking that requires significant research and data collection. However, recent efforts show that significant efforts are shaping up or taking place. It therefore stands to reason that accounting for water in an adequate manner will be increasingly present in planning and design, as well as the AEC sector.

Soil is a ubiquitous yet frequently disregarded material in the AEC sector. Sites are frequently leveled in preparation of construction and soil is excavated and removed to make space for underground constructions, such as garages and basements. Moreover, the surface of soil is often sealed with impervious materials such as concrete or asphalt to provide various types of gray infrastructure. This is generally different for green sites, such as public parks etc. where soil is evidently an important material to facilitate the growth of plants, to provide ecosystem services, etc. Two current developments are likely to change the way soil is regarded and used in cities. Firstly, sustainable planning and design places an increasing emphasis on accomplishing greener cities and architectures, which requires substantial amounts of healthy soil. Secondly, increasing urban agriculture and food production also requires substantial amounts of healthy soil. Therefore, it is likely that planners and designers need to account for local soil on given sites in ways that will be quite different from how this is done today. The emphasis on utilizing local soil and conducting well planned soil management constitutes a third major development need.

Lal et al. elaborated the relationship between soil and the Sustainable Development Goals of the United Nations United Nations (2024b) as follows: "Sustainable management of soil health is important to achieving several SDGs. Pertinent SDGs intricately connected with soil health include SDG 1 (End Poverty), 2 (Zero Hunger), 3 (Good Health and Wellbeing), 5 (Gender Equality), 6 (Clean Water and Sanitation), 7 (Affordable and Clean Energy), 9 (Industry Innovation and Infrastructure), 11 (Sustainable Cities and Communities), 12 (Responsible Consumption and Production), 13 (Climate Action), and 15 (Life on Land) [...] Soil health is becoming a central element of the research and innovation program of the EU, aiming to reach 75 percent of healthy soils by 2030." (Lal et al., 2021, p. 1) As mentioned before soil plays a pivotal role in critical zone research which concerns "the heterogeneous, near-surface environment in which complex interactions involving, rock, soil, water, air and living organisms regulate the natural habitat and determine the availability of life-sustaining resources" (National Research Council, 2001, p. 2).

Van Es defined soil as follows: "The layer(s) of generally loose mineral and/or organic material that are affected by physical, chemical, and/or biological processes at or near the planetary surface and usually hold liquids, gasses, and biota and support plants" (Van Es, 2017, p. 21). Furthermore, Kovda elaborated "that soil cover could emerge on the Earth only after life had appeared, even though only in primitive forms. The soil cover is a product of organisms' activities and their interaction with mineral surroundings; therefore, it could not appear on the Earth in the absence of living matter." (Kovda, 1993, p. 199)

A recent report by the European Commission Directorate-General for Research and Innovation stated that soil degradation is essentially affected by how humans choose to live. Moreover, continued soil degradation can accelerate numerous sustainability problems faced by the European Union. Therefore, taking care of the condition of soils is indispensable for accomplishing the tasks set out by the United Nations Sustainable Development Goals and Europe's New Green Deal, especially counteracting environmental and ecological degradation, biodiversity loss, and pollution (European Commission, 2020).

As discussed before, soil and its functions constitute one of the key systems and resources of the Earth's critical zone which supports life. It serves as "an interface between the solid and fluid envelopes. These envelopes are the atmosphere, the hydrosphere, the biosphere, and the lithosphere. It is at this juncture between the spheres that soil forms." (Jónsson and Davíðsdóttir, 2016, p. 26)

Soil in urban contexts is frequently in a particularly poor condition due to permanent disturbance, pollution, compaction, sealing, etc. (Fig. 92). Yang et al. pointed out that in cities "soil horizons are often irregularly established, with anthropogenic layers and a high degree of heterogeneity owing to human disturbance and infill. Soil structure is often under degradation due to artifacts and technogenic substrata, mechanical compaction, and human trampling. Physical degradation, such as compaction and destruction of structure, may reduce the ability of urban soils in infiltrating water and storing capacity, thus causing a higher runoff and pollutant load to the receiving water bodies. Soil compaction is also believed to worsen the urban heat island effect by reflecting more radiation, and seriously reduce the soil gas capacity and exchange. However, soil sealing fully loses its service function, further deteriorating urban ecology and environment." (Yang et al., 2015, p. 30)

Currently, major efforts are taking shape to address soil improvement, especially in cities, but also for agriculture and other land uses. To facilitate this development, multi-scalar data are required, as well as knowledge on soil management and improvement. Regarding the former, various databases that focus

Fig. 92
Urban soils are typically contaminated in various ways, including by construction materials and pollutants. Photography: Michael Hensel, 2024.

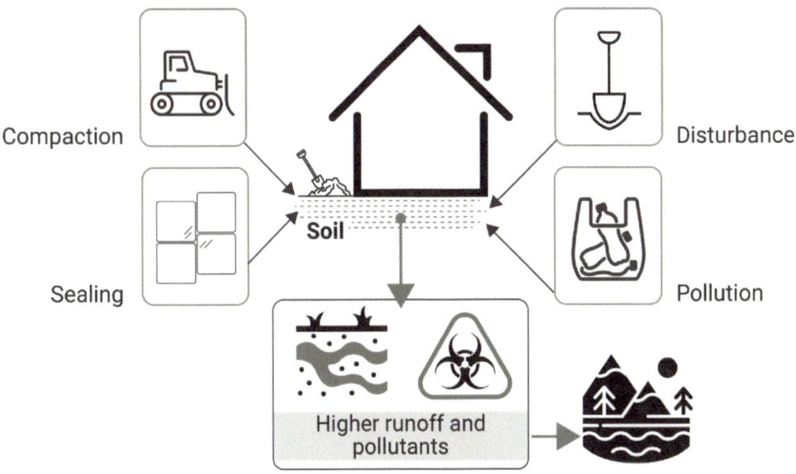

Fig. 93
Urban soils often suffer impacts leading to reduced water infiltration and storage capacity followed by increased runoff and pollutant loads in water bodies.

Figs. 92, 93

on larger scales either exist already or are being developed. For instance, The *FAO – Harmonized World Soil Database* provides a "a comprehensive global soil inventory that offers detailed insights into soil properties, including their morphology, chemistry, and physical characteristics, with a focus on a one-kilometer resolution. It's a valuable tool for research in areas like agriculture, food security, and climate change impacts. [... It was] developed in 2008 by the International Institute for Applied Systems Analysis (IIASA)

Fig. 94
Construction sites in areas of urban densification are often characterized by complete removal of soil one or several stories deep to make space for underground parking. What happens to the excavated soil is not typically of any specific interest and not typically accounted for in material flows. However, soil is a key resource for developing green and livable cities and for meeting the Sustainable Development Goals in urban areas. Photography: Michael Hensel, 2022.

Fig. 95
Construction sites in areas of urban densification are also often characterized by underground construction across the entire plot, thereby affording no opportunity to absorb rainwater locally or to replant larger plants that require more rooting depth. The shallow soil distributed on top of underground construction is frequently only planted with roll-out lawn and smaller plants. Photography: Michael Hensel, 2022.

Figs. 94, 95

and the Food and Agriculture Organization of the United Nations (FAO) [... and] data was compiled and organized using Geographic Information Systems (GIS) at IIASA. This collaborative effort ensured that the database was comprehensive and accurate. Subsequent updates were made in 2013 (HWSD v1.2) and in 2023 (HWSD v2.0) [...] HWSD v2.0 expands on its previous versions by including data from various national soil databases, offering detailed soil attributes for seven different soil layers (a significant increase from the two layers in HWSD v1.2), and adopting a consistent soil reference system combining FAO1990 standards with the World Reference Base for Soil Resources." (FAO – Harmonized World Soil Database, 2024)

Another important resource is *SoilWise*. The International Soil Reference and Information Centre (ISRIC) states that 60 to 70 percent of European soils are not healthy (ISRIC World Soil Information, 2024). The goal of the Soil Deal for Europe is to reach 75 percent significantly improved or healthy soils across the European Union by 2030. Given the current condition of soils, this is a steep task that requires soil data that are harmonized across the EU to enable informed decision making. In this context, *SoilWise* offers "an integrated and actionable access point to scattered and heterogeneous soil data and knowledge in Europe [...] The *SoilWise* repository and community are designed to be a starting point and common ground for countries, the European Commission, and other stakeholders to jointly guide soil and related spatial policy. An overall aim is to support informed decision-making towards the 2030 goals of the Green Deal, achieve healthy soils in 2050 and ensure broad use of the project by land managers, policy, research, and industry." (ISRIC World Soil Information, 2024)

An increasing number of countries worldwide maintain national soil databases, which are often pooled into larger regional networks. The European Soil Bureau Network (ESBN) and its Land Management Unit (LMU), for instance, links European national soil science institutions, and collects, harmonizes, organizes, and distributes soil information for Europe (ESDAC, 2024). Many cities today also provide soil data on their municipal cadaster websites even though such data are often still coarse. Data surveys are necessary but costly to conduct. In this context, citizen science can play an important role in addressing gaps in urban soil knowledge and data by acquiring soil-related data across urban areas and cities through citizen engagement, while also tapping into local knowledge (Paltseva, 2024). Moreover, data-based methods utilizing machine learning for the purpose of predicting soil properties can play a key role (Li et al., 2022).

Fig. 96
The slope shown in this photograph is stabilized using a combination of different slope stabilization methods, ranging from concrete surfaces and ring anchors in the lower part of the slope where it is the steepest, to individual concrete soil anchors, to soil nails and geotextiles, and vegetation. Photography: Michael Hensel, 2022.

Fig. 97
Detailed view of Fig. 96 showing a close-up of slope stabilization methods including concrete surfaces and ring anchors in the lower part of the slope where it is steepest, to individual concrete soil anchors and vegetation. Photography: Michael Hensel, 2022.

Various current research activities focus on the scale of individual buildings and how soil can be incorporated into building designs beyond the addition of planters or thin green roofs or façades. This can be accomplished by utilizing construction methods from landscape architecture and landscape engineering (Figs. 96–98). Hensel proposed an approach to hybridizing architecture and landscape architecture entitled 'geomorphic tectonics.' This is a novel way of designing and constructing buildings, envisaged as architectures that provide terrain through construction, keeping existing soil on site to articulate the architecture, in multifunctional and even structural terms. Different actors or species can then colonize these architectures due to the conditions created by a tectonic system that blends construction and landscape architecture (Hensel, 2023).

Figs. 96, 97

Fig. 98

Fig. 98
Slope stabilizing concrete grid in a forest with non-sealed grid fields that allow vegetation to grow in the grid fields. Photography: Milko Vasa, 2017 (Adobe Stock).

An increasing number of hybrid architecture and landscape architecture typologies are currently emerging that use a significant amount of soil relative to the architectural volume of a building. This includes, for instance, the design for the Abu Dhabi Flamingo Visitor Centre by OCEAN net. Located in the Al Wathba Wetland Reserve, the site is characterized by lakes that are home to 250 bird species including Greater Flamingos, as well as numerous aquatic, amphibious, insect, and plant species. The proposed scheme organizes the site as transition between the Al Wathba Wetlands ecosystem and a future afforestation scheme for the surrounding area (Figs. 99–102). In this project, the blending of architecture and landscape creates an ecological transition that supports local plant and animal biodiversity. A sequence of architectural, landscape and microclimatic experiences characterize the scheme: a tree grove, the landscape that extends over the building and continues to the south into the wetlands, and the cavernous interior of the building. To make this possible, the northern and southern elevations of the center are designed as a sloped terrain covered by selected soil types with the necessary depth to support the transition from a forest ecosystem to the wetland ecosystem.

Fig. 99
Rendered aerial view of the Flamingo Visitor Centre in the Al Wathba Wetland Reserve, Abu Dhabi. This unbuilt project is designed as a hybrid architecture and landscape architecture typology. Courtesy of OCEAN net, 2020.

Fig. 100
Site plan of the Flamingo Visitor Centre showing the ecological transition from the afforested area in the north to wetlands in the south. Courtesy of OCEAN net, 2020.

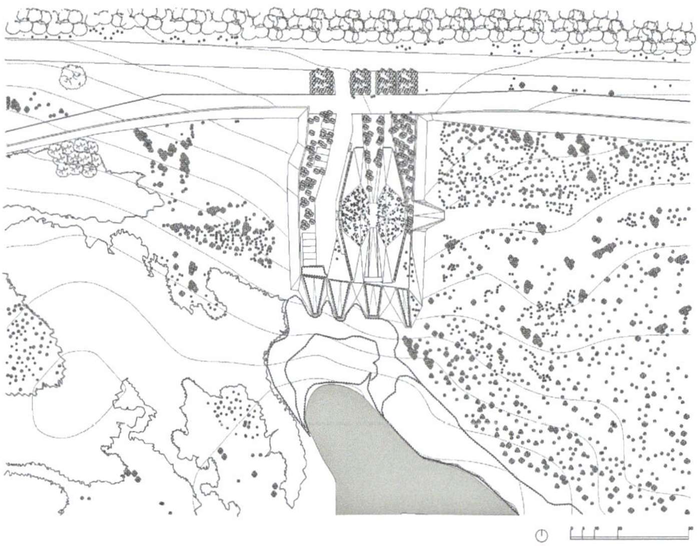

Figs. 99, 100

The European research project *ECOLOPES (ECOlogical building enveLOPES)* takes a similar approach but extends it to multi-species design for buildings and developing data-driven computational methods that incorporate architectural and ecological domain knowledge, including data-generating ecological models, decision support via computational ontologies and a knowledge graph, and algorithmic processes for design generation and optimization (Weisser et al., 2022; ECOLOPES, 2024).

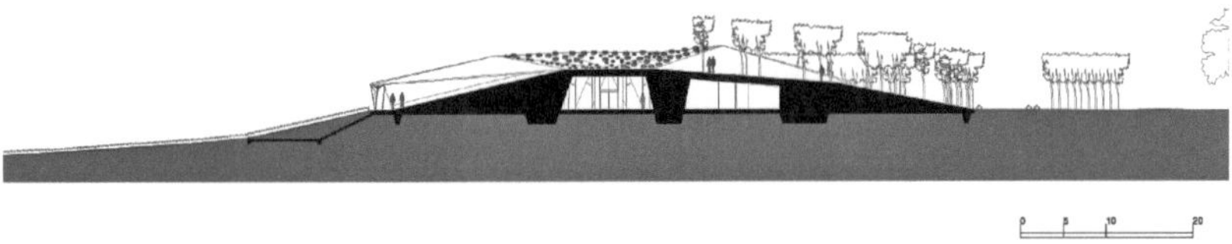

Fig. 101
Longitudinal section of the Flamingo Visitor Centre showing the landform of the building, emulating a dune as a transition area from the afforested area (right) to the wetland (left). Courtesy of OCEAN net, 2020.

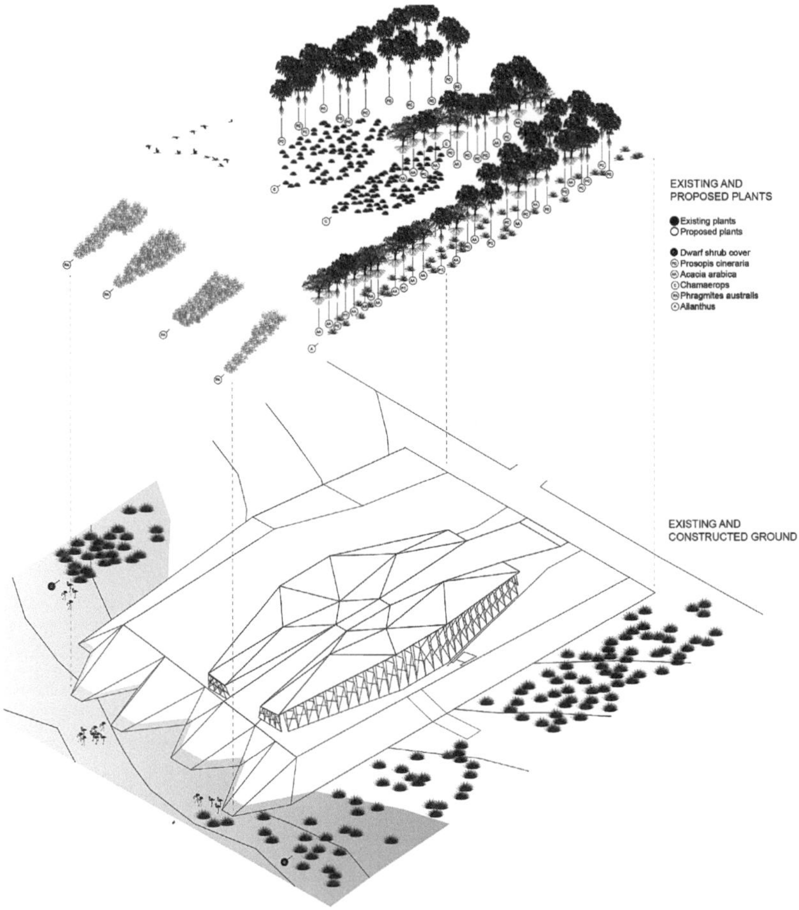

Fig. 102
Exploded axonometric view of the Flamingo Visitor Centre showing the extensive use of soil to minimize sealed surfaces and enable an ecological transition from forest to wetlands. Courtesy of OCEAN net, 2020.

Figs. 101, 102

Additionally, traditional methods for incorporating soil and biomass into constructions to support agriculture and horticulture are underway leading to the development of novel ecological prototypes for urban food production (Sunguroğlu Hensel, 2020, 2022b). The 'lemon houses' at Lake Garda (Figs. 103 and 104), for instance, served the purpose of growing lemon trees in a location much further north than the area of their natural occurrence. The lemon houses were built on steep slopes, converting them into

Fig. 103 Representation of a Lake Garda lemon house drawn by the German merchant and botanist J.C. Volkamer (Spectaculum Hortus Hesperidum Salodienses, 1713). Available via license: CC BY-NC-ND 4.0.

terraces that are framed on three sides by stone walls. The stone walls and terraces protect the soil from erosion, provide effective water management, and store solar heat gained during the day to maintain a suitable temperature for the lemon trees at night and during colder seasons. The lemon houses feature a removable front wall and roof that rests on 10-meter-tall pillars, which form a grid. The removable walls in front of these constructions consist of timber and glass panels, while the timber roofs are made from individual planks. In a closed state the lemon houses provide climate-controlled shelter for the trees during the cold season. During the warm season the front walls and roof are removed to maximize solar exposure. The dimensions of the trees and the construction, soil management, irrigation methods, and pruning techniques were all adjusted to one another. The lemon houses not only incorporated soil to support the growth of lemon trees but required considerable effort in terms of soil conservation and management to assure the required soil quality to support the growth of lemon trees (Sunguroğlu Hensel, 2020, 2022b).

Soil management has a range of purposes, for instance enabling ecosystem stability and services provided by soil (Schwilch et al., 2018; Thiele-Bruhn et al., 2012), enabling sustainable agro-ecosystems (Komatsuzaki and Ohta, 2007) and preserving soil biodiversity (Thiele-Bruhn et al., 2012), etc.

Urban soils are frequently impoverished and polluted, resulting in considerable negative impact for ecosystems and human health. Experts have stressed the need to gain a better

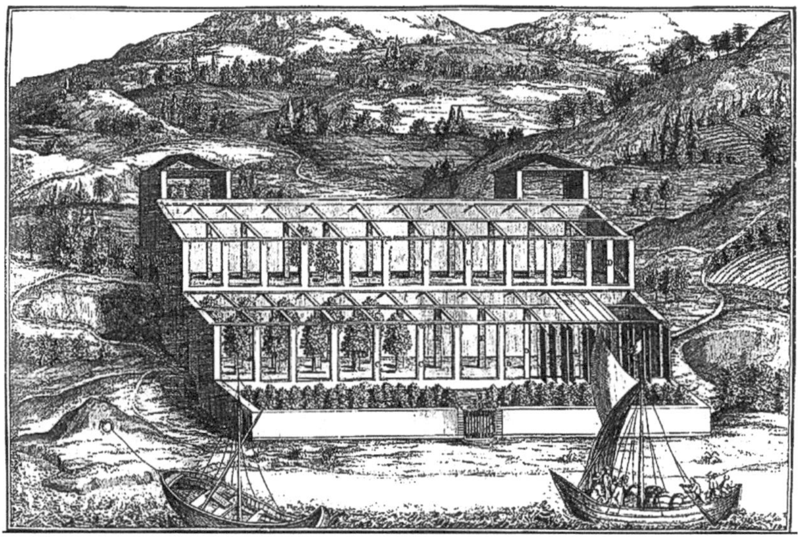

Fig. 103

Figs. 104–106

Fig. 104
Pra de la Fam lemon house, Lake Garda, Italy, with one part of the building enclosed with movable walls and roof (left) and the other part with walls and roof removed (right). Photography: Defne Sunguroğlu Hensel, 2021.

Fig. 105
Exterior façade of the lemon house at Castello Scaligero, Torri Del Benaco, Lake Garda, Italy. The lower part of the façade is closed with removable elements made from timber and glass. At the upper part of the construction the façade panels and roof cladding are removed. Photography: Defne Sunguroğlu Hensel, 2020.

Fig. 106
View of the half-closed interior the lemon house at Castello Scaligero, Torri Del Benaco, Lake Garda, Italy, showing the large soil volume for the lemon trees. Photography: Defne Sunguroğlu Hensel, 2020.

understanding of the relationship between soil microbial diversity, green areas, and human health and wellbeing in urban environments (Li et al., 2018) Urban soil science only emerged as a field of study in recent decades. Urban soil research follows two trajectories, as Norra and Stüben explained: "one approach is the research on genesis of urban soils and its meaning as part of an ecosystem, the other is the research on contamination and harmful disturbances of urban soils with negative consequences on the quality of life" (Norra and Stüben, 2003, p. 230).

Various data-based methods and tools have been proposed and developed for urban soil science and management, including Geographic Information Systems (Li and Feng, 2012) coupled with Web-based decision support (Hossack et al., 2004), Cloud-based spatio-temporal databases (Green et al., 2016), data mining (Hong et al., 2022), machine learning (Zhang et al., 2020), etc. Growing

Fig. 107
Urban soil research helps to understand the impact of industrialization and urbanization on soil pollution, ecosystems, and human health.

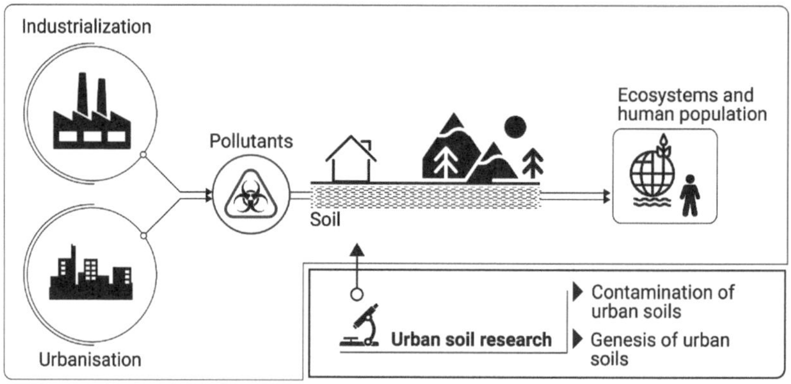

Fig. 107

efforts to build urban soil databases and develop data-driven methods for analysis, planning and urban soil management purposes indicate far greater attention given to urban soils across different disciplines and knowledge domains. It is only a question of time before this development has considerable impact on urban planning, architectural design, and the broader AEC sector.

5.6 BIOMASS

From the perspective of critical zone research, the topics of water, soil, and biomass are inextricably linked, though in this chapter we address them separately. The intention is not to disregard their linkages but to examine the different points of entry to each of these vital resources. The interesting thing about biomass is that it comprises materials that were living before being harvested for other purposes and decompose to support a new cycle of growth. Thus, biomass also belongs in the category of regenerative materials.

In the context of material and data, material agency and material flows, biomass is relevant for three main reasons: (1) to engender green cities, providing habitat and the delivery of ecosystem services, (2) for urban agriculture and food production, and (3) as regenerative material for the purpose of construction and adaptation of the built environment (see Chapter 3.6).

An increasing number of designs are emerging that focus on hybrid architecture and landscape architecture typologies and involve a significant amount of both soil and biomass relative to the architectural volume of a building. These include the design for the Langley Vale Visitor Hub by OCEAN net. Located in Surrey, UK, the site is located between ancient woodland and grassland ecosystems. To reflect this ecological transition, the scheme blends on the eastern elevation with the landscape via a densely vegetated slope that extends the woodland, and gradually transitions into a local grassland ecosystem on top of the building (Figs. 108–114). The slope enables wildlife to access the green roof, and the dense vegetation of the slope provides ample protection and helps replenish the soil of the slope over time. Once the vegetation is fully mature, especially the various tree species, the building will likely reach its end of life and needs to be replaced. What

Fig. 108
Rendered aerial view of the Langley Vale Visitor Hub. This unbuilt project is designed as a hybrid architecture and landscape architecture typology located at the transition between local woodland ecology and grassland ecology. Courtesy of OCEAN net, 2016.

Fig. 109
Rendered view of the Langley Vale Visitor Hub, showing the integration of built volume and the landscaped slope that facilitates a transition between local woodland ecology and grassland ecology. Courtesy of OCEAN net, 2016.

Figs. 108, 109

remains is not an empty site but a part of a maturing woodland. The soil that needs to be excavated for the foundations of the building will remain on site to form the sloping terrain, making possible the densely vegetated eastern elevation of the construction. Plant selection is based on promoting local biodiversity and regeneration of building materials, especially the timber cladding of the façade of the visitor hub.

Research on data and data-integrated approaches to biomass for the purpose of engendering green cities, providing habitat and the delivery of ecosystem services, includes urban green systems. This also involves the introduction of novel urban green systems or adaptation of traditional green systems to urban contexts (Höpfl et al., 2021; Ludwig et al., 2024), urban ecosystems and delivery of ecosystem services (Perini, 2022), urban trees (Yang et al., 2022) and urban forests (Pauleit et al., 2022), etc. Furthermore, an increasing amount of research focuses on data-driven intensified integration of biomass into constructions for the purpose of enhanced human-nature interaction and supporting urban ecosystems (Ludwig et al., 2021; Weisser et al., 2022).

One resource of interest is the *Urban Atlas*, provided by Copernicus Land Monitoring Service, which "gives users access to detailed land cover/land use maps for 788 Functional Urban Areas across Europe, in addition to street tree maps, building block height measurements, and population estimates. These products provide information necessary for urban planners to make informed, data-driven decisions about things like green spaces, transportation networks, and emergency response plans" which includes "a separate layer of Urban Atlas 2018 showing contiguous rows or patches of trees covering 500 square meters or more and with a Minimum Mapping Width (MMW) of 10 meter over 'Artificial surfaces' [...] inside each Functional Urban Area (FUA)" (Copernicus Land Monitoring Service, 2024). The cadastral websites of European cities also frequently include data on various aspects of urban green infrastructure, often at the resolution of the location of individual trees. A further important development is the preparation of databases containing spatio-temporal data on the morphology of urban green infrastructure (Zhu et al., 2021), and the preparation of classification systems that enable evaluation of ecosystem services (Wallace, 2007; Finisdore, 2020; Morpurgo et al., 2023), as well as on decision support (Pelizaro et al., 2009; Stessens et al., 2017; Feng, 2024).

A considerable amount of research has been conducted on data and data-integrated approaches to biomass in the context of rural and urban agriculture and food production, whereby typically data on rural agriculture is ahead of data on urban agricul-

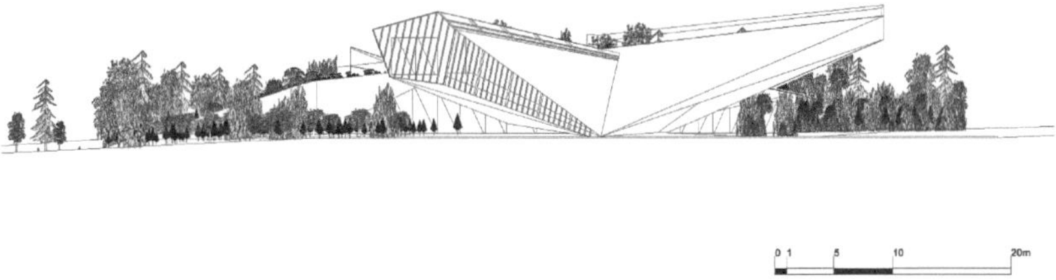

Fig. 110
West elevation of the Visitor Hub showing the more architectural façade of the scheme. Courtesy of OCEAN net, 2016.

Fig. 111
North elevation showing the transition from architecture to landscape architecture. Courtesy of OCEAN net, 2016.

Fig. 112
South elevation showing the transition from architecture to landscape architecture. Courtesy of OCEAN net, 2016.

Fig. 113
East elevation showing the densely vegetated slope. Courtesy of OCEAN net, 2016.

Fig. 114
Cross section of the building showing the transition from landscape architecture to architecture. Courtesy of OCEAN net, 2016.

Figs. 110–114

ture, with transfer and adaptation of insights from the former to the latter, though also with an increasing amount of research directly focused on data in urban agriculture. Research topics include Big Data (Bronson and Knezevic, 2016; Sunguroğlu Hensel, 2022), data acquisition (Atzberger, 2013; Tyc et al., 2021), the use of Geographic Information Systems (Bill et al., 2011), data integration (Tyc et al., 2021), decision support (Benis, 2017; Castrignanó et al., 2020; Sunguroğlu Hensel, 2022), Cloud computing and climate smart agriculture (Anandhi et al., 2020), and the Internet of Things (Castrignanó et al., 2020). A growing body of research focuses on data-driven intensified integration of agriculture and construction,

Fig. 115
Research on data related to urban and rural agriculture demonstrates the transfer of insights from rural to urban contexts and utilizes big data, data integration, cloud computing, data acquisition, geographic information systems (GIS), decision support systems, and the Internet of Things (IoT)

Fig. 116
Biomass plays a key role in green cities by supporting ecosystem services, urban agriculture, food production, and providing regenerative materials for construction and adaptation of the built environment.

(e.g., building integrated agriculture, BIA; Gould and Caplow, 2012; Katalari et al., 2017) including BIM (Khan et al., 2018), the development of ecological prototypes based on adapting traditional methods (Sunguroğlu Hensel, 2020, 2012), as well as data-driven design methods for traditional agricultural constructions (Tyc et al., 2022). Regarding urban agriculture, the available data are still sparse. Nevertheless, focused local efforts are underway to address this gap (Young et al., 2018; Sunguroğlu Hensel, 2022).

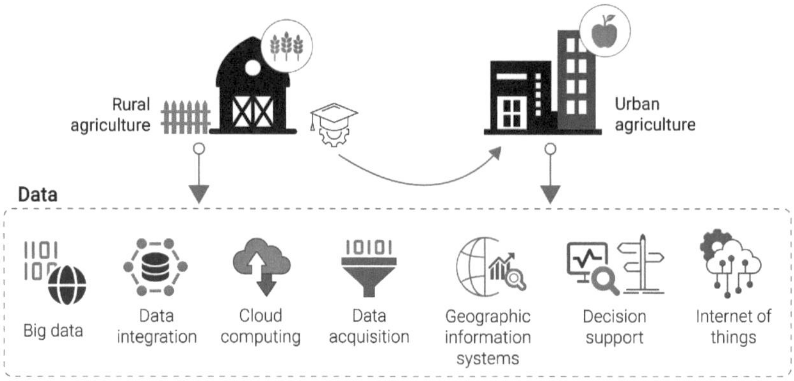

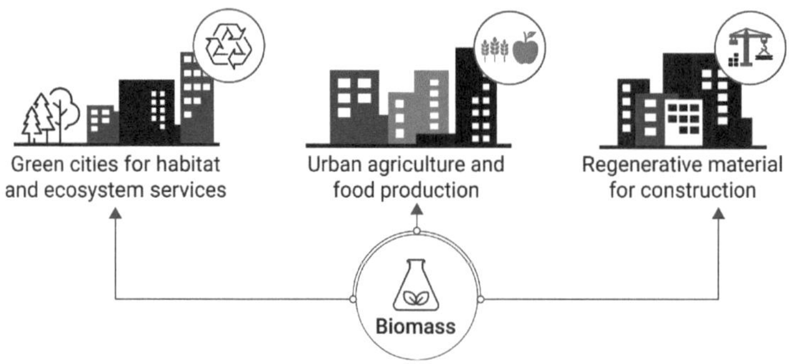

Figs. 115, 116

Arguably, the most significant potential lies in the linkage between biomass for the purpose of engendering green cities, providing habitat and the delivery of ecosystem services, biomass in the context of urban agriculture and food production, and biomass providing regenerative materials for the purpose of construction and adaptation of the built environment. This entails a multi-scale approach to biomass that considers both material flows and material performance across scales. Research efforts are already underway with a focus on urban agriculture and regenerative cities (Clarke, 2014; Rashed, 2018).

Biomass mainly relates to soil in a two-fold manner: (1) soil enables the growth of plants; and (2) biomass as organic waste can be composted and used to improve soil properties. The composting process entails two stages: the first involves microbial processes that drive the decomposition of many biodegradable materials (Azim et al., 2018); while the second stage involves the transformation of remaining organic material into so-called humic substances (Adani et al., 1999; 2018). The process of humification constitutes the major driver of improving soil quality, soil fertility, and soil structure (Chen and Aviad, 1990; Chen et al., 1994). As Azim et al. pointed out, numerous parameters are key to starting and monitoring compost process and quality and it is still difficult to upscale to field and industrial scales (Azim et al., 2018) However, some larger-scale composting processes are already at hand in peri-urban areas (Figs. 117 and 118). Nevertheless, composting offers a key process for improvement and soil management of urban soils, with the ability to effectively support urban agriculture and horticulture, green spaces, regenerative design based on utilization of biomass, and cycles of local circularity.

Fig. 117
Rural composting site in Germany. Source: Wikimedia Commons, Creative Commons Attribution-Share Alike 3.0 Unported. Photography: Crystalclear, 2007.

Fig. 118
Large composting site. Source: Wikimedia Commons, National Archives Identifier: 5999807. Photography: Environmental Protection Agency, 2007.

Figs. 117 , 118

Tapping into available and in some ways ubiquitous material resources has, as shown, several conceptual drivers. These include general sustainability, circularity (Chapter 4.7) and regeneration (Chapter 3.6), as well as material flows (Chapter 4.6), urban metabolism (Chapter 4.5), and advanced waste management. As discussed in Chapter 5.2, urban mining is a topic of increasing importance. In the context of advancing sustainability, especially regarding sustainable and green cities and green architectures, another set of materials comes to the fore. These are not typically regarded as primary architectural materials and hence not accounted for in a related manner. This, however, is currently changing across multiple scales of observation and analysis, as well as across numerous expert domains including the AEC sector and will necessarily require adequate data and correlating processes and related data across scales and domains. As this is taking shape, planners and architects need to rethink and upskill to be able to work with interdisciplinary data related to processes typically considered outside of the remit of architectural design and, at least in part, of urban design. It is important to recognize that various research fields within Earth and environmental science, such as critical zone research, will play a key role. Various research gaps will need to be addressed (Hensel and Sunguroğlu Hensel, 2023, 2024) for which data and data-driven methods are required (Sunguroğlu et al., 2022).

This development will foreground questions of architectural science in relation to other domains, such as urban science and sustainability science (Hensel 2022), as well as correlating various data-related research areas across scales (Chokhachian et al., 2022). This involves re-integrating expert domains within and across disciplines. For instance, Chokhachian et al. sought to address data-integrated approaches across the interrelated themes and domains of urban adaptation, urban morphology, urban mobility, urban climate, urban ecosystems, urban forests, and urban agriculture. "These [...] themes are related to current research on cities and urbanization based on Big Data, data science related methods, data-driven design, and analyses. Recent advances in these focal areas facilitate an improved understanding of linked urban (systems and processes) through multi-domain and trans-scalar approaches to urban planning and architectural design (Sunguroğlu Hensel et al., 2022)." (Chokhachian et al., 2022b, p. 3)

Several recent research projects indicate the emergence of data-driven approaches to novel urban green systems (Höpfl et al., 2021; Ludwig et al., 2024), novel ecological prototypes for urban food production (Sunguroğlu Hensel, 2020), and ecological building envelopes (Ludwig et al., 2021; Weisser et al., 2022). What can be gleaned from these types of projects is a move towards hybridizing architecture, landscape architecture, and urban design. It is in this context that materials like water, soil, and biomass come to the fore as integral parts of the built environment, whereby the latter term requires rethinking. Here, again, questions of material agency and material performance are key, engaging issues such as microclimate modulation, human-nature interaction, ecosystem support, and ecosystem services as integral parts of data-driven processes in planning and design. In this way, the projects highlight the required competence and skills to operate in interdisciplinary teams with the purpose of correlating domain specific datasets across a range of knowledge domains, including Earth, environmental and life sciences. This development on its own requires and is likely to foster a more holistic rethinking not only of the built environment, but also of architectural design and the AEC sector, as well as urban design, planning, management, and governance.

CHAPTER

6

INDUSTRY 4.0, 5.0, ...

As discussed in the previous chapters, industrialization fundamentally changed the way materials are thought of, designed, and utilized, and, moreover, how data are experienced and instrumentalized. This process has fostered a productive linkage of material and data across disciplines, including materials science and materials engineering, sustainability science, waste management, as well as planning and design in the context of cities, urbanization, and construction. While this development has been momentous it is far from concluded as the process of industrialization continues. Currently, humanity is in the process of progressing to a stage of industrial evolution that has been termed the *Fourth Industrial Revolution* or *Industry 4.0* (4IR). The German Federal Ministry for Economic Affairs and Climate Action defines Industry 4.0 as "the intelligent networking of machines and processes for industry with the help of information and communication technology [...]. For Industry 4.0, it is not the computer that is the core technology, but rather the Internet. Digitalizing production is gaining a new level of quality with global networking across corporate and national borders: the Internet of Things, machine-to-machine communication and manufacturing facilities that are becoming ever more intelligent are heralding a new era: the fourth industrial revolution, Industry 4.0." (Federal Ministry for Economic Affairs and Climate Action – Platform Industry 4.0, 2024) Combined with a set of novel technologies this constitutes a new paradigm shift. Klaus Schwab, who introduced the term Industry 4.0, stated that humanity stands "on the brink of a technological revolution that will fundamentally alter the way we live, work, and relate to one another. In its scale, scope, and complexity, the transformation will be unlike anything humankind has experienced before. We do not yet know just how it will unfold, but one thing is clear: the response to it must be integrated and comprehensive, involving all stakeholders of the global polity, from the public and private sectors to academia and civil society." (Schwab, 2015) Philbeck and Davis further elaborated that "The Fourth Industrial Revolution builds upon the rapid exchange of information made possible by the data-centric foundations of the Third Industrial Revolution's digital technologies, which in turn relied on the electricity and telecommunication systems at the heart of the Second Industrial Revolution. The layering of dependencies matters because it shows that 4IR is best suited to examining technologies and systems that take the digital world for granted [...]. Digital technologies are part of the fabric of daily life and, as they give rise to a new layer of physical and biological technologies, it is paramount to consider the ways that newer technologies emerging atop them are extending capabilities beyond the immediate functionality of being able to transmit, store, and process exponentially greater amounts of data." (Philbeck and Davis, 2018, p. 18) This shows that 4IR builds on the assumption that data are widely available, though the previous chapters have shown this is not fully the case regarding material aspects. Nevertheless, it is useful to examine trajectories of development that operate on this assumption, ushering in the next step in industrial development.

As Industry 4.0 unfolds, it is already exerting a significant impact on the AEC sector. The question that must be asked now is how materials thinking, design and engineering will further evolve. This is likely to involve, on the one hand, advancing the links between materials science and data science in the context of 4IR (Sajid et al., 2021), and on the other, developing networking technology via the internet, the Internet of Things (Qazi et al., 2022) (see Chapter 1.8), artificial intelligence, machine learning (Chodbury, 2021), digital twins (Qazi et al., 2022), advanced robotics, etc. Another key question is how materials and material data are experienced and instrumentalized in planning and design involving material flows and material agency. This chapter focuses on examining some of the innovative data-driven methods and novel technologies that have emerged and that promise to take or

Fig. 119
Data-driven methods and emerging technologies, including extended reality, haptic feedback, and gamification, are becoming increasingly important in materials science.

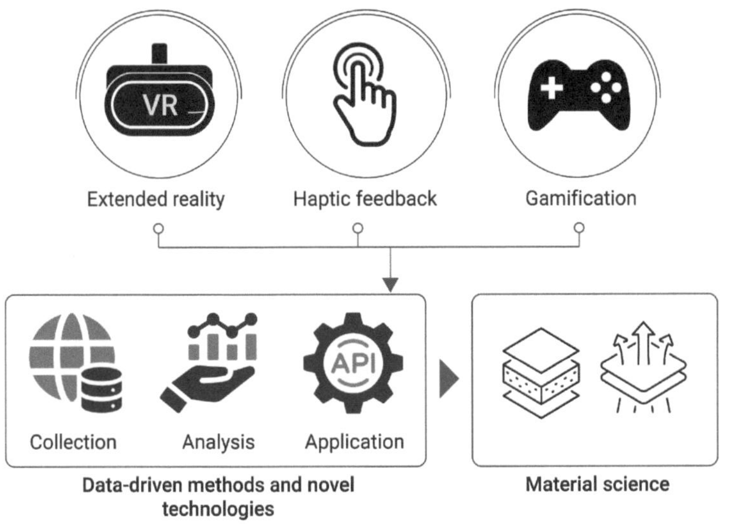

Fig. 119

have taken prominent roles in the field of materials science, and the way planning and design instrumentalizes material flows and material agency. These technologies include Extended Reality (XR) (virtual, augmented, mixed reality) (Stanney et al., 2021), the provision of haptic feedback in Extended Reality (MacLean, 2000; Stone, 2001; Danieau et al., 2013; See et al., 2022), as well as gaming and gamification (Deterding et al., 2011) (Fig 119).

6.2 EXTENDED REALITY

Extended Reality technology includes Augmented Reality, Mixed Reality, Virtual Reality, and XR blended. These are computer-generated immersive environments that provide a range of different experiences to the user (Stanney et al., 2021).

Virtual Reality provides "shared, simulated spaces which are inhabited and shaped by their inhabitants who are represented as avatars" (Girvan, 2018, p. 1099) and is based on telepresence, interactivity, and immersion (Walsh and Pawlowski, 2002). Augmented Reality entails "real-time combination of digital and physical information through different technological devices" (Cabero and Barroso, 2016, p. 44). Extended Reality entails "all real-and-virtual combined environments and human-machine interactions generated by computer technology and wearables." (Fast-Berglund et al., 2018, p. 32) Biswas and Visell point out that "emerging virtual and augmented reality technologies can transform human activities in myriad domains, lending tangible, embodied form to digital data, services, and information" (Biswas and Visell, 2021, p. 1). Furthermore, Cárdenas-Robledo et al. (2020) explain that "Extended Reality technologies such as Virtual Reality, Augmented Reality, and Mixed Reality represents a paradigm that enhances and supports industry 4.0 in diverse settings [...]." The combination of such technologies reduces the gap between the physical and digital world, allowing the direct interaction of remote physical locations, where the work of the Operator 4.0, "a smart and skilled operator who may perform not only cooperative work with robots but also work aided by machines and if needed by means of human cyber-physical systems, advanced human-machine interaction technologies and adaptive automation towards achieving human-automation symbiosis work systems" (Romero et al., 2016a, p. 678), leads to faster real-time decision making (Berg and Vance, 2017) and new knowledge generation (Romero et al., 2016b; Romero et al., 2016a; Romero et al., 2017).

Extended Reality technology has been extensively used in architectural design and architectural design education (Hensel and Sørensen, 2013, 2014; Kharvari and Kaiser, 2022), and urban design and planning (Hajrasouliha, 2023; Matthys et al., 2023). Extended Reality utilization has also been proposed for the AEC sector (Han and Leite, 2022). Alizadehsalehi et al. state that in the AEC sector "Extended Reality technologies that simulate a construction project in a multidimensional digital model and present multiple aspects of a project can be a tremendous help in all stages of a project" (Alizadehsalehi et al., 2020, p. 1). They also highlight different methods for converting BIM models to virtual, augmented, and mixed reality. (ibid.)

Extended Reality can serve to render visible material performance that are known but not normally visible. For example, the Islamic wooden latticework screen walls, so-called *mashrabīyas*, are building elements that regulate light, air flow, temperature, humidity of the air current, and visual access and control from the inside to the outside and vice versa (see Chapter 2.5). As described above, this is accomplished by a controlled articulation of the sizes of the balusters that make up the latticework and the interstices between them. Extended Reality can be used to render visible not only the material object but also the airflow, adding a color gradient that indicates, for instance, the velocity of airflow. Likewise, the hygroscopic behavior of the *mashrabīyas* can be visualized. This can be done by changing the sizes of the balusters that make up the latticework and the interstices between them, and by extension the changing velocity of airflow or changes in ambient humidity or moisture content of the wooden balusters. This produces a direct visual validation of changes in material behavior and material performance. The same logic can also be applied to larger scales, for the purpose of analyzing and altering material flows. Given the possibilities of creating different overlays of visual data on different performances and at different scales in Virtual Reality, Augmented Reality, and Mixed Reality, these represent a powerful toolset for material scientists, material engineers, architects, and planners.

Extended Reality technologies are currently used for teaching and learning in materials science and materials engineering (Extremera et al., 2022). Vegara et al. identified "a growing trend to use virtual reality learning environments (VRLEs) in education to enhance the student learning process and course learning

Fig. 120
Extended reality technologies - encompassing virtual, mixed, and augmented realit - are widely applied in architectural design and education, urban planning, and construction simulation.

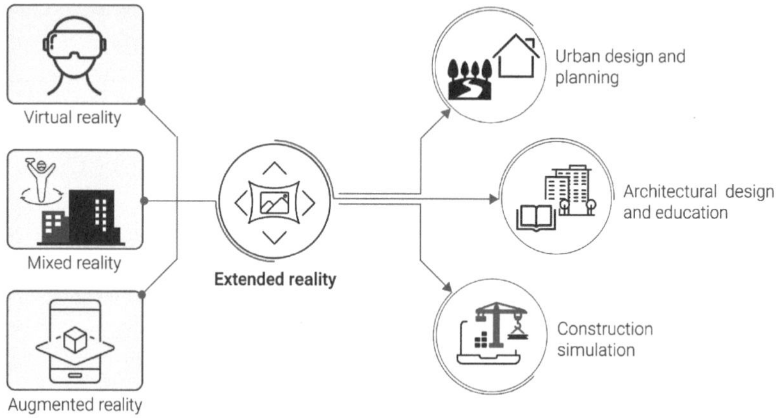

Fig. 120

outcomes (Vegara et al., 2017a). This fact is also reflected in the instruction of materials science and engineering (MSE) in higher education (Vegara et al., 2017b; Le, 2024)." (Vegara, 2019, p. 1) This constitutes a major extension from learning through physical experiments in laboratories to learning in virtual or augmented environments. In some instances, the latter even fully replaces the former, especially when physical facilities are not at hand or when physical experiments are too resource-intensive.

6.3 HAPTIC FEEDBACK

Different types of feedback are under development in the context of Extended Reality, especially in media, medical and biological sciences. One focus of technical development is placed on haptic feedback, which adds a powerful element to the virtual design of materials or to virtual material experiments. Biswas and Visell point out that "emerging Virtual and Augmented Reality technologies can transform human activities in myriad domains, lending tangible, embodied form to digital data, services, and information. Haptic technologies will play a critical role in enabling humans to touch and interact with the contents of these virtual environments. The immense variety of skilled manual tasks that humans perform in real environments are only possible through the coordination of touch sensation, perception, and movement that together comprise the haptic modality." (Biswas and Visell, 2021, p. 1) Stone notes that "haptic feedback systems have evolved much faster than their visual display counterparts and are, today, delivering impressive peripheral devices that are truly usable by non-specialist users of computing technology" (Stone, 2001, p. 1). Danieau et al. explain that "haptic technology has been widely employed in applications ranging from teleoperation and medical simulation to art and design, including entertainment, flight simulation, and virtual reality. Today there is a growing interest among researchers in integrating haptic feedback into audiovisual systems. A new medium emerges from this effort: haptic-audiovisual (HAV) content." (Danieau et al., 2013, p. 193) Haptic feedback can serve a variety of different workflows, for instance in combination with advanced and often remote robotic technologies (Minami et al., 2023).

Haptic rendering is one way of providing haptic feedback (Salisbury et al., 2004; Höver et al., 2009; Xia, 2018). Salisbury et al. explain that "interactions can be between a human hand and a real object; a robot end-effector and a real object; a human hand and a simulated object (via haptic interface devices); or a variety of combinations of human and machine interactions with real, remote or virtual objects. Rendering refers to the process by which desired stimuli are imposed on the user to convey information about a virtual haptic object." (Salisbury et al. 2004, p. 24) Current research includes data-driven haptic rendering for different types of material behavior, including visco-elasticity (Höver et al., 2008; Abdulali et al., 2020; Cha et al., 2022) and plasticity (Abdulali and Jeon, 2021). Data-driven approaches facilitated by neural networks and Deep Learning have been proposed and explored for the purpose of haptic rendering (Chen, 2016; Joolee and Jeon, 2022). Furthermore, different approaches to haptic sensing and feedback are under development, such as wearable technologies (Yin et al., 2021). Yin et al. describe "devices fabricated from flexible and elastic bio-compatible materials have significantly greater compatibility with the human body and could lead to a more natural VR/AR experience [...] soft materials for wearable sensing and haptic feedback in VR/AR applications, explores emerging soft technologies for on-body devices, and identifies current challenges and future opportunities toward seamless integration of the virtual and physical world." (Yin et al., 2021) Various research groups are exploring the topic, for instance in the context of the Special Research Area project Advanced Computational Design at Vienna University of Technology. In this context, one "goal is to develop a mobile, remotely controlled, safe robot platform that provides haptic feedback of elastic materials in large walkable VR, so that users can interact with larger surfaces that react to physical pressure. The major scientific contributions are (1) the establishment of a new platform that supports safe large-scale haptic interaction, (2) research and development of novel algorithms, safety concepts and interaction metaphors for human-robot interaction in immersive VEs and (3) near real-time mechanical simulation of elastic structural response for haptic interaction with 3D virtual structural elements. In a range of future VR applications such as architectural design (e.g., stage design SP2), industrial simulation, training, entertainment and rehabilitation, large areas and haptic interaction are of crucial importance." (Advanced Computational Design, 2024) Still, while a few similar efforts are currently underway, there remains a large research gap on the topic of haptic feedback.

In summary, haptic feedback can not only extend the possibilities and potentials of teaching and learning in materials science and materials engineering using virtual or augmented environments, but also constitutes a major contribution to conducting virtual experiments extending the possibilities of virtual material design.

6.4 GAMIFICATION

Serious games are characterized by an "defined educational intent and are meant primarily for entertainment" (Abt, 1987). Deterding et al. define gamification as "using game design elements in non-game contexts", explaining that "recent years have seen a rapid proliferation of mass-market consumer software that takes inspiration from video games. Usually summarized as 'gamification', this trend connects to [...] existing concepts and research in human-computer interaction and game studies, such as serious games, pervasive games, alternate reality games, or playful design." (Deterding et al., 2011, p. 9) Furthermore, Morsi and Jackson pointed out that games can serve to develop various abilities including the rapid processing of information, training visual processing techniques, and improving skills in data organization, critical thinking and problem solving (Morsi and Jackson, 2007).

Simulation-based games have received considerable attention in the context of urban planning and governance. Duke and Geurts define a simulation as “a conscious endeavor to reproduce the central characteristics of a system in order to understand, experiment with and/or predict the behavior of a system” (Duke and Geurts, 2004, p. 36). A prominent example of a simulation game on urban scales is *SimCity*, the educational value of which has been broadly reflected upon (Adams, 1998; Gaber, 2007; Bereitschaft, 2015; Arnold et al., 2019). The potential use of gaming simulations in architecture has been under examination for some time already (May, 1979). Recently, Yan et al. proposed the integration of Building Information Modelling with gaming applications to enable real-time interactive visualization for architecture, focusing on “interoperability between games and building models to enhance architectural visualization and education [...] with the capability for simulations of physical dynamics and user activities” (Yan et al., 2011, p. 446). Furthermore, aspects of immersion, interaction and collaboration in architectural design based on utilizing gaming engines are investigated (Hoon et al., 2003). Barham et al. reported the use of game-based laboratory simulation for the purpose of teaching and learning about material strengths in the context of civil engineering (Barham et al., 2012). Further research into serious games applications and gaming engines and their implementation in the AEC sector and in materials science and engineering is underway.

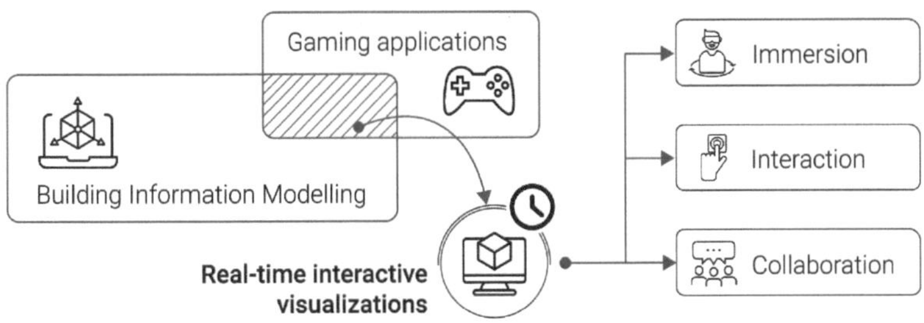

Fig. 121

Fig. 121
Combining Building Information Modeling (BIM) with gaming applications enhances real-time architectural visualization, including simulations and interactive design.

Artificial Intelligence (AI) and machine learning (ML) have been mentioned in various instances in the previous chapters, alluding to their increasing importance in numerous sectors, and more specifically in the AEC sector and in materials science and engineering. Nevertheless, as a key element of Industry 4.0 the topic of AI requires a more detailed examination, as both AI (Li et al., 2020) and ML (Vasudevan et al., 2019; DeCost et al., 2020) are rapidly taking center stage in materials science and materials engineering.

Li et al. have found that "advances in artificial intelligence (AI), especially machine learning (ML), provide enormous tools for processing complex data generated from experimental and computational materials research. With the rapid development of AI methods and the complex nature of interdisciplinary research, a challenge is posed as for which methods to choose for different material systems or context and which steps of the material discovery process would stand to benefit [...]. AI can assist in each step through the whole life cycle of material discovery (including characterization, property prediction, synthesis, and theory paradigm discovery)." (Li et al., 2020, p. 393) Furthermore, DeCost et al. explain that ML "applications to materials science have exploded, spanning data analysis, knowledge extraction, and experiment selection (Agrawal and Choudhary, 2016; Holdren et al., 2014). The numerous reasons for this trend are related to the omnipresence of ML systems in our everyday lives, the free availability software, and the demonstrated successes in materials discovery and on-the-fly data acquisition inspired by the Materials Genome Initiative (MGI; Agrawal and Choudhary, 2016; Aziza, 2018; Lookman et al., 2016)." (DeCost et al., 2020, p. 1) The Materials Genome Initiative serves the purpose of "discovering, manufacturing, and deploying advanced materials twice as fast and at a fraction of the cost compared to traditional methods [...]. Advanced materials are essential to economic security and human well-being, with applications in industries aimed at addressing challenges in clean energy, national security, and human welfare, yet it can take 20 or more years to move a material after initial discovery to the market. Accelerating the pace of discovery and deployment of advanced material systems will therefore be crucial to achieving global competitiveness in the 21st century." (Materials Genome Initiative, 2024) Another development of interest is the AI-based materials knowledge system (AI-MKS) framework, which seeks to utilize “emergent AI/ML (machine learning) toolsets in conjunction with [...] experimental and physics-based simulation toolsets employed currently by the domain experts in the materials field” for the purpose of engineering features of heterogeneous materials (Kalidini, 2020, p. 1).

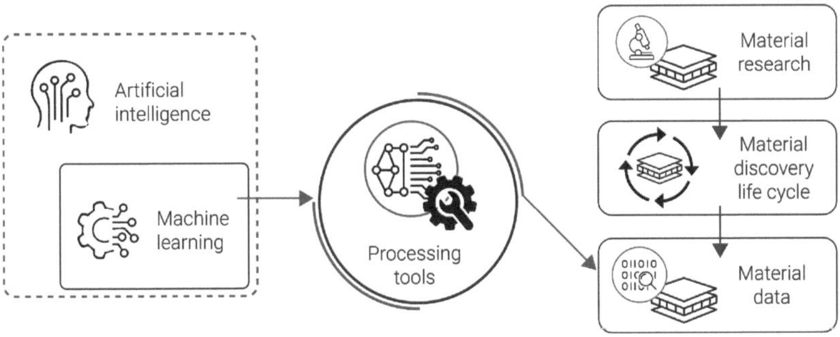

Fig. 122

Fig. 122 Artificial intelligence (AI), especially machine learning (ML), provides powerful tools for processing complex data in materials research and supports each step of the material discovery process

More generally, most current efforts at utilizing AI in materials science are focused on material design and materials engineering rather than on knowledge discovery through fundamental scientific insight from data. Therefore, to tap into the potential of AI more fully it is necessary to utilize scientific AI for the purpose of scientific inquiry and knowledge discovery (Cost et al., 2020). Furthermore, there is a research gap in materials science and materials engineering regarding AI systems that can be part of inferring physical principles from data and probabilistic methods (DeCost et al., 2020). This indicates that the promising aspects of AI not only include methods of material design and optimization that are already being developed, but even more importantly scientific inquiry and knowledge discovery, not only in materials science, but also involving further knowledge domains.

6.6 ADVANCED MANUFACTURING

Cyber-Physical Systems (CPS) play a key role in the development of advanced manufacturing. Monostori et al. explain that “cyber-physical systems [...] are systems of collaborating computational entities which are in intensive connection with the surrounding physical world and its on-going processes, providing and using, at the same time, data-accessing and data-processing services available on the Internet." (Monostori et al., 2016, p. 621) Cyber-physical production systems (CPPS) utilize Cyber-Physical Systems in the context of production and manufacturing. Arinez et al. claim that "manufacturing is entering a period of substantial innovation and change driven by the increased integration of sensors and the Internet of Things (IoT), increased data availability, and advances in robotics and automation. This leads to pervasive digitalization of the factory and challenges manufacturing enterprises to reconsider, reexamine, and reevaluate their present operations and future strategic directions in the new era known as Smart Manufacturing and Industry 4.0 (Monostori et al., 2016) [...]. The factory operations face challenges of highly nonlinear and stochastic activity due to the countless uncertainties and interdependencies that exist. Recent developments in artificial intelligence (AI), especially machine learning (ML) have shown great potential to transform the manufacturing domain through advanced analytics tools for processing the vast amounts of manufacturing data generated." (Arinez et al., 2020, p. 1). The notion of smart manufacturing implies converting "data acquired across the product lifecycle into manufacturing intelligence to yield positive impacts on all aspects of manufacturing [...]. The emergence of New IT as the Internet of Things (IoT), Cloud computing, mobile Internet, and artificial intelligence (AI), can be strategically leveraged and effectively integrated in support of data-driven manufacturing." (Tao et al., 2018, p. 157) Smart additive manufacturing implies the use of data-driven methods and tools, for instance in materials design (Tian et al., 2021).

Construction 4.0 is based on the utilization of BIM, GIS, AI, ML, Extended Reality, advanced manufacturing, and robotics, IoT, as well as Big Data (Wang et al., 2022). Various advanced manufacturing technologies have been considered and developed for the AEC sector. These include additive manufacturing technologies such as 3D printing, producing objects by successive layers of material, 4D printing (involving property-changing materials, thereby enabling self-assembly and adaptability), and 5D printing, incorporating cost and time dimensions (Rane, 2023). The scope of efforts regarding development implementation of advanced technologies in the AEC sector includes off-site production and assembly, on-site construction, design, and construction of experimental prototypes that demonstrate potential applications of advanced manufacturing or use of novel materials. A key driver of innovation is the research-driven use and development of manufacturing technologies and materials. These have been investigated in academic contexts, especially with a focus on emergent technologies and their role in design (Hensel et al., 2010) and the production of prototypes for material systems or full-scale constructions (Hensel and Menges, 2006; Menges et al., 2017; Yuan and Menges, 2019).

In summary, advanced manufacturing and construction in the AEC sector and the utilization of advanced and smart manufacturing in material design are well underway, even though many research gaps exist. Data play a key role in all the technologies that are directly involved in advanced manufacturing. In the process new expert fields and skills emerge and will be required for further development and application of advanced manufacturing.

6.7 THE INTERNET OF THINGS

The Internet of Things (IoT) is a network of connected physical devices that communicate and exchange data over the internet, enabling real-time monitoring, control, automation, and advanced manufacturing. IoT as digital materiality of physical objects implies that "physical materiality refers to artifacts that can be seen and touched, that are generally hard to change, and that connote a sense of place and time [...] Digital materiality, in contrast, refers to what the software incorporated into an artifact can do by manipulating digital representations." (Yoo et al., 2012, p. 1398) Physical objects with digital materiality can be characterized by seven properties:

/ '*Senseability*' (context-awareness): the ability of a digitalized artifact to sense and respond to changes in its environment.

/ '*Addressability*' and '*traceability*': the ability to be identified and located in real time.

/ '*Associability*': the ability to be associated, and therefore coordinated, with other objects to enable inferences about future states and conditions.

/ '*Communicability*': the ability to send and receive digitized messages.

/ '*Programmability*': the ability to accept new sets of instructions and to modify its behaviors.
/ '*memorability*': the ability to store information and historical logs of its state and interactions.
(Ng and Wakenshaw, 2017)

Industrial IoT (IIoT) entails machine-to-machine and industrial communication technologies with automation applications for the purpose of enabling efficient and sustainable production. Sisinni et al. explain that "the IIoT (the basic pillar of digital manufacturing) is about connecting all the industrial assets, including machines and control systems, with the information systems and the business processes. Therefore, the large amount of data collected can feed analytic solutions and lead to optimal industrial operations. On the other hand, Smart Manufacturing [...] focuses on the manufacturing stage of (smart) product life cycle, with the goal of quickly and dynamically responding to demand changes. Therefore, the IIoT affects all the industrial value chain and is a requirement for smart manufacturing." (Sisinni et al., 2018, p. 4725).

Currently IoT is gaining prominence in architectural design and urban planning. Rathore et al. proposed the development of an "IoT-based system for smart city development and urban planning using Big Data analytics [...] consisting of various types of sensor deployment, including smart home sensors, vehicular networking, weather and water sensors, smart parking sensors, and surveillance objects. A four-tier architecture is proposed that includes [...] IoT sources and data generation and collection, [...] communication between, for instance, sensors, relays, base stations, and the Internet, [...] data management and processing [... and] application and usage of the data analysis and the results generated. The system implementation consists of various steps that begin with data generation and move to collection, aggregation, filtration, classification, preprocessing, computing, and decision making." (Rathore et al., 2016, p. 63)

Proposed or implemented IoT applications in the AEC sector include, for instance, BIM and IoT data, as well as relational databases to advance construction and operational activities (Tang et al., 2019; Biswas et al., 2024), the combination of AI and IoT-based sensors for monitoring and control (Rane et al., 2023), and linking BIM, AI and IoT for the purpose of prefabricated construction (Rangasamy and Yang, 2024). Linking BIM and IoT data can "offer complementary views of the project that together supplement the limitations of each. BIM models offer high fidelity representations of the project at the component level. By incorporating geometry, spatial location and a scalable set of metadata properties, BIM models provide a high-fidelity operable dataset capturing the as-designed building objects, properties, and spatial organization as a set of virtual assets. IoT data enhance this information set by providing real-time and recordable status from the actual operations in construction and operations." (Tang et al., 2019, p. 127)

IoT is proposed in combination with AI and smart materials in a wide range of sectors including the medical sector (Fatima et al., 2021), in energy applications (Kolhe et al., 2022), in the automotive sector (Ammar et al., 2022), to support the advancement of nano-materials (Vasoya, 2023), to enable smart materials, smart textiles and smart clothing (Ramaiah, 2021; Han, 2023), as well as in architecture (Wang et al., 2018).

This indicates that IoT in conjunction with AI and smart materials has gained or is in the process gaining a foothold across industries as a one of the key aspects and technologies of Industry 4.0. Again, data play a fundamental role in this development, involving direct data acquisition in which material agency and material flows can directly impact on design and operational decisions. The importance of IoT can therefore not be overstated and will increasingly impact data-driven processes in design, planning, and operation especially in the context of the built environment.

6.8 OUTLOOK

Industry 5.0 develops in parallel to Industry 4.0, foregrounding the transition to a human-centric and sustainable industry (European Commission – Research and Innovation, 2024). Industry 5.0 contributes to several European Commission priorities including "an economy that works for people", the "European Green Deal" and "Europe fit for the digital age", by way of:

/ "Adopting a human-centric approach to digital technologies including artificial intelligence.

/ Up-skilling and reskilling workers, particularly in digital skills.

/ Modern, resource-efficient, and sustainable industries and the transition to a circular economy (Green Deal).

/ A globally competitive and world-leading industry, speeding up investment in research and innovation." (European Commission – Research and Innovation, 2024)

Key aspects of Industry 5.0 include *the democratization of knowledge* (Özdemir and Hekim, 2018), *human-robot collaboration* (Nahavandi, 2019), and *smart consumption* (Rosemann et al., 2021). Regarding the latter, Roseman et al. explain that "(Industry) 5.0 focuses on the time and the experiences during the consumption of a product. Digital technologies like sensors and Cloud computing have facilitated a 'continuous connectivity' between a product's provider and its consumer (Siggelkow and Terwiesch, 2019) such that selling a product is no longer the end of a relationship [...] products can instead follow a *make-to-evolve paradigm*. These products are upgradeable and continue to develop new capabilities tailored to a changing context and the users' profiles." (Rosemann et al., 2021, p. 71)

Many of the technological advancements of Industry 4.0 and 5.0 are already underway. While these are not yet fully implemented on a global scale and in many sectors, the consequences are nevertheless clear as can be seen in many regions and industries, including materials science and materials engineering, as well as the AEC sector. The combination of Big Data, data-driven research, planning and design, advanced data analytics, artificial intelligence, advanced manufacturing, the Internet of Things, the transition to a circular economy ('Green Deal'), a rapid increase in digital skills of scientists, researchers and workers, investment in research and innovation, are separately and jointly driving fundamental change.

All this begs the question as to the next step in the development. UBS has stated that "such is the elevated pace of technological progress that just as many enterprises feel they have begun adapting to Industry 5.0, the latest upgrade is already on the horizon. Industry 4.0 was powered by the integration of IoT, Cloud computing, advanced analytics, AI and machine learning into manufacturing processes and enterprise workflows [...] Industry 5.0 emerged as a concept looking to complement the technologies of industry 4.0 with an added focus on human, social and environmental value. And now Industry 6.0 looks to create intelligent systems that can operate with little need for human intervention [...]." (UBS, 2023). Furthermore, Carayannis et al. note that "in Industry 6.0, artificial intelligence permeates all sectors of the economy and society, and [...] enables a comprehensive acceleration of innovation processes [...] This includes resources, such as food, water, steel, education, robotics, and energy. A significant portion of industrial tools and physical goods are produced using 3-D printing techniques, utilizing nanotechnologies and CAM processes (Carayannis, 2023) [...] Within the context of Industry 6.0, machines are primarily designed and manufactured by other machines. Materials and manufacturing processes become too complex for much of the population to comprehend from one generation to another [...] In addition, it can be assumed that new technologies, such as quantum computing, will allow for the creation of copies of all things. For every individual, it will be possible, at any time and location, to access the accumulated knowledge of the world through suitable human interfaces. In such a scenario, research, exploration, and creativity will become the highest human endeavors (Carayannis, 2023)." (Carayannis et al., 2024, p. 11244)

The full implementation of Industries 4.0, 5.0, and 6.0 will likely change on a fundamental level how the built environment is thought of and how planning and design on architectural, urban, and larger scales operates, especially in relation to material agency and material flows, as the make-up and performative capacities of materials will be exploited in unprecedented ways. This ground-breaking transition will probably not fully eradicate traditional and craft-based approaches as most developments tend to foster a countertrend of appreciating the 'old' ways. However, how traditional solutions are perceived and studied will likely be affected and altered in the context of material performance and data-driven methods and technologies. As an example, one might think of traditional green roofs in vernacular timber buildings. In many parts of the Global North such roofs utilized birch bark as a waterproof layer to keep rainwater out. This is only possible with birch bark that is not entirely dry, as dryness would lead to cracks and therefore loss of function. Typically, the birch bark was topped with a layer of soil and a low growth green vegetation. The soil serves to retain humidity to prevent the birch bark from drying out. The vegetation can be seen as a sensor that indicates whether the soil contains an adequate level of humidity or whether it is getting too dry. When the vegetation turns yellow for too long action is required. It does not seem far-fetched to imagine similar material agency (albeit technical rather than natural) will allow different layers of a material system to actively communicate and adjust performances in a smart way. Moreover, traditional solutions used natural and frequently regenerative materials, a trend that is likely to be of great importance in relation to building livable cities and implementing the Green Deal. The design and utilization of materials are already multi-domain and trans-scalar in character, whereby local, regional, and global aspects are linked on issues of material performance and material flows. As the transition towards Industries 4.0, 5.0, and 6.0 takes shape, the type of involvement of humans in material design and manufacturing, operation and management, material circular economy, etc. will likely change too on a fundamental level or at least add an entirely novel range of involvement or non-involvement. This book can only offer an initial glimpse of this development. Further frequent examinations of the developments described herein will need to take place to establish the specific trajectories of developments as they unfold.

CONCLUSION

As stated in the preceding chapters, the continued integration of material data resources, advanced materials, smart sensors, and digital modeling technologies promises a transformative future for the AEC sector. Material data resources and repositories are foundational for materials science and materials engineering research, offering valuable information on properties, behaviors, and performance. Building Information Systems (BIS) and Building Information Modelling (BIM) store and manage building-related information, while facilitating collaboration among architects, engineers, and contractors, leading to more efficient and sustainable building designs. Improved decision-making and effectiveness results from the continuous flow of structured material data throughout the planning, design, construction, and reuse and adaptation processes.

Data-driven approaches to designing material performance tap into expert databases that will likely be significantly expanded with data on *material behavior* and *material performance* and *material systems performance*. Multivariate and spatio-temporal data, data mining and analysis, data-driven modeling, and simulations for the purpose of design and multi-criteria optimization will play a role. Regarding *material properties, focus* needs to be placed on (i) *material variation*, (ii) the *hierarchical organization* of materials across scales, and (iii) the *correlation of material properties*. Regarding *material behavior,* focus needs to be placed on (i) instrumentalizing the *correlation between material properties and their interactions with the surrounding environment*, (ii) combining *knowledge-driven* and *data-driven* modeling, (iii) and employing *multivariate spatio-temporal data* methods and tools. Regarding *material performance* and *material systems performance,* focus will need to be placed on: (i) linking the abovementioned aspects of material properties and material behavior into a *data-driven design* approach to *design variety generation* in which each design output can be analyzed and ranked, and (ii) sharing data on *material performance* and *material systems performance* in a dedicated open-source expert database. Furthermore, future research will need to focus on the development of visual programming-based tools that facilitate both extensive system mapping, as well as computational ontologies for decision support with focus on material and material systems performance(s). The increasing utilization of spatio-temporal data and multi-scalar data in planning and design, as well as in materials science and materials informatics, will change architectural design and urban planning at a fundamental level. Furthermore, data-driven computational simulations are increasingly taking center stage in urban planning and architectural design.

Novel resource and waste management processes, including reuse, recycling, upcycling, circularity, and regeneration, have become central topics in urban planning and design as well as in architectural design. Circular material flows require data that consider variable circumstances in terms of spatial locations and stakeholder needs. On the one hand, this necessitates geospatial reference data; on the other, specific collated product-related data are essential to provide materials, products – including buildings – with an identity. As with all data applications, the extent to which any claim of *retaining circularity potential* is justified depends on the quality and accessibility of the data. This is fundamental in relation to geographically dispersed flows of materials in a circular value network, specifically regarding the control over these materials. Sustainability and industrial ecology offer several invaluable tools and methods for quantifying and qualifying the sustainability impact of interventions at various scale levels, in particular relating to lifecycle performances. Moreover, the sheer complexity inherent in rigorous analytical Life Cycle Assessment studies has ushered in the development of simplified methods and fast tracks, cutting off specific aspects that may be crucial to assess geographically distributed environmental impacts of a circular economy. Proposals for material passports have been developed that usually adhere to aspects such as material composition, Life Cycle Assessment, traceability, due diligence efforts, and associated circular economy services such as repair, redistribution, and remanufacturing. The innovation of passports for buildings and building materials has been coupled with the potential of digital technologies, such as georeferenced building information modeling, 360° photography, and virtual or augmented digital surroundings. Such technologies can help improve the accuracy of building orientations, enhance material orders and associated transport miles, reduce waste, and cut costs.

Tapping into ubiquitous material resources requires several conceptual drivers, including general sustainability, circularity, regeneration, as well as material flows, urban metabolism, and advanced waste management, and urban mining. Furthermore, in the context of advancing sustainability through green cities and green architectures, another set of other materials has come to the fore that is not typically regarded as primary architectural materials. This is currently changing across multiple scales of observation and analysis, as well as across numerous expert domains including the AEC sector. This development will necessarily require adequate data and correlating processes and related data across scales and domains. As this is taking shape planners and architects need to rethink and upskill to be able to work with interdisciplinary data related to processes typically seen as outside the remit of architectural design and, at least in part, of urban design. It is vital to recognize that Earth and environmental sciences will play a key role. Various research gaps exist that will need to be addressed and for which data and data-driven methods are required, tackling issues such as microclimate modulation, human-nature interaction, ecosystem support, and ecosystem services as an integral element of data-driven processes in planning and design. Competence and skills development needs to focus on interdisciplinary work with the purpose of correlating domain-specific datasets across a range of knowledge domains. This development is likely to foster more holistic rethinking of the built environment, architectural design, and the AEC sector, as well as of urban design, planning, management, and governance.

Finally, as Industry 4.0 rapidly unfolds it will fundamentally affect materials thinking and material design. The combination of Big Data, Extended Reality, Artificial Intelligence, advanced manufacturing, and the Internet of Things have already ushered in tremendous change across many sectors, including materials science, and gradually yet persistently in architectural design and urban planning. While this transformation still needs to run its course, developments towards Industry 5.0 are already underway bringing about key changes that complement Industry 4.0 and promote a sustainable and human-centric industry. Beyond this, Industry 6.0 will add intelligent systems that can operate with little need for human involvement, especially through a high degree of AI implementation across industrial sectors and society, thereby enabling an enormous acceleration of innovation processes. Some experts suggested that in the context of Industry 6.0 material and manufacturing process will be too complex for most people to comprehend (Carayannis et al., 2024). This can be seen as both an exciting and disturbing outlook, suggesting dystopian out-of-control processes. At this stage the key question is how societies and individuals will relate to this development, especially concerning the future evolution of material culture and knowledge, which undergoes a fundamental transition towards a forecasted independence of intelligent systems that will further alter material and manufacturing processes. It is likely that, in future, the relationship between material and data will necessarily require a new and more holistic examination of how this relationship continues to restructure material thinking and design in architecture, urban and larger scales, both for human, non-human and machinic actors.

INTRODUCTION

Altafini, D., Pezzica, C., Bleil De Souza, C., Gagarin, A., Rosenberg, G., Gunner, S., and Tryfonas, T. (2024) 'DECIDE: An outcome-driven decision support system for urban-regional planning', *Networks, Markets & People (NMP) International Symposium: Communities, Institutions and Enterprises towards post-humanism epistemologies and AI challenges*, Reggio Calabria, Italy, 22–24 May 2024. Available at: https://orca.cardiff.ac.uk/id/eprint/168179/ (Accessed 13 August 2024)

Ashby, M. (2014) 'Foreword: Materials Experience – Fundamentals of Materials and Design', in Karana, E., Pedgley, O., and Rognoli, V. (eds.) *Materials Experience – Fundamentals of materials and design*. Oxford: Butterworth-Heinemann, Elsevier, pp. xvii–xxii.

Ball, D.W. (2015) *The Nature of Matter: Understanding the Physical World*. Chantilly, VA: The Great Courses.

Batty, M. (2013) 'Big data, smart cities, and city planning', *Dialogues in Human Geography*, 3(3), pp. 274–279. doi:10.1177/2043820613513390.

Bokolo, A.J. (2023) 'Data driven approaches for smart city planning and design: a case scenario on urban data management', *Digital Policy, Regulation and Governance*, 25 (4), pp. 351–367. doi:10.1108/DPRG-03-2022-0023.

Chokhachian, A., Hensel, M., and Perini, K. (eds.) (2022) Informed Urban Environments: Data-integrated Design for Human and Ecology-centered Perspectives. Cham: Springer. doi:10.1007/978-3-031-03803-7.

Deutsch R. (2016) *Data-Driven Design and Construction – 25 Strategies for Capturing, Analysing, and Applying Building Data*. Hoboken NJ: Wiley.

Engin, Z., van Dijk, J., Lan, T., Longley, P.A., Treleaven, P., Batty, M., and Penn, A. (2020) 'Data-driven urban management: Mapping the landscape', *Journal of Urban Management*, 9(2), pp. 140–150. doi:10.1016/j.jum.2019.12.001.

Federal Ministry for Economic Affairs and Climate Action – Platform Industry 4.0 (2024) What is Industry 4.0. Available at: www.plattform-i40.de/IP/Navigation/EN/Industrie40/WhatIsIndustrie40/what-is-industrie40.html (Accessed 24 August 2024).

Geldermans, B. (2020) 'Securing healthy circular material flows in the built environment,' *DOAJ (DOAJ: Directory of Open Access Journals)* [Preprint]. doi:10.7480/abe.2020.06.5038.

Hensel, M. and Bier, H.H. (eds.) (2022) Interdisciplinary Data-integrated Approaches, *Spool 9*(1). doi:10.47982/spool.2022.1.00.

Hensel, M. and Sunguroğlu, D. (2008) 'Material Performance', *Architectural Design*, 78(2), pp. 34–38. doi:10.1002/ad.639.

Hensel, M. (2022) 'The Bigger Picture en Route to Informed Urban Environments – Initiating Linkages Between Sustainability Science, Urban Science, and Architectural Science Through an Inter- and Transdisciplinary Data-Integrated Approach', in Chokhachian, A., Hensel, M., and Perini, K. (eds.) *Informed Urban Environments – Data-Integrated Design for Human and Ecology-Centered Perspectives*, Cham: Springer, pp. 11–25.

Himanen, L., Geurts, A., Foster, A.S., and Rinke, P. (2019) 'Data-Driven Materials Science: Status, Challenges, and Perspectives', *Advanced Science*, *6*(21), 1900808. doi:10.1002/advs.201900808.

Kelleher, J.D. and Tierney, B. (2018) *Data Science*. Cambridge Mass: The MIT Press.

Kendall, S. (1990) *The ecology of production, and the significance of distributed control*. PhD dissertation. Stephen Kendall. Available at: https://drstephenkendall.com/wp-content/uploads/2017/01/Mapping-Control-in-Production-Chains.pdf. (Accessed 23 August 2023).

Kitchin, R. (2015) 'Data-Driven, Networked Urbanism'. Available at: http://dx.doi.org/10.2139/ssrn.2641802 (Accessed 13 August 2024).

Kitchin, R., Lauriault, T.P., and McArdle, G. (eds.) (2018) *Data and the City*. London: Routledge, pp. 44–46.

Krause, J. (2011) *Unsichtbare Architektur*. Altenberg: Druckerei zu Altenberg.

Lönberg-Holm, K. and Sutnar, L. (1950) *Catalogue Design Progress – Advancing Standards in Visual Communication*. New York: Sweets's Catalogue Services, F.W. Dodge Corporation.

Neutra, R. (1954) *Survival through Design*. New York: Oxford University Press.

Petrova, E., Pauwels, P., Svidt, K., and Jensen, R.L. (2018) 'Towards data-driven sustainable design: decision support based on knowledge discovery in disparate building data', *Architectural Engineering and Design Management*, 15(5), pp. 334–356. doi:10.1080/17452007.2018.1530092.

Ramos, R.A.R. and Silva, A.N.R.D. (2003) 'A data-driven approach for the definition of metropolitan regions', in *Proceedings of the 8th International Conference on Computers in Urban Planning and Urban Management*, pp. 1–15.

Schwab, K. (2015) 'The Fourth Industrial Revolution – What it Means and How to Respond', *Foreign Affairs*, Available at: www.foreignaffairs.com/world/fourth-industrial-revolution (Accessed 24 August 2024).

Shaken, A.M. (2005) 'From the Gospel of Efficiency to Modernism: A History of Sweet's Catalogue, 1906–1947', *Design Issues*, 21(2), pp. 28–47.

Sunguroğlu Hensel, D., Tyc, J., and Hensel, M. (2022) 'Data-driven Design for Architecture and Environment Integration: Convergence of data-integrated workflows for understanding and designing environments', *Spool*, 9(1), pp.19–34. doi:10.47982/spool.2022.1.02.

Turner II, B.L., Clark, W.C., Kates, R.W., Richards, J.F., Mathews, J.T., and Meyer W.B. (1990) The Earth as Transformed by Human Action – Global and Regional Changes in the Biosphere over the Past 300 Years. Cambridge: Cambridge University Press.

Vincent J.F.V., Bogatyreva O.A., Bogatyrev N.R., Bowyer, A., and Pahl, A.-K. (2006) 'Biomimetics: its practice and theory', *Journal of the Royal Society Interface*, *3*(9), pp. 471–482. doi:10.1098/rsif.2006.0127.

Wegst, U.G.K. and Ashby, M.F. (2004) 'The mechanical efficiency of natural materials', *Philosophical Magazine*, *84*(21), pp. 2167–2186. doi:10.1080/14786430410001680935.

CHAPTER 1

Abanda, F.H. and Byers, L. (2016) 'An investigation of the impact of building orientation on energy consumption in a domestic building using emerging BIM (Building Information Modelling)', *Energy*, *97*, pp. 517–527. doi:10.1016/j.energy.2015.12.135.

Abdalazeem, M.E., Hassan, H., Asawa, T., and Mahmoud, H. (2022) Review on integrated photovoltaic-green roof solutions on urban and energy-efficient buildings in hot climate. *Sustainable Cities and Society*, *82*, 103919. doi:10.1016/j.scs.2022.103919.

Abreha, B.G., Agarwal, S., Foster, I., Blaiszik, B., and Lopez, S.A. (2019) 'Virtual excited state reference for the discovery of electronic materials database: An open-access resource for ground and excited state properties of organic molecules', *The Journal of Physical Chemistry Letters*, *10*(21), pp. 6835–6841. doi:10.1021/acs.jpclett.9b02577.

Aburas, M., Soebarto, V., Williamson, T., Liang, R., Ebendorff-Heidepriem, H., and Wu, Y. (2019) 'Thermochromic smart window technologies for building application: A review', *Applied Energy*, *255*, 113522. doi:10.1016/j.apenergy.2019.113522.

Akhter, F., Khadivizand, S., Siddiquei, H.R., Alahi, M.E.E., and Mukhopadhyay, S. (2019) 'IoT enabled intelligent sensor node for smart city: pedestrian counting and ambient monitoring', *Sensors*, *19*(15), 3374. doi:10.3390/s19153374.

Alablani, I. and Alenazi, M. (2020) 'EDTD-SC: An IoT sensor deployment strategy for smart cities', *Sensors*, *20*(24), 7191. doi:10.3390/s20247191.

Ali, K.N., Alhajlah, H.H., and Kassem, M.A. (2022) 'Collaboration and risk in building information modeling (BIM): a systematic literature review', *Buildings*, *12*(5), 571. doi:10.3390/buildings12050571.

Ashby, M.F. (1989) 'Materials selection in conceptual design', *Materials Science and Technology*, *5*(6), pp. 517–525. doi:10.1179/mst.1989.5.6.517.

Ashby M.F. (2011) 'Chapter 4 - Material property charts, in Ashby MFBT-MS in MD, 4th ed. Oxford: Butterworth-Heinemann, pp. 57–96. doi:10.1016/B978-1-85617-663-7.00004-7.

Ashino, T. (2010) 'Materials Ontology: An Infrastructure for exchanging materials information and knowledge', *Data Science Journal*, 9, pp. 54–61. doi:10.2481/dsj.008-041.

Badour, Y., Danto, S., Albakour, S., Mornet, S., Penin, N., Hirsch, L., and Gaudon, M. (2023) 'Low-cost WO3 nanoparticles/PVA smart photochromic glass windows for sustainable building energy savings', *Solar Energy Materials and Solar Cells*, *255*, 112291. doi:10.1016/j.solmat.2023.112291.

Bahl, S., Nagar, H., Singh, I., and Sehgal, S. (2020) 'Smart materials: types, properties and applications: A review', *Materials Today: Proceedings*, *28*, pp. 1302–1306. doi:10.1016/j.matpr.2020.04.505.

Bajpai, R., Choudhary, K., Srivastava, A., Sangwan, K.S., and Singh, M. (2020) 'Environmental impact assessment of fly ash and silica fume based geopolymer concrete', *Journal of Cleaner Production*, *254*, 120147. doi:10.1016/j.jclepro.2020.120147.

Belussi, L., Barozzi, B., Bellazzi, A., Danza, L., Devitofrancesco, A., Fanciulli, C., Ghellere, M., Guazzi, G., Meroni, I., Salamone, F., and Scamoni, F. (2019) 'A review of performance of zero energy buildings and energy efficiency solutions', *Journal of building engineering*, *25*, 100772. doi:10.1016/j.jobe.2019.100772.

Bigdeli, M. and Monfared, V. (2021) 'The prediction of stress and strain behaviors in composite gears using FEM', *International Journal of Engineering*, *34*(2), pp. 556–563. doi:10.5829/IJE.2021.34.02B.29.

Blaiszik, B., Chard, K., Pruyne, J., Ananthakrishnan, R., Tuecke, S., and Foster, I. (2016) 'The materials data facility: data services to advance materials science research', *Jom*, *68*(8), pp. 2045–2052. doi:10.1007/s11837-016-2001-3.

Brandt, N., Griem, L., Herrmann, C., Schoof, E., Tosato, G., Zhao, Y., Zschumme, P., and Selzer, M. (2021) 'Kadi4Mat: A Research Data Infrastructure for Materials Science', *Data Science Journal*, 20(8), pp. 1–14. doi:10.5334/dsj2021-008.

Cai, J., Du, M., and Li, Z. (2022) 'Flexible temperature sensors constructed with fiber materials', *Advanced Materials Technologies*, *7*(7), 2101182. doi:10.1002/admt.202101182.

Camero, A. and Alba, E. (2019) 'Smart City and information technology: A review. *cities*, *93*, pp. 84–94. doi:10.1016/j.cities.2019.04.014.

Cerovsek, T. (2011) 'A review and outlook for a "Building Information Model" (BIM): A multi-standpoint framework for technological development', *Advanced engineering informatics*, *25*(2), pp. 224–244. doi:10.1016/j.aei.2010.06.003.

Cheung, K., Drennan, J., and Hunter, J. (2008) 'Towards an Ontology for Data-driven Discovery of New Materials', *Semantic Scientific Knowledge Integration AAAI/SSS Workshop*, Stanford University, Palo Alto, CA, 26–28 March. California, USA: The Association for the Advancement of Artificial Intelligence (AAAI), pp. 1–6.

Chong, K.P. and Garboczi, E.J. (2002) 'Smart and designer structural material systems', *Progress in Structural Engineering and Materials*, *4*(4), pp. 417–430. doi:10.1002/pse.134.

Dave, B., Buda, A., Nurminen, A., and Främling, K. (2018) 'A framework for integrating BIM and IoT through open standards', *Automation in construction*, *95*, pp. 35–45. doi:10.1016/j.autcon.2018.07.022.

Baas, A. de, Del Nostro, P., Friis, J., Ghedini, E., Goldbeck, G., Paponetti, I.M., Pozzi, A., Sarkar, A., Yan, L., Zaccarini, F.A., and Toti, D. (2023) 'Review and Alignment of Domain-Level Ontologies for Materials Science', *IEEE Access*, *11*, pp. 120372–120401. doi:10.1109/ACCESS.2023.3327725.

Demircilioğlu, E., Teomete, E., Schlangen, E., and Baeza, F.J. (2019) 'Temperature and moisture effects on electrical resistance and strain sensitivity of smart concrete', *Construction and Building Materials*, *224*, pp. 420–427. doi:10.1016/j.conbuildmat.2019.07.091.

Ding, S., Dong, S., Ashour, A., and Han, B. (2019) 'Development of sensing concrete: Principles, properties and its applications', *Journal of Applied Physics*, *126*(24), 241101. doi:10.1063/1.5128242.

EMMO (2020) European Materials Modelling Ontology. Available at: https://emmo-repo.github.io/versions/1.0.0-beta/emmo.html (Accessed 25 June 2024).

Fensel, D. (2001). *Ontologies*. Berlin, Heidelberg: Springer.

Gao, H., Koch, C., and Wu, Y. (2019) 'Building Information Modelling Based Building Energy Modelling: A Review', *Applied Energy*, 238, pp. 320–343. doi:10.1016/j.apenergy.2019.01.032.

Gates-Rector, S. and Blanton, T. (2019) 'The powder diffraction file: a quality materials characterization database', *Powder Diffraction*, *34*(4), pp. 352–360. doi:10.1017/S0885715619000812.

Geilhufe, R. (2019) 'The Organic Materials Database-OMDB: a novel framework for functional materials prediction', in *APS March Meeting Abstracts*, pp. S43–003.

Ghazal, T.M., Hasan, M.K., Alshurideh, M.T., Alzoubi, H.M., Ahmad, M., Akbar, S.S., Al Kurdi, B., and Akour, I.A. (2021) 'IoT for smart cities: Machine learning approaches in smart healthcare – A review', *Future Internet*, *13*(8), 218. doi:10.3390/fi13080218.

Ghiringhelli, L.M., Carbogno, C., Levchenko, S., Mohamed, F., Huhs, G., Lüders M., Oliveira, M., and Scheffler M. (2017) 'Towards efficient data exchange and sharing for big-data driven materials science: metadata and data formats', *npj Computational Materials*, 3, 46. doi:10.1038/s41524-017-0048-5.

Ghiringhelli, L.M., Baldauf, C., Bereau, T., Brockhauser, S., Carbogno, C., Chamanara, J., Cozzini, S., Curtarolo, S., Draxl., C., Dwaraknath, S., Fekete, A., Kermode, J., Koch, C.T., Kühbach, M., Ladines, A.N., Lambrix, P., Himmer, M.O., Levchenko, S.V., Oliveira, M., Michalchuk, A., Miller, R.E., Onat, B., Pavone, P., Pizzi, G., Regler, B., Rignanese, G.M., Schaarschmidt, J., Scheidgen, M., Schneidewind, A., Sheveleva, T., Su, C., Usvyat, D., Valsson, O., Wöll, C., and Scheffler, M. (2023) 'Shared metadata for data-centric materials science', *Scientific Data* 10, 626. doi:10.1038/s41597-023-02501-8.

Glick, J. (2013) 'Chapter 8 – Ontologies and Databases – Knowledge Engineering for Materials Informatics', in Rajan, K. (ed.) *Informatics for Materials Science and Engineering*. Oxford: Elsevier Butterworth-Heinemann, pp. 147–187. doi:10.1016/B978-0-12-394399-6.00008-4.

Gohil, P.P., Malek, M., Bachwani, D., Patel, D., Upadhyaya, D., and Hathiwala, A. (2022) 'Application of 5D Building Information Modeling for Construction Management', *ECS Transactions*, *107*(1), 2637. doi:10.1149/10701.2637ecst.

Grassi, P., Lefkovitz, N., Nadeau, E., Galluzzo, R., and Dinh, A. (2018) 'Attribute metadata: A proposed schema for evaluating federated attributes', Tech. Rep., National Institute of Standards and Technology. doi:10.6028/NIST.IR.8112.

Hao, Y., Zhang, S., Fang, B., Sun, F., Liu, H., and Li, H. (2022) 'A review of smart materials for the boost of soft actuators, soft sensors, and robotics applications', *Chinese Journal of Mechanical Engineering*, *35*(1), 37. doi:10.1186/s10033-022-00707-2.

Hassani, F.A., Shi, Q., Wen, F., He, T., Haroun, A., Yang, Y., Feng, Y., and Lee, C. (2020) 'Smart materials for smart healthcare-moving from sensors and actuators to self-sustained nanoenergy nanosystems', *Smart Materials in Medicine*, *1*, pp. 92–124. doi:10.1016/j.smaim.2020.07.005.

Hayashi, H., Hayashi, K., Kouzai, K., Seko, A., and Tanaka, I. (2019) 'Recommender system of successful processing conditions for new compounds based on a parallel experimental data set', *Chemistry of Materials*, *31*(24), pp. 9984–9992. doi:10.1021/acs.chemmater.9b01799.

Hearley, B.L., Arnold, S.M., and Stuckner, J. (2023) 'A Robust Schema for Machine Learning Data and Models Within the Granta MI Information Management System', in *AIAA SCITECH 2023 Forum*, 1266. doi:10.2514/6.2023-1266.

Hey, T., Tansley, S., and Tolle, K. (2009) *The Fourth Paradigm: Data-Intensive Scientific Discovery*. Redmont: Microsoft Research.

Himanen, L., Geurts, A., Foster, A.S., and Rinke, P. (2019) 'Data-driven materials science: status, challenges, and perspectives', *Advanced Science*, *6*(21), 1900808. doi:10.1002/advs.201900808.

Hill, J., Mulholland, G., Persson, K., Seshadri, R., Wolverton, C., and Meredig, B. (2016) 'Materials science with large-scale data and informatics: Unlocking new opportunities', *Mrs Bulletin*, *41*(5), pp. 399–409. doi:10.1557/mrs.2016.93.

Ismagilova, E., Hughes, L., Rana, N.P., and Dwivedi, Y.K. (2022) 'Security, privacy and risks within smart cities: Literature review and development of a smart city interaction framework', *Information Systems Frontiers*, pp. 1–22. doi:10.1007/s10796-020-10044-1.

Jain, A., Montoya, J., Dwaraknath, S., Zimmermann, N.E., Dagdelen, J., Horton, M., Huck, P., Winston, D., Cholia, S., Ong, S.P., and Persson, K. (2020) 'The materials project: Accelerating materials design through theory-driven data and tools', *Handbook of Materials Modeling: Methods: Theory and Modeling*, pp. 1751–1784. doi:10.1007/978-3-319-44677-6_60.

Jain, A., Ong, S.P., Hautier, G., Chen, W., Richards, W.D., Dacek, S., Cholia, S., Gunter, D., Skinner, D., Ceder, G., and Persson, K.A. (2013) 'Commentary: The Materials Project: A materials genome approach to accelerating materials innovation'. *APL materials*, *1*(1), 011002, doi:10.1063/1.4812323.

Jani, J.M., Leary, M., Subic, A., and Gibson, M.A. (2014) 'A review of shape memory alloy research, applications and opportunities', *Materials & Design (1980–2015)*, *56*, pp. 1078–1113. doi:10.1016/j.matdes.2013.11.084.

Khan, A., Tayara, H., and Chong, K.T. (2023) 'Prediction of organic material band gaps using graph attention network', *Computational Materials Science*, *220*, 112063. doi:10.1016/j.commatsci.2023.112063.

Kirimtat, A., Krejcar, O., Kertesz, A., and Tasgetiren, M.F. (2020) 'Future trends and current state of smart city concepts: A survey', *IEEE access*, *8*, pp. 86448–86467. doi:10.1109/ACCESS.2020.2992441.

Kirova, N., Markopoulou, A., Mahdi, H., and Jalodia, S. (2020) 'A Smart Material System for Real-Time Urban Flow Data Collection Toward Responsive Environments and Informed Decision Making in Urban Spaces', in *Impact: Design With All Senses: Proceedings of the Design Modelling Symposium*, Springer International Publishing: Berlin, pp. 699–713. doi:10.1007/978-3-030-29829-6_54.

Lee, G., Sacks, R., and Eastman, C.M. (2006) 'Specifying parametric building object behavior (BOB) for a building information modeling system', *Automation in Construction*, *15*(6), pp. 758–776. doi:10.1016/j.autcon.2005.09.009.

Li, H., Armiento, R., and Lambrix, P. (2020). 'An Ontology for the Materials Design Domain', in Pan, J.Z., Tamma, V., d'Amato, C., Janovic, K., Fu, B., Polleres, A., Seneviratne, O., and Kagal, L. (eds.) *The Semantic Web – ISWC 2020. ISWC 2020. Lecture Notes in Computer Science*, 12507. Cham: Springer. doi:10.1007/978-3-030-62466-8_14.

Li, W., Qu, F., Dong, W., Mishra, G., and Shah, S.P. (2022) 'A comprehensive review on self-sensing graphene/cementitious composites: A pathway toward next-generation smart concrete', *Construction and Building Materials*, *331*, 127284. doi:10.1016/j.conbuildmat.2022.127284.

Lützkendorf, T. and Speer, T.M. (2005) 'Alleviating asymmetric information in property markets: building performance and product quality as signals for consumers', *Building Research & Information*, *33*(2), pp. 182–195. doi:10.1080/0961321042000323815.

Lu, W., Xiao, R., Yang, J., Li, H., and Zhang, W. (2017) 'Data mining-aided materials discovery doi:10.1016/j.jmat.2017.08.003.

Lv, C., Zhou, X., Zhong, L., Yan, C., Srinivasan, M., Seh, Z.W., Liu, C., Pan, H., Li, S., Wen, Y., and Yan, Q. (2022) 'Machine learning: an advanced platform for materials development and state prediction in lithium-ion batteries', *Advanced Materials*, *34*(25), 2101474. doi:10.1002/adma.202101474.

Ma, B., Finan, N.J., Jany, D., Deagen, M.E., Schadler, L.S., and Brinson, L.C. (2023) 'Machine-Learning-Assisted Understanding of Polymer Nanocomposites Composition-Property Relationship: A Case Study of NanoMine Database', *Macromolecules, 56*(11), pp. 3945–3953. doi:0.1021/acs.macromol.2c02249.

Mahapatra, S.D., Mohapatra, P.C., Aria, A.I., Christie, G., Mishra, Y.K., Hofmann, S., and Thakur, V.K. (2021) 'Piezoelectric materials for energy harvesting and sensing applications: Roadmap for future smart materials', *Advanced Science*, *8*(17), 2100864. doi:10.1002/advs.202100864.

Makul, N. (2020) 'Advanced smart concrete – A review of current progress, benefits and challenges', *Journal of Cleaner Production*, *274*, 122899. doi:10.1016/j.jclepro.2020.122899.

Maiorov, V.A. (2019) 'Electrochromic glasses with separate regulation of transmission of visible light and near-infrared radiation', *Optics and Spectroscopy*, *126*, pp. 412–430 doi:10.1134/S0030400×19040143.

Mangalika, U. (2021) 'A Detailed review on Applications of Smart Materials in Structural Engineering', *Journal of Machine and Computing*, pp. 57–67. doi:10.53759/7669/jmc202101007.

McMasters, R.L. and Schlussel, E. (2023) 'Thermal Performance of Additively Manufactured Aircraft Structure Material with Geometric Voids', In *AIAA AVIATION 2023 Forum*, 4278. doi:10.2514/6.2023-4278.

Mir, B.A. (2017) 'Smart materials and their applications in civil engineering: An overview. *International Journal of Civil Engineering and Construction Science*, *4*, pp. 11–20.

Napolitano, R., Reinhart, W., and Gevaudan, J.P. (2021) 'Smart cities built with smart materials', *Science*, *371*(6535), pp. 1200–1201. doi:10.1126/science.abg4254.

Nguyen, T.D., Yeo, L.P., Ong, A.J., Zhiwei, W., Mandler, D., Magdassi, S., and Tok, A.I.Y. (2020) 'Electrochromic smart glass coating on functional nano-frameworks for effective building energy conservation', *Materials Today Energy*, *18*, 100496. doi:10.1016/j.mtener.2020.100496.

Ontotext (2024) What are Ontologies? Available at: www.ontotext.com/knowledgehub/fundamentals/what-are-ontologies/ (Accessed 25 June 2024).

Oliveira, J., Correia, V., Castro, H., Martins, P., and Lanceros-Mendez, S. (2018) 'Polymer-based smart materials by printing technologies: Improving application and integration', *Additive Manufacturing*, *21*, pp. 269–283. doi:10.1016/j.addma.2018.03.012.

O'Mara, J., Meredig, B., and Michel, K. (2016) 'Materials data infrastructure: a case study of the citrination platform to examine data import, storage, and access', *Jom*, *68*(8), pp. 2031–2034. doi:10.1007/s11837-016-1984-0.

Pásztory, Z. (2021) 'An overview of factors influencing thermal conductivity of building insulation materials', *Journal of Building Engineering*, *44*, 102604. doi:10.1016/j.jobe.2021.102604.

Plageras, A.P., Psannis, K.E., Stergiou, C., Wang, H., and Gupta, B.B. (2018). 'Efficient IoT-based sensor BIG Data collection-processing and analysis in smart buildings', *Future Generation Computer Systems*, *82*, pp. 349–357. doi:10.1016/j.future.2017.09.082.

Rickman, J.M., Lookman, T., and Kalinin, S.V. (2019) 'Materials informatics: From the atomic-level to the continuum', *Acta Materialia*, 168, pp. 473–510. doi:10.1016/j.actamat.2019.01.051.

Rumor, L. and Andrade-Campos, A. (2022) 'On the need for material model databases: A state-of-the-art review', *Advances in Mechanical Engineering*, *14*(10), 16878132221130575. doi:10.1177/16878132221130575.

Sbailò, L., Fekete, Á., Ghiringhelli, L.M., and Scheffler, M., 2022. The NOMAD Artificial-Intelligence Toolkit: turning materials-science data into knowledge and understanding. *npj Computational Materials*, *8*(1), p. 250.

Shen, S., Lv, C.X., Zhu, H., Sun, L.J., and Wang, R.C. (2022) 'Potentials and prospects of bicycle sharing system in smart cities: A review', *IEEE Sensors Journal*, *22*(8), pp. 7519–7533. doi:10.1109/JSEN.2022.3160178.

Siadkowska, K. (2021) 'November. Smart materials technologies in composite structures of aerial vehicles', in *AIP Conference Proceedings*, *2429*(1), 020035. AIP Publishing. doi:10.1063/5.0070427.

Sofi, A., Regita, J.J., Rane, B., and Lau, H.H. (2022) 'Structural health monitoring using wireless smart sensor network – An overview', *Mechanical Systems and Signal Processing*, *163*, 108113. doi:10.1016/j.ymssp.2021.108113.

Spaggiari, A., Castagnetti, D., Golinelli, N., Dragoni, E., and Scirè Mammano, G. (2019) 'Smart materials: Properties, design and mechatronic applications', *Proceedings of the institution of mechanical engineers, part l: journal of materials: design and applications*, *233*(4), pp. 734–762. doi:10.1177/1464420716673671.

Sun, M., Staszewski, W.J., and Swamy, R.N. (2010) 'Smart sensing technologies for structural health monitoring of civil engineering structures', *Advances in Civil Engineering*, *2010*. doi:10.1155/2010/724962.

Sung, D. (2016) 'Smart geometries for smart materials: taming thermobimetals to behave', *Journal of Architectural Education*, *70*(1), pp. 96–106. doi:10.1080/10464883.2016.1122479.

Sunguroğlu Hensel, D. and Vincent, J.F.V. (2015) 'Evolutionary inventive problem-solving in biology and architecture: ArchiTRIZ and Material-Ontology', *Intelligent Buildings International*, *8*(2), pp. 118–137. doi:10.1080/17508975.2015.1014462.

Tan, Y., Fang, Y., Zhou, T., Wang, Q., and Cheng, J.C.P. (2017) 'Improve indoor acoustics performance by using building information modeling', in *ISARC – Proceedings of the International Symposium on Automation and Robotics in Construction*, 34. IAARC Publications.

Teng, Y., Xu, J., Pan, W., and Zhang, Y. (2022) 'A systematic review of the integration of building information modeling into life cycle assessment', *Building and Environment*, *221*, 109260. doi:10.1016/j.buildenv.2022.109260.

Thuraisingham, B. (2000) 'A primer for understanding and applying data mining', *IT Professional*, 2(1), pp. 28–31. doi:10.1109/6294.819936.

Turner, A.P. (2013) 'Biosensors: sense and sensibility', *Chemical Society Reviews*, *42*(8), pp. 3184–3196. doi:10.1039/C3CS35528D.

Tzou, H.S., Lee, H.J., and Arnold, S.M. (2004) 'Smart materials, precision sensors/actuators, smart structures, and structronic systems', *Mechanics of Advanced Materials and Structures*, *11*(4–5), pp. 367–393. doi:10.1080/15376490490451552.

Vaitkus, A., Merkys, A., Sander, T., Quirós, M., Thiessen, P.A., Bolton, E.E., and Gražulis, S. (2023). 'A workflow for deriving chemical entities from crystallographic data and its application to the Crystallography Open Database', *Journal of Cheminformatics*, *15*, 123 doi:10.1186/s13321-023-00780-2.

Voigt, S.P. and Kalidindi, S.R. (2021). 'Materials graph ontology', *Materials Letters*, *295*, 129836. doi:10.1016/j.matlet.2021.129836.

Volk, R., Stengel, J., and Schultmann, F. (2014) 'Building Information Modeling (BIM) for existing buildings – Literature review and future needs', *Automation in Construction*, *38*, pp. 109–127. doi:10.1016/j.autcon.2013.10.023.

Ward, L., Dunn, A., Faghaninia, A., Zimmermann, N.E.R., Bajaj, S., Wang, G., Montoya, J., Chen, J., Bystrom, K., Dylla, M., Chard, K., Asta, M., Persson, K.A.,Snyder, G.J., Foster, I., and Jain, A. (2018) 'Matminer: An open source toolkit for materials data mining', *Computational Materials Science*, 152, pp. 60–69. doi:10.1016/j.commatsci.2018.05.018.

Wentker, M., Greenwood, M., and Leker, J. (2019) 'A bottom-up approach to lithium-ion battery cost modeling with a focus on cathode active materials', *Energies*, *12*(3), 504. doi:10.3390/en12030504.

Wisniewski, D., Potoniec, J., Ławrynowicz, A., and Keetc, C.M. (2018) 'Competency Questions and SPARQL-OWL Queries Dataset and Analysis', Preprint *arXiv:1811.09529*. doi:10.48550/arXiv.1811.09529.

Xia, H., Liu, Z., Efremochkina, M., Liu, X., and Lin, C. (2022) 'Study on city digital twin technologies for sustainable smart city design: A review and bibliometric analysis of geographic information system and building information modeling integration', *Sustainable Cities and Society*, *84*, 104009. doi:10.1016/j.scs.2022.104009.

Ye, W., Chen, C., Dwaraknath, S., Jain, A., Ong, S.P., and Persson, K.A. (2018) 'Harnessing the Materials Project for machine-learning and accelerated discovery', *MRS Bulletin*, *43*(9), pp. 664–669. doi:10.1557/mrs.2018.202.

Yu, M. (2022) 'Construction of regional intelligent transportation system in smart city road network via 5G network', *IEEE Transactions on Intelligent Transportation Systems*, *24*(2), pp. 2208–2216. doi:10.1109/TITS.2022.3141731.

Yuan, M., Paradiso, S., Meredig, B., and Niezgoda, S.R. (2018) 'Machine learning-based reduce order crystal plasticity modeling for ICME applications', *Integrating Materials and Manufacturing Innovation*, *7*(4), pp. 214–230. doi:10.1007/s40192-018-0123-x.

Zagorac, D., Müller, H., Ruehl, S., Zagorac, J., and Rehme, S. (2019) 'Recent developments in the Inorganic Crystal Structure Database: theoretical crystal structure data and related features', *Journal of applied crystallography*, *52*(5), pp. 918–925. doi:10.1107/S160057671900997X.

Zhao, X., Askari, H., and Chen, J. (2021) 'Nanogenerators for smart cities in the era of 5G and Internet of Things', *Joule*, *5*(6), pp. 1391–1431. doi:10.1016/j.joule.2021.03.013.

CHAPTER 2

Abdelmohsen, S., Adriaenssens, S., El-Dabaa, R., Gabriele, S., Olivieri, L., and Teresi, L. (2019) 'A multi-physics approach for modeling hygroscopic behavior in wood low-tech architectural adaptive systems', *Computer-Aided Design*, *106*, pp. 43–53. doi:10.1016/j.cad.2018.07.005.

Addington, M. and Schodek, D. (2005) *Smart Materials and Technologies for the architecture and design professions*. Oxford: Elsevier, Architectural Press.

AL-Oqla, F.M. and Salit, M.S. (2017) 'Chapter 3 – Materials selection', in AL-Oqla, F.M. and Salit, M.S. (eds.) Materials Selection for Natural Fiber Composites. Sawston: Woodhead Publishing (Elsevier), pp. 49–71. doi:10.1016/B978-0-08-100958-1.00003-7.

ANSYS Granta (2024) Material Property Charts. Available at: www.grantadesign.com/education/students/charts/ (Accessed 9 August 2024).

Ashby, M.F. (1989) 'Materials selection in conceptual design', *Materials Science and Technology*, *5*(6), pp. 517–525. doi:10.1179/mst.1989.5.6.517.

Ashby M.F. (2011) 'Chapter 4 – Material property charts', in Ashby MFBT-MS in MD, 4th ed. Oxford: Butterworth-Heinemann, pp. 57–96. doi:10.1016/B978-1-85617-663-7.00004-7.

Atkins, P. (2010) *The Laws of Thermodynamics*. Oxford: Oxford University Press.

Balaras, C.A. and Argiriou, A.A. (2002) 'Infrared thermography for building diagnostics', *Energy and Buildings*, 34(2), pp. 171–183. doi:10.1016/S0378-7788(01)00105-0.

Ball, P. (1997) *Made to Measure: New Materials for the 21st Century*. Princeton: Princeton University Press.

Chew, P.Y. and Reinhardt, A. (2023) 'Phase diagrams – Why they matter and how to predict them', *The Journal of Chemical Physics*, 158(3), 030902. doi:10.1063/5.0131028.

Cross, N. (2006) *Designerly Ways of Knowing*. London: Springer.

Cross, N. and Dorst, K. (1998) 'Coevolution of Problem and Solution Spaces in Creative Design: observations from an empirical study', in Gero, J. and Maher, M.L. (eds.) *Computational Models of Creative Design IV*. Sydney: University of Sydney.

Cui, Y., Xie, J., Liu, J., Wang, J., and Chen, S. (2017) 'A review on phase change material application in building', *Advances in Mechanical Engineering*, 9(6). doi:10.1177/1687814017700828.

Deilami, K., Kamruzzaman, M., and Liu, Y. (2018) 'Urban heat island effect: A systematic review of spatio-temporal factors, data, methods, and mitigation measures', *International Journal of Applied Earth Observation and Geoinformation*, *67*, pp. 30–42. doi:10.1016/j.jag.2017.12.009.

Dinwoodie, J.M. (2000) *Timber: Its nature and behavior* (2nd Ed.). London: E&FN Spon.

Dwiartama, A. and Rosin, C. (2014) 'Exploring agency beyond humans: the compatibility of Actor-Network Theory (ANT) and resilience thinking', *Ecology & Society*, 19(3), 28. Available at: http://dx.doi.org/10.5751/ES-06805-190328 (accessed 15 January 2024).

Elsevier (2024) *Calphad*. Available at: www.sciencedirect.com/journal/calphad (Accessed 31 July 2024).

Esbensen, K.H. (2002) *Multivariate Data Analysis in Practice – An introduction to multivariate data analysis and experimental design* (5th Ed.) Oslo: Camo Software.

Fathy, H. (2008) *Natural Energy and Vernacular Architecture – Principles and Examples with Reference to Hot Arid Climates*. Chicago: University of Chicago Press.

Fordham, M. (2024) 'The Physics of Freezing at the Iranian Yakhchal'. Available at: www.maxfordham.com/practice-people/journal/the-physics-of-freezing-at-the-iranian-yakhchal (Accessed 27 September 2024).

Furrer, D.U., Dimiduk, D.M., and Ward, C.H. (2024) 'Evolution of Model-Based Materials Definitions', *Integrating Materials and Manufacturing Innovation, 13*, pp. 474–487. doi:10.1007/s40192-024-00353-7.

Ganti, T. (2003) *The Principles of Life*. Oxford: Oxford University Press.

Gaskell, D.R. and Laughlin, D.E. (2017) *Introduction to the Thermodynamics of Materials*. 7th edn. Boca Raton: CRC Press. doi:10.1201/9781315119038.

Giffaut, E., Grivé, M., Blanc, P. Vieillard, P., Colàs, E., Gailhanou, H., Gaboreau, S., Marty, N., Madé, B., and Duro, L. (2014) 'Andra thermodynamic database for performance assessment: ThermoChimie', *Applied Geochemistry*, 49, pp. 225–236. doi:10.1016/j.apgeochem.2014.05.007.

Hensel, M. (2008) 'Performance-oriented Design – Precursors and Potentials', in Hensel, M. and Menges, A. (eds.) *Versatility and Vicissitude, AD 78(2)*, pp. 48–53.

Hensel, M. (2009) 'Material Capacities and Variable Behavior – Potentials for the Design Disciplines', in *Nordes 2009 Conference Engaging Artifacts*, 30 August–1 September, Oslo School of Architecture and Design, Oslo, Norway. Available at: https://archive.nordes.org/index.php/n13/article/view/71 (Accessed 15 January 2024).

Hensel, M. (2010a) 'Performance-oriented Architecture: Towards a Biological Paradigm for Architectural Design and the Built Environment', *FORMAkademisk 3*(1), pp. 36–56. doi:10.7577/formakademisk.138.

Hensel, M. (2010b) 'Material Systems and Environmental Feedback Dynamics', in Hensel, M., Menges, A., and Weinstock, M. (eds.) *Emergent Technologies and Design: A Biological Paradigm for Architecture*. London: Routledge, pp. 63–81.

Hensel, M. (2011) 'Performance-oriented Architecture and the Spatial and Material Organization Complex – Rethinking the Definition, Role and Performative Capacity of the Spatial and Material Boundaries of the Built Environment', *FORMAkademisk, 4*(1), pp. 3–23. doi:10.7577/formakademisk.125.

Hensel, M. (2012) 'Performance-oriented Design from a Material Perspective – Domains of Agency and the Spatial Material Organization Complex', in Grobman, Y.J., Neuman, E. (eds.) *Performalism: Form and Performance in Digital Architecture*. London: Routledge, pp. 43–48.

Hensel, M. (2013) *Performance-oriented Architecture – Rethinking Architectural Design and the Built Environment*. London: AD Wiley.

Hensel, M. (2022) 'The Bigger Picture en Route to Informed Urban Environments – Initiating linkages between sustainability science, urban science, and architectural science through an inter- and transdisciplinary data-integrated approach', in Chokhachian, A., Hensel, M., and Perini, K. (eds.) *Informed Urban Environments: Data-integrated Design for Human and Ecology-centered Perspectives*. Cham: Springer (The Urban Book Series), pp. 11–26. doi:10.1007/978-3-031-03803-7_2.

Hensel, M. and Menges, A. (eds.) (2006) *Morpho-Ecologies*. London: AA Publications.

Hensel, M. and Menges, A. (2006) 'Material and Digital Design Synthesis: Integrating material self-organization, digital morphogenesis, associative parametric modeling, and computer-aided manufacturing', *Architectural Design 76*(2), pp. 88–95. doi:10.1002/ad.244.

Hensel, M. and Menges, A. (2008a) 'Form- und Materialwerdung – Das Konzept der Materialsysteme', *Arch +, 188*, pp. 18–19.

Hensel, M. and Menges, A. (eds.) (2008b) *Versatility and Vicissitude, AD 78(2)*.

Hensel, M., Menges, A., and Weinstock, M. (2010) *Emergent Technologies and Design – Towards a biological paradigm for architecture*. Milton Park: Routledge.

Hensel, M. and Sunguroğlu Hensel D. (2006) 'Smart Material Conditioning', *XXI, 12*, pp. 76–79.

Hensel, M. and Sunguroğlu Hensel D. (2011) 'Paper-thin Architectures', *XXI, 2*, pp. 14–15.

Hensel, M. and Sunguroğlu Hensel, D. (2020) 'Performances of Architectures and Environments – A Framework', in Kanaani M (ed.) *The Routledge Companion to Performativity in Design and Architecture: Using Time to Craft an Enduring, Resilient and Relevant Architecture*. London: Routledge, pp. 1–17.

Hensel, M., Sunguroğlu, D., and Menges A. (2008) 'Material Performance', *Architectural Design*, 78(2), pp. 34–38. doi:10.1002/ad.639.

Hensel, M., Sunguroğlu Hensel, D., Gharleghi, M., and Craig, S. (2012) 'Towards an Architectural History of Performance: Auxiliarity, Performance and Provision in Historical Persian Architectures', *Architectural Design*, 82(3), pp. 26–37. doi:10.1002/ad.1402.

HZDR (2024) *Thermodynamic Reference Database (THEREDA)*. Available at: www.hzdr.de/db/Cms?pOid=49901&pNid=0&pLang=en (Accessed 31 July 2024).

ICD (2012a) Institute for Computational Design and Construction. Available at: www.icd.uni-stuttgart.de/projects/hygroscope-meteorosensitive-morphology/ (Accessed 4 July 2024).

ICD (2012b) Institute for Computational Design and Construction. Available at: www.icd.uni-stuttgart.de/projects/hygroskin-meteorosensitive-pavilion/ (Accessed 4 July 2024).

Ingold, T. (2013) *Making – Anthropology, Archaeology, Art, and Architecture*. Milton Park: Routledge.

Klein, S. and Nellis, G. (2012) *Thermodynamics*. Cambridge: Cambridge University Press.

Kroupa, A. (2013) 'Modelling of phase diagrams and thermodynamic properties using Calphad method – Development of thermodynamic databases', Computational Materials Science, 66, pp. 3–13, doi:10.1016/j.commatsci.2012.02.003.

Law, J. (1992) 'Notes on the theory of the actor-network: ordering, strategy, and heterogeneity', *Systems Practice*, 5, pp. 379–393. Available at: http://dx.doi.org/10.1007/BF01059830 (accessed 02 April 2024).

Laureano, P. (1999) *Traditional Knowledge – The system of traditional knowledge in the Mediterranean and its classification with reference to different social groupings*. Report prepared for the Secretariat of the Convention to Combat Desertification. Available at: www.unccd.int/sites/default/files/sessions/documents/ICCD_COP3_1/cstmisc1eng.pdf (Accessed 24 July 2024).

Liu, Z.K. and Wang, Y. (2016) *Computational Thermodynamics of Materials*. Cambridge: Cambridge University Press.

Masanes, L. and Oppenheim, J. (2017) 'A general derivation and quantification of the third law of thermodynamics', *Nature Communications*, 8, 14538. doi:10.1038/ncomms14538.

Menges, A. (ed.) (2012) 'Material Computation – Higher Integration in Morphogenetic Design', *Architectural Design, 82*(2).

Menges, A. (ed.) (2015) 'Material Synthesis – Fusing the Physical and the Computational', *Architectural Design, 85*(5).

Monat, J.P. and Gannon, T.F. (2015) 'What is systems thinking? A Review of Selected Literature Plus Recommendations'. *American Journal of Systems Science, 4*(1), pp. 11–26 doi:10.5923/j.ajss.20150401.02.

Nuclear Energy Agency (2024) *Thermochemical Database (TDB) Project*. Available at: www.oecd-nea.org/jcms/pl_22166/thermochemical-database-tdb-project (Accessed 31 July 2024).

Oke, T.R. (1987). *Boundary layer climates*. Oxon, Routledge.

Panshal, J.H., Kalidini, S.R., and McDowell, D.L. (2013) 'Key computational modeling issues in Integrated Computational Material Engineering, Computer-Aided Design, 45(1), pp. 4–25. doi:10.1016/j.cad.2012.06.006.

Qing, J. and Zi, W. (2011) *Thermodynamics of Materials*. Berlin: Springer.

Raoux, S. (2009) 'Phase Change Materials', Annual Review of Materials Research, 39, pp. 25–48. doi:10.1146/annurev-matsci-082908-145405.

Rittel, H.W.J. (1970) 'Der Planungsprozess als iterativer Vorgang von Varietätserzeugung und Varietätseinschränkung', in Joedicke, J. (ed.) *Arbeitsberichte zur Planungsmethodik 4 – Entwurfsmethoden in der Bauplanung*. Stuttgart: Karl Krämer Verlag, pp. 17–32.

Rittel, H.W.J. and Webber, M.M. (1973) 'Dilemmas in a General Theory of Planning', *Policy Science, 4*, pp. 155–169. doi:10.1007/BF01405730.

Santamouris M. (ed.) (2001) *Energy and climate in the urban built environment*. London, James and James, London.

Sevaldson, B. (2022) *Designing Complexity – The Methodology and Practice of Systems Oriented Design*. Champaign IL: Common Ground.

Solomatine, D.P. and Ostfeld, A. (2008) 'Data-driven modeling: some past experiences and new approaches', *Journal of Hydroinformatics*, 10(1), pp. 3–22. doi:10.2166/hydro.2008.015.

Sunguroğlu Hensel, D. and Baraut Bover, G. (2013) 'Nested Catenaries', *Journal of the International Association for Shell and Spatial Structures*, 54(1), pp. 39–55.

Sunguroğlu Hensel, D. and Baraut Bover, G. (2015) 'A Developmental Route to Local Specificity: Nested Catenaries', *AD Architectural Design*, 85(2), pp. 120–127. doi:10.1002/ad.1886.

Sunguroğlu Hensel, D. (2020) 'Ecological Prototypes: Initiating Design Innovation in Green Construction', *Sustainability*, 12, 5865. doi:10.3390/su12145865.

Sunguroğlu Hensel, D., Tyc, J., and Hensel, M. (2022) 'Data-driven Design for Architecture and Environment Integration: Convergence of data-integrated workflows for understanding and designing environments', *Spool* 9(1): pp. 19–34. doi:10.47982/spool.2022.1.02.

Tschoegel, N.W. (2000) *Fundamentals of Equilibrium and Steady-State Thermodynamics*. Amsterdam: Elsevier.

Ulrich W. (1983) *Critical Heuristics of Social Planning – A New Approach to Practical Philosophy*. Chichester: John Wiley & Sons.

Van der Giessen, E., Schultz, P.A., Bertin, N., Bulatov, V.V., Cai, W., Csányi, G., Foiles, S.M., Geers, M.G.D., González, C., Hütter, M., Kim, W.K., Kochmann, D.M, LLorca, J., Mattsson, A.E., Rottler, J., Shluger, A., B Sills, R.S., Steinbach, I., Strachan, A., and Tadmor, E.B. (2020) 'Roadmap on multiscale materials modeling', *Modelling and Simulation in Materials Science and Engineering, 28*, 043001. doi:10.1088/1361-651X/ab7150.

Vincent J.F.V., Bogatyreva O.A., Bogatyrev N.R., Bowyer, A., and Pahl, A.-K. (2006) Biomimetics: its practice and theory. *Journal of the Royal Society Interface, 3*(9), pp. 471–482. doi:10.1098/rsif.2006.0127.

Wagenführ, A. (2008) *Die strukturelle Anisotropie von Holz als Chance für technische Innovation*. Leipzig: Verlag der Sächsischen Akademie der Wissenschaften zu Leipzig.

Wegst, U.G.K. and Ashby, M.F. (2004) 'The mechanical efficiency of natural materials', *Philosophical Magazine, 84*, pp. 2167–2186. doi:10.1080/14786430410001680935.

CHAPTER 3

Amato, F., Guignard, F., Robert, S., and Kanevski, M. (2020) 'A novel framework for spatio-temporal prediction of environmental data using deep learning', *Scientific Reports, 10*, 22243. doi:10.1038/s41598-020-79148-7.

Ashby, M.F. (2022) *Materials and sustainable development*. Oxford: Butterworth-Heinemann.

Attia, S. (2018) Regenerative and Positive Impact Architecture – Learning from Case Studies. Cham. Springer. Available online: https://link.springer.com/content/pdf/10.1007/978-3-319-66718-8.pdf (Accessed 22 July 2024).

Batsakis, S., Petrakis, E.G.M (2010) 'SOWL: spatio-temporal representation, reasoning and querying over the semantic web'. *I-SEMANTICS '10: Proceedings of the 6th International Conference on Semantic Systems, 15*, pp. 1–9. doi:10.1145/1839707.1839726.

Bishara, D., Xie, Y., Liu, W.K., and Li, S. (2023) 'A State-of-the-Art Review on Machine Learning-Based Multiscale Modeling, Simulation, Homogenization and Design of Materials', *Archives of Computational Methods in Engineering*, 30, pp. 191–222. doi:10.1007/s11831-022-09795-8.

Bocken, N.M., Pauw, I. de, Bakker, C., and van Der Grinten, B. (2016) 'Product design and business model strategies for a circular economy,' *Journal of Industrial and Production Engineering*, 33(5), pp. 308–320. doi:10.1080/21681015.2016.1172124.

Brand, S. (1994) *How Buildings Learn – What happens after they are built.* New York: Viking Press.

Butler, K.T., Davies, D.W., Cartwright, H., Isayev, O., and Walsh, A. (2018) 'Machine learning for molecular and materials science', *Nature*, *559*(7715), pp. 547–555. doi:10.1038/s41586-018-0337-2.

Carpenter, S.R. (2002) 'Ecological Futures: Building an ecology of the long now,' *Ecology*, 83(8), 2069. doi:10.2307/3072038.

Cole, R.J. (2011) 'Regenerative design and development: current theory and practice', *Building Research & Information*, 40(1), pp. 1–6. doi:10.1080/09613218.2012.617516.

Cox, H.G. (1968) *The Secular City: Secularization and Urbanization in theological perspective*. London: Penguin Books.

Cramer J. (2014) *Milieu, Elementaire Deeltjes 16*. Amsterdam: University Press.

Duffy, F. and Hannay, P. (1992) *The changing workplace*. New York: Phaidon Press.

du Plessis, C. (2011) 'Towards a regenerative paradigm for the built environment', *Building Research & Information*, *40*(1), pp. 7–22. doi:10.1080/09613218.2012.628548.

ECOLOPES (2024) Available at: https://ecolopes.org/ (Accessed 14 August 2024).

Einstein, A. (1905) 'On the electrodynamics of moving bodies,' *Annalen der Physik*, *17*(10), pp. 891–921.

Geldermans, R.J. (2016) 'Design for Change and Circularity – Accommodating Circular Material & Product Flows in Construction,' *Energy Procedia*, 96, pp. 301–311. doi:10.1016/j.egypro.2016.09.153.

Gibbons, L.V., Cloutier, S.A., Coseo, P.J., and Barakat, A. (2018) 'Regenerative development as an integrative paradigm and methodology for landscape sustainability', *Sustainability*, 10, 1910. doi:10.3390/su10061910.

Gibbons, L.V. (2020) 'Regenerative – The New Sustainable?', *Sustainability*, 12(13), 5483. doi:10.3390/su12135483.

Gosnell, H., Grimm, K., and Goldstein, B.E. (2020) 'A half century of Holistic Management: what does the evidence reveal?,' *Agriculture and Human Values*, 37(3), pp. 849–867. doi:10.1007/s10460-020-10016-w.

Han, J., Kamber, M., and Pei, J. (2012) '13 Data Mining Trends and Research Frontiers', in Han, J., Kamber, M., and Pei, J. (eds.) The Morgan Kaufmann Series in Data Management Systems (3. ed.) Burlington: Morgan Kaufmann, Elsevier, pp. 585–631 doi:10.1016/B978-0-12-381479-1.00013-7.

Hansen, R.F. (1998) 'Continuity and Disjunction: The Pre-Classic Antecedents of Classic Maya Architecture,' in Houston S.D. (ed.) *Function and Meaning in Classic Maya Architecture*. Dumbarton Oaks Research Library and Collection, Washington, D.C.

Heavy AI (2024) Spatio-temporal Definition. Available at: www.heavy.ai/technical-glossary/spatial-temporal#:~:text=refers%20to%20space.-,Temporal%20refers%20to%20time.,(see%20above%20example%20image (Accessed 25 May 2024).

Hill, J. et al. (2016) 'Materials science with large-scale data and Informatics: Unlocking New Opportunities', *MRS Bulletin*, 41(5), pp. 399–409. doi:10.1557/mrs.2016.93.

Ingólfsson, H.I., Bhatia, H., Aydin, F., Oppelstrup, T., López, C.A., Stanton, L.G., Carpenter, T.S., Wong, S., Di Natale, F., Zhang, X., Moon, J.Y., Stanley, C.B., Chavez, J.R., Nguyen, K., Dharuman, G., Burns, V., Shrestha, R., Goswami, D., Gulten, G., Van, Q.N., Ramanathan, A., Van Essen, B., Hengartner, N.W., Stephen, A.G., Turbyville, T., Bremer, P.T., Gnanakaran, S., Glosli, J.N., Lightstone, F.C., Nissley, D.V., and Streitz, F.H. (2023) 'Machine Learning-Driven Multiscale Modeling: Bridging the Scales with a Next-Generation Simulation Infrastructure', *Journal of Chemical Theory and Computation*, 19(9), pp. 2658-2675. doi:10.1021/acs.jctc.2c01018.

Kalina, K.A., Linden, L., Brummund, J., and Kästner, M. (2023) 'FEANN: an efficient data-driven multiscale approach based on physics-constrained neural networks and automated data mining', *Computational Mechanics*, 71, pp. 827–851. doi:10.1007/s00466-022-02260-0.

Keoleian, G.A. and Spitzley, D.V. (2006) 'Life cycle-based sustainability metrics', *Sustainability science and engineering*, *1*, pp. 127–159. doi:10.1016/S1871-2711(06)80014-0.

Lee, D., Chen, W., Wang, L., Chan, Y.C., and Chen, W. (2024) 'Data-driven Design for Metamaterials and Multiscale Systems: A Review', Advanced Materials, 36(8), 2305254. doi:10.1002/adma.202305254.

Lu, G. and Kaxiras, E. (2004) 'An Overview of Multiscale Simulations of Materials', arXiv:cond-mat/0401073v1. doi:10.48550/arXiv. cond-mat/0401073.

Ludwig, F., Hensel, M., and Weisser, W. (2021) 'ECOLOPES Gebäudehüllen als biodiverse Lebensräume', in Bundesinstitut für Bau-, Stadt- und Raumforschung', in BBSR (eds.) *Bauen von morgen – Zukunftsthemen und Szenarien*. Bundesamt für Bauwesen und Raumordnung, Bonn, pp 84–89.

Lv, C. et al. (2021) 'Machine learning: An advanced platform for materials development and state prediction in lithium-Ion Batteries', *Advanced Materials*, 34(25), 2101474. doi:10.1002/adma.202101474.

Lynch, K. (1972) *What Time is This Place?* Cambridge: MIT Press.

Malinov, S. and Sha, W. (2003) 'Software products for modeling and simulation in materials science', *Computational Materials Science*, 28 (2), pp. 179–198. doi:10.1016/S0927-0256(03)00106-X.

Mang, P. and Reed, B. (2011) 'Designing from place: a regenerative framework and methodology', *Building Research & Information*, 40(1), pp. 23–38. doi:10.1080/09613218.2012.621341.

Mang, P. and Reed, B. (2012) 'Regenerative development and design', in *Springer eBooks*, pp. 8855–8879. doi:10.1007/978-1-4419-0851-3_303.

Martins, P. (2006) 'Sustainability: science or fiction?', Sustainability: Science, Practice and Policy, 1(2), pp. 36–41. doi:10.1080/15487733.2006.11907976.

Materiom (2024) Available at: https://materiom.org/ (Accessed 22 July 2024).

Meagher, M. (2015) 'Designing for change: The poetic potential of responsive architecture,' *Frontiers of Architectural Research*, 4(2), pp. 159–165. doi:10.1016/j.foar.2015.03.002.

Mouton, L., Allacker, K., and Röck, M. (2023) 'Bio-based building material solutions for environmental benefits over conventional construction products – Life cycle assessment of regenerative design strategies', *Energy and Buildings*, 282, 112767. doi:10.1016/j.enbuild.2022.112767.

Muhammad, R., Zhang, W., Abbas, Z., Guo, F., and Gwiazdzinski, L., (2022) 'Spatiotemporal change analysis and prediction of future land use and land cover changes using QGIS MOLUSCE plugin and remote sensing big data: a case study of Linyi', China. *Land*, *11*(3), 419. doi:10.3390/land11030419.

National Research Council (2001) *Basic Research Opportunities in Earth Science*. Washington: The National Academies Press. doi:10.17226/9981.

Oxford Dictionaries. Definition of "Time". Available at: https://web.archive.org/web/20120704084938/http://oxforddictionaries.com/definition/time (Accessed 20 September 2023).

O'Mara, J., Meredig, B., and Michel, K. (2016) 'Materials Data Infrastructure: A Case Study of the citrination platform to examine data import, storage, and access', *JOM*, 68(8), pp. 2031–2034. doi:10.1007/s11837-016-1984-0.

Pagoropoulos, A., Pigosso, D.C., and McAloone, T.C. (2017) 'The emergent role of digital technologies in the Circular Economy: A review,' *Procedia cirp*, *64*, pp. 19–24.

Peuquet, D.J., 1994. 'It's about time: A conceptual framework for the representation of temporal dynamics in geographic information systems' *Annals of the Association of American Geographers*, *84*(3), pp. 441–461.

Potting, J., Hekkert, M.P., Worrell, E., and Hanemaaijer, A. (2017) *Circular Economy: Measuring innovation in the product chain*. https://dspace.library.uu.nl/handle/1874/358310 (Accessed 29 April 2024).

ReMat – Regenerative Materials Knowledge Platform (2024) Available at: www.regenerativematerials.org/ (Accessed 20 July 2024).

Rotmans, J. and Loorbach, D. (2009) 'Complexity and transition management,' *Journal of Industrial Ecology*, 13(2), pp. 184–196. doi:10.1111/j.1530-9290.2009.00116.x.

Savory, A. and Butterfield, J. (1999) *Holistic management: A New Framework for Decision Making*, 2nd edition. Washington: Island Press.

Shehata, N., Mohamed, O.A., Sayed, E.T., Abdelkareem, M.A., and Olabi, A.G. (2022) 'Geopolymer concrete as green building materials: Recent applications, sustainable development and circular economy potentials', *Science of the Total Environment*, *836*, 155577. doi:10.1016/j.scitotenv.2022.155577.

Soh, M. (2019) *Time: a four-dimensional approach to urban design.* Available at: www.nadigroup.com/insights/time-a-four-dimensional-approach-to-urban-design (Accessed 30 April 2024).

Sunguroğlu Hensel, D., Tyc, J., and Hensel, M. (2022) 'Data-driven Design for Architecture and Environment Integration: Convergence of data-integrated workflows for understanding and designing environments', *Spool*, 9(1), pp. 19–34. doi:10.47982/spool.2022.1.02.

Tange, K. and Kawazoe, N. (1965) *Ise: prototype of Japanese architecture.* Cambridge: MIT press.

Till, J. (2013) *Architecture depends*. Cambridge: MIT Press.

Tyc, J., Sunguroğlu Hensel, D., Parisi, E.I., Tucci, G., and Hensel, M. (2021) 'Integration of remote sensing data into a composite voxel model for environmental performance analysis of terraced vineyards in Tuscany, Italy', *Remote Sensing*, 13(17), 3483. doi: 10.3390/rs13173483.

Tyc, J., Parisi, E.I., Tucci, G., Sunguroğlu Hensel, D., and Hensel, M. (2022) 'A Data-integrated and Performance-oriented Parametric Design Process for Terraced Vineyard', *Journal of Digital Landscape Architecture* 7, pp. 504–521.

Van Tendeloo, G., Bals, S., Van Aert, S., Verbeeck, J., and Van Dyck, D. (2012) 'Advanced electron microscopy for advanced materials', *Advanced materials*, *24*(42), pp. 5655-5675. doi:10.1002/adma.201202107.

Venkateswara Rao, K., Govardhan, A., and Chalapati Rao, K.V. (2012) 'An Architecture Framework for Spatio-temporal Data Mining System'. *International Journal of Software Engineering & Applications* (*IJSEA*), *3*(5), pp. 125–146.

Wang, S., Cao, J., and P.S. Yu, P.S. (2022) 'Deep Learning for Spatio-Temporal Data Mining: A Survey', *IEEE Transactions on Knowledge and Data Engineering*, *34*(8), pp. 3681–3700. doi:10.1109/TKDE.2020.3025580.

Weisser, W., Hensel, M., Barath, S., Grobman, Y.J., Hauck, T.E., Joschinski, J., Ludwig, F., Mimet, A., Perini, K., Roccotiello, E., Schloter, M., Shwartz, A., Sunguroğlu Hensel, D., and Vogler, V. (2022) 'Creating ecologically sound buildings by integrating ecology, architecture, and computational design', *People & Nature*, 5(1), pp. 4–20. doi:10.1002/pan3.10411.

Wilson, M.R. (2007) 'Molecular simulation of liquid crystals: progress towards a better understanding of bulk structure and the prediction of material properties' *Chemical Society Reviews*, *36*(12), pp. 1881–1888. doi:10.1039/B612799C.

Woods, L. (2009) 'Storm Watch'. Available at: https://lebbeuswoods.wordpress.com/2009/12/19/storm-watch/ (Accessed 15 August 2023)

Xia, X., Spadaccini, C.M., and Greer, J.R. (2022) 'Responsive materials architected in space and time,' *Nature Reviews Materials*, *7*(9), pp. 683–701.

CHAPTER 4

Abel, C. (2000) *Architecture and Identity: Responses to cultural and technological change* (2nd ed.). Boston: Architectural Press.

Achterberg, E., Hinfelaar, J., and Bocken, N. (2016) 'Master circular business models with the Value Hill,' Sustainable Finance Lab, Nuovalente, Het Groene Brein, TU Delft, Circle Economy. https://hetgroenebrein.nl/wp-content/uploads/2017/08/finance-white-paper-20160923.pdf (Accessed 21 August 2023).

Alexander, C., Ishikawa, S., and Silverstein, M. (1977) *A pattern language: towns, buildings, construction*, New York: Oxford University Press.

Amenta, L., Attademo, A., Remøy, H., Berruti, G., Cerreta, M., Formato, E., and Russo, M. (2019) 'Managing the Transition towards Circular Metabolism: Living Labs as a Co-Creation Approach,' *Urban Planning*, 4(3), pp. 5–18. doi:10.17645/up.v4i3.2170.

Arciniegas, G., Šilerytė, R., Dąbrowski, M., Wandl, A., Dukai, B., Bohnet, M., and Gutsche, J.M. (2019) 'A geodesign decision support environment for integrating management of resource flows in spatial planning,' *Urban Planning*, 4(3), pp. 32–51. doi:10.17645/up.v4i3.2173.

Arora, M., Raspall, F., Cheah, L., and Silva, A. (2019) 'Residential building material stocks and component-level circularity: The case of Singapore,' *Journal of Cleaner Production*, *216*, pp. 239–248. doi:10.1016/j.jclepro.2019.01.199.

Bansard, J. and Schroder, M. (2021) 'The Sustainable Use of Natural Resources: The Governance Challenge,' *IISD Earth Negotiations Bulletin*, Brief, 16. www.iisd.org/system/files/2021-04/still-one-earth-natural-resources.pdf (Accessed 17 July 2023).

Bar-Yam, Y. (2002) 'General Features of Complex Systems,' New England Complex Systems Institute, Cambridge, MA, USA. www.eolss.net/Sample-Chapters/C15/E1-29-01-00.pdf (Accessed 23 August 2023).

Bellstedt, C., Ezequiel Martin Carreno, G., Athanassiadis, A., and Chaudhry, S. (2022) *Urban Circularity Assessment Method*. CityLoops Deliverable 4.4. https://cityloops.eu/fileadmin/user_upload/Materials/UCA/CityLoops_WP4_D4.4_Urban_Circularity_Assessment_Method_Metabolism_of_Cities.pdf (Accessed 25 August 2023).

Berger, M., Sonderegger, T., Alvarenga, R., Bach, V., Cimprich, A., Dewulf, J., Frischknecht, R., Guinée, J., Helbig, C., Huppertz, T., Jolliet, O., Motoshita, M., Northey, S., Peña, C., Rugani, B., Sahnoune, A., Schrijvers, D., Schulze, R., Sonnemann, G., and Young, S. (2020) 'Mineral resources in life cycle impact assessment: part II – recommendations on application-dependent use of existing methods and on future method development needs,' *International Journal of Life Cycle Assessment*, 25(4), pp. 798–813. doi:10.1007/s11367-020-01737-5.

Bocken, N.M.P., Pauw, I. de, van der Grinten, B., and Bakker, C. (2016) 'Product design and business model strategies for a circular economy,' *Journal of Industrial and Production Engineering*, *33*(5), pp. 308–320. doi:10.1080/21681015.2016.1172124.

Boulding, K.E. (1966) 'The Economics of the Coming Spaceship Earth,' in Jarett, H. (ed.) *Environmental quality in a growing economy*. Baltimore: Johns Hopkins University Press, pp. 3–14.

Brand, S. (1994) *How Buildings Learn – What happens after they are built.* New York: Viking Press.

Braungart, M. and McDonough, W. (2002) *Cradle to Cradle: Remaking the way we make things.* Berkeley: North Point Press.

Broto, V.C., Allen, A., and Rapoport, E. (2012) 'Interdisciplinary perspectives on urban metabolism,' *Journal of Industrial Ecology*, *16*(6), pp. 851–861. doi:10.1111/j.1530-9290.2012.00556.x.

Bruel, A., Kronenberg, J., Troussier, N., and Guillaume, B. (2019) 'Linking Industrial Ecology and Ecological Economics: A theoretical and Empirical foundation for the circular economy,' *Journal of Industrial Ecology*, 23(1), pp. 12–21. doi:10.1111/jiec.12745.

Brunner, P.H. and Rechberger, H. (2003) *Practical Handbook of Material Flow Analysis, CRC Press eBooks.* doi:10.1201/9780203507209.

Bucci Ancapi, F.E., Van den Berghe, K.B.J., and Van Bueren, E. (2022) 'A Policy Coherence Framework for Circular Built Environment Implementation: The Case of a Campus Development', in Shahnoori, S. and Mohammadi, M. (eds.) *The state of circularity: The content of the 2nd International Conference on Circular Systems for the Built Environment.* Eindhoven: Technische Universiteit Eindhoven, pp. 120–136.

Buchanan, M. (2017) 'The thermodynamics of Earth,' *Nature Physics*, *13*(2), 106. doi:10.1038/nphys4031.

Cáceres, N.R., Garcia-Martinez, A., and Cózar, J.C.G. de (2023) 'Use of GIS and BIM tools in determining the life cycle impact of urban systems. Case study: Residential buildings which apply the Eco-Efficiency Matrix in the city of Quito, Ecuador,' *Journal of Cleaner Production*, *383*, 135485. doi:10.1016/j.jclepro.2022.135485.

CBE Hub (2023) Scale Matters. Circularity in the Built Environment Hub, Delft University of Technology. Available at: www.tudelft.nl/bk/onderzoek/onderzoeksthemas/circular-built-environment/scale-matters (Accessed 15 August 2023).

Circle Economy (2021) *The key elements of the circular economy. Circle Economy Foundation.* Available at: www.circle-economy.com/circular-economy/key-elements (Accessed 3 August 2023).

City of Amsterdam (2020) *Policy: Circular economy*. Available at: .www.amsterdam.nl/en/policy/sustainability/circular-economy/ (Accessed 26 July 2023).

Cramer J. (2014) *Milieu, Elementaire Deeltjes 16*. Amsterdam: University Press.

Cramer, J. (2020) *How network governance powers the circular economy. 10 Guiding Principles for Building a Circular Economy, based on Dutch Experiences.* Amsterdam Economic Board. https://amsterdameconomicboard.com/app/uploads/2020/12/How-Network-Governance-Powers-the-Circular-Economy-Ten-Guiding-Principles-for-a-Circular- Economy-Jacqueline-Cramer-1.pdf (Accessed 22 August 2023).

Curl, J.S. (2006) *A Dictionary of Architecture and Landscape Architecture.* Oxford: Oxford University Press.

Duvigneaud, P., Denaeyer-De Smet, S., and Tanghe, M. (1977) *Carte écologique de l'occupation du sol et des degrés de verdurisation de l'agglomération Bruxelloise. Situation mars 75. Notice explicative.* Brussels: Service de l'environnement.

Ellen MacArthur Foundation (2013) *Towards the circular economy Vol. 1: an economic and business rationale for an accelerated transition.* Available at: https://emf.thirdlight.com/file/24/xTyQj3oxiYN-MO1xTFs9xT5LF3C/Towards%20the%20circular%20economy%20Vol%201%3A%20an%20economic%20and%20business%20rationale%20for%20an%20accelerated%20transition.pdf (Accessed 22 August 2024).

European Central Bank (2003) *Annual Report 2002.* ECB, Frankfurt am Main, Germany. Available at: www.ecb.europa.eu/pub/pdf/annrep/ar2002en.pdf (Accessed 18 July 2023).

European Commission, Directorate-General for Internal Market, Industry, Entrepreneurship and SMEs, Bobba, S., Claudiu, P., Huygens, D. et al. (2018) *Report on critical raw materials and the circular economy.* Publications Office. Available at: https://data.europa.eu/doi/10.2873/167813 (Accessed 18 July 2023).

European Commission, Directorate-General for Internal Market, Industry, Entrepreneurship and SMEs, Grohol, M., Veeh, C. (2023) *Study on the critical raw materials for the EU 2023: final report*. Publications Office of the European Union. Available at: https://data.europa.eu/doi/10.2873/725585 (Accessed 18 July 2023).

Eurostat (2023) 'Circular economy – Material flows'. Available at: https://ec.europa.eu/eurostat/statistics-explained/index.php?title=Circular_economy_-_material_flows (Accessed 15 August 2023).

Fischer-Kowalski, M., Krausmann, F., Giljum, S., Lutter, S., Mayer, A., Bringezu, S., Moriguchi, Y., Schütz, H., Schandl, H., and Weisz, H. (2011) 'Methodology and indicators of economy-wide material flow accounting,' *Journal of Industrial Ecology*, *15*(6), pp. 855–876. doi:10.1111/j.1530-9290.2011.00366.x.

Foster, J.B. (2000) *Marx's Ecology: Materialism and Nature.* New York: University Press.

Furlan, C., Wandl, A., Geldermans, B., and Sileryte, R. (2020) 'A refined waste flow mapping method: Addressing the material and spatial dimensions of waste flows in the urban territory through big data: the case of the Amsterdam Metropolitan Area,' *Contesti Città, Territori, Progetti*, 1. doi:10.13128/contest-11909.

Geldermans, B. (2020) 'Securing healthy circular material flows in the built environment,' *DOAJ (DOAJ: Directory of Open Access Journals)* [Preprint]. doi:10.7480/abe.2020.06.5038.

Geldermans, B., Wandl, A., Steenmeijer, M., and Furlan, C. (2018) *REPAiR: REsource Management in Peri-urban AReas: Going Beyond Urban Metabolism: D3.3 Process model for the two pilot cases: Amsterdam, the Netherlands & Naples, Italy*. Delft: Delft University of Technology.

Gouvernement du Grand-Duché de Luxembourg. *PCDS Product Circularity Data Sheet.* Available at: https://pcds.lu/pcds-system/#pcds (Accessed 15 August 2023).

Graedel, T.E., Reck, B.K., Ciacci, L., and Passarini, F. (2019) 'On the Spatial Dimension of the Circular Economy,' *Resources*, *8*(1), p. 32. doi:10.3390/resources8010032.

Haberl, H., Fischer-Kowalski, M., Krausmann, F., Weisz, H., and Winiwarter, V. (2004) 'Progress towards sustainability? What the conceptual framework of material and energy flow accounting (MEFA) can offer,' *Land Use Policy*, *21*(3), pp. 199–213. doi:10.1016/j.landusepol.2003.10.013.

Habraken, J. (2000) *Structure of the ordinary – Form and Control in the Built Environment.* Cambridge: MIT Press.

Hagelüken, C, Lee-Shin, J.U., Carpentier, A., and Heron, C. (2016) 'The EU circular economy and its relevance to metal recycling,' *Recycling*, 1(2), pp. 242–253. doi:10.3390/recycling1020242.

Hale, R.C., Seeley, M.E., La Guardia, M.J., Mai, L., and Zeng, E.Y. (2020) 'A Global Perspective on Microplastics,' *Journal of Geophysical Research. Oceans*, 125(1). doi:10.1029/2018jc014719.

Harvard's Growth Lab (2023) *The Atlas of Economic Complexity*. Available at: https://atlas.cid.harvard.edu (Accessed 23 August 2023).

Heinrich, M. and Lang, W. (2019) *Materials Passports – Best Practice. Innovative Solutions for a Transition to a Circular Economy in the Built Environment*. Munich: Technische Universität München. doi:10.5281/zenodo.2556515.

Heynen, N., Kaika, M., and Swyngedouw, E. (2006) *In the Nature of Cities: Urban political ecology and the politics of urban metabolism*. London: Routledge.

Hmood, K. (ed.) (2019) *Urban and Architectural Heritage Conservation within Sustainability.* London: InTech.

Hynes, P.H. (1989) *The Recurring Silent Spring*. Oxford: Pergamon Press.

IEA (2008) *World Energy Outlook 2008*, Paris: OECD Publishing. doi:10.1787/weo-2008-en.

IEA (2019) *Global Status Report for Buildings and Construction 2019*. IEA, Paris Available at: www.iea.org/reports/global-status-report-for-buildings-and-construction-2019 (Accessed 24 July 2023).

IEA (2023) *Renewable energy market update – June 2023 – analysis.* International Energy Agency. Available at: www.iea.org/reports/renewable-energy-market-update-june-2023 (Accessed 9 August 2023).

Ioannou, O., Geldermans, B., Wandl, A., and Klein, T. (2022) 'Planning for change: A methodological framework for integrating circularity into Tu Delft's Faculty of Architecture and the Built Environment's curricula,' *SAJ. Serbian Architectural Journal*, *12*(3), pp. 234–269. doi:10.5937/saj2003234i.

Intergovernmental Panel on Climate Change (2022) *Climate Change 2022 – Mitigation of climate change*. Cambridge University Press eBooks. doi:10.1017/9781009157926.

International Organization for Standardization. *ISO/DIS 59040 Circular Economy – Product circularity data sheet.* Available at: www.iso.org/standard/82339.html (Accessed 15 August 2023).

Jacobs, J. (1961) *The Death and Life of Great American Cities*. New York: Random House.

Ferm, J. and Jones, E. (2016) 'Mixed-use 'regeneration' of employment land in the post-industrial city: challenges and realities in London,' *European Planning Studies*, *24*(10), pp. 1913–1936. doi:10.1080/09654313.2016.1209465.

Kendall, S. (1990) *The ecology of production, and the significance of distributed control.* PhD dissertation. Stephen Kendall. Available at: https://drstephenkendall.com/wp-content/uploads/2017/01/Mapping-Control-in-Production-Chains.pdf. (Accessed 23 August 2023).

Kennedy, C., Cuddihy, J., and Engel-Yan, J. (2007) 'The changing metabolism of cities,' *Journal of Industrial Ecology*, *11*(2), pp. 43–59. doi:10.1162/jie.2007.1107.

Kennedy, J.F. (2004) *Building without borders: sustainable construction for the global village.* Available at: http://ci.nii.ac.jp/ncid/BA82017982 (Accessed 1 August 2023).

Lucertini, G. and Musco, F. (2020) 'Circular Urban Metabolism Framework,' *One Earth*, 2(2), pp. 138–142. doi:10.1016/j.oneear.2020.02.004.

Lyle, J.T. (1985) *Design for human ecosystems: landscape, land use, and natural resources.* Available at: https://ci.nii.ac.jp/ncid/BA00511499 (Accessed 19 July 2023).

Meadows, D.H., Randers, J., and Meadows, D.L. (2004) *The limits to growth: The 30-year Update*. Vermont: Chelsea Green Publishing Company.

Meadows, D.H., Randers, J., and Meadows, D.L. (2004) *The limits to growth: The 30-year Update*. Vermont: Chelsea Green Publishing Company.

Meath, C., Karlovšek, J., Navarrete, C., Eales, M., and Hastings, P. (2022) 'Co-designing a multi-level platform for industry level transition to circular economy principles: A case study of the infrastructure CoLab,' *Journal of Cleaner Production*, *347*, 131080. doi:10.1016/j.jclepro.2022.131080.

Meglin, R., Kytzia, S., and Habert, G. (2021) 'Regional circular economy of building materials: Environmental and economic assessment combining Material Flow Analysis, Input-Output Analyses, and Life Cycle Assessment,' *Journal of Industrial Ecology*, *26*(2), pp. 562–576. doi:10.1111/jiec.13205.

Moreno, B. and García-Álvarez, M.T. (2018) 'Measuring the progress towards a resource-efficient European Union under the Europe 2020 strategy,' *Journal of Cleaner Production*, *170*, pp. 991–1005. doi:10.1016/j.jclepro.2017.09.149.

Mulhall, D., Ayed, A.C., Schroeder, J., Hansen, K., and Wautelet, T. (2022) 'The Product Circularity Data Sheet – A Standardized Digital Fingerprint for Circular Economy Data about Products,' *Energies*, *15*(9), 3397. doi:10.3390/en15093397.

Neves, S.A. and Marques, A.C. (2022) 'Drivers and barriers in the transition from a linear economy to a circular economy,' *Journal of Cleaner Production*, *341*, 130865. doi:10.1016/j.jclepro.2022.130865.

Norberg-Schulz, C. (1980) *Genius Loci: Towards a Phenomenology of Architecture*. New York: Rizzoli.

OECD (2021) *OECD Work on Trade and the Environment, a retrospective 2008–2020*. Available at: https://one.oecd.org/document/COM/TAD/ENV/JWPTE(2020)3/FINAL/en/pdf (Accessed 1 August 2023).

OECD (2023) *OECD SME and entrepreneurship outlook*. OECD Publishing, Paris. doi.org/10.1787/342b8564-en.

Oliver, P. (ed.) (1997) *Encyclopedia of vernacular architecture of the world*. Cambridge: Cambridge University Press, Cambridge.

Parkinson, M. (2017) *GIS Enhances Construction Surveying*. Available at: www.esri.com/about/newsroom/arcuser/gis-enhances-construction-surveying/ (Accessed 1 August 2023).

Pincetl, S., Bunje, P., and Holmes, T. (2012) 'An expanded urban metabolism method: Towards a systems approach for assessing urban energy processes and causes,' *Landscape and Urban Planning*, *107*(3), pp. 193–202. https://doi.org/10.1016/j.landurbplan.2012.06.006.

Potting, J., Hekkert, M., Worrell, E., and Hanemaaijer, A. (2017) *Circular Economy: Measuring innovation in the product chain*. Available at: https://dspace.library.uu.nl/handle/1874/358310 (Accessed 21 August 2023).

Ranta, V., Aarikka-Stenroos, L., Ritala, P., and Mäkinen, S.J. (2018) 'Exploring institutional drivers and barriers of the circular economy: A cross-regional comparison of China, the US, and Europe,' *Resources, Conservation and Recycling*, *135*, pp. 70–82. doi:10.1016/j.resconrec.2017.08.017.

Raugei, M. and Ulgiati, S. (2009) 'A novel approach to the problem of geographic allocation of environmental impact in Life Cycle Assessment and Material Flow Analysis,' *Ecological Indicators*, *9*(6), pp. 1257–1264. doi:10.1016/j.ecolind.2009.04.001.

Reike, D., Vermeulen, W.J.V., and Witjes, S. (2018) 'The circular economy: New or Refurbished as CE 3.0? – Exploring Controversies in the Conceptualization of the Circular Economy through a Focus on History and Resource Value Retention Options,' *Resources, Conservation and Recycling*, *135*, pp. 246–264. doi:10.1016/j.resconrec.2017.08.027.

Remoy, H., Wandle, A., Ceric, D., and Van Timmeren, A. (2019) 'Facilitating circular economy in urban planning,' *Urban Planning*, *4*(3), pp. 1–4. doi:10.17645/up.v4i3.2484.

Rockström, J., Steffen, W., Noone, K., Persson, Å., Chapin III, F.S., Lambin, E.F., Lenton, T.M., Scheffer, M., Folke, C., Schellnhuber, H.J., Nykvist, B., Wit, C.A. de, Hughes, T., van der Leeuw, S., Rohde, H., Sörlin, S., Snyder, P.K., Costanza, R., Sevdin, U., Falkenmark, M., Karlberg, L., Corell, R.W., Fabry, V.J., Hansen, J., Walker, B., Liverman, D., Richardson, K., Crutzen, P., and Foley, J.A. (2009) 'A safe operating space for humanity,' *Nature*, *461*(7263), pp. 472–475. doi:10.1038/461472a.

Rood, T. and Hanemaaijer, A. (2014) *Reflectie op programma Van Afvalstof Naar Grondstof (Reflection on the Programme from Waste to Resource)*. The Hague: PBL Netherlands Environmental Assessment Agency.

Salman, M. (2019) 'Sustainability and Vernacular Architecture: Rethinking what identity is,' in Hmood, K. (ed.) *Urban and Architectural Heritage Conservation within Sustainability*. London: IntechOpen. doi:10.5772/intechopen.82025.

Sargut, G. and McGrath, R. (2011). Learning to live with Complexity. *Harvard Business Review*, *89*(9): pp. 68–76.

Schrijvers, D., Hool, A., Blengini, G.A., Chen, W.Q., Dewulf, J., Eggert, R., van Ellen, L., Gauss, R., Goddin, J., Habib, K., Hagelüken, C., Hirohata, A., Hofmann-Amtenbrink, M., Kosmol, J., Le Gleuher, M., Grohol, M., Ku, A., Lee, M.H., Liu, G., Nansai, K., Nuss, P., Peck, D., Reller, A., Sonnemann, G., Tercero, L., Thorenz, A., and Wäger, P.A. (2020) 'A review of methods and data to determine raw material criticality,' *Resources, Conservation and Recycling*, *155*, 104617. doi:10.1016/j.resconrec.2019.104617.

Sileryte, R., Sabbe, A., Bouzas, V., Meister, K., Wandl, A., and Van Timmeren, A. (2022) 'European Waste Statistics data for a Circular Economy Monitor: Opportunities and limitations from the Amsterdam Metropolitan Region,' *Journal of Cleaner Production*, *358*, 131767. doi:10.1016/j.jclepro.2022.131767.

Sonderegger, T., Berger M., Alvarenga, R., Bach, V., Cimprich, A., Dewulf, J., Frischknecht, R., Guinée, J., Helbig, C., Huppertz, T., Jolliet, O., Motoshita, M., Northey, S., Rugani, B., Schrijvers, D., Schulze, R., Sonnemann, G., Valero, A., Weidema, B.P., and Young, S.B. (2020) 'Mineral resources in life cycle impact assessment-part I: a critical review of existing methods,' *The International Journal of Life Cycle Assessment*, *25*(4), pp. 784–797. doi:10.1007/s11367-020-01736-6.

Stahel, W.R. and Reday-Mulvey, G. (1981) *Jobs for Tomorrow: The Potential for Substituting Manpower for Energy*. New York: Vantage Press.

Stahel, W. (1981) 'The product-life factor', in Grinton Orr S. (ed.) *An Inquiry into the Nature of Sustainable Societies: The Role of the Private Sector*, Houston: HARC, pp. 72–96.

Steinitz, C. (2012) *A framework for geodesign: Changing Geography by Design*. Redlands: ESRI Press.

Su, B., Heshmati, A., Geng, Y., and Yu, X. (2013) 'A review of the circular economy in China: moving from rhetoric to implementation,' *Journal of Cleaner Production*, *42*, pp. 215–227. doi:10.1016/j.jclepro.2012.11.020.

Suppipat, S., Teachavorasinskun, K., and Hu, A.H. (2021) 'Challenges of applying simplified LCA tools in sustainable design pedagogy,' *Sustainability*, *13*(4), 2406. doi:10.3390/su13042406.

Tanzer, J. and Rechberger, H. (2019) 'Setting the common ground: a generic framework for material flow analysis of complex systems,' *Recycling*, *4*(2), 23. doi:10.3390/recycling4020023.

Tapia, C., Bianchi, M., Pallaske, G., and Bassi, A.M. (2021) Towards a territorial definition of a circular economy: exploring the role of territorial factors in closed-loop systems. *European Planning Studies*, *29*(8), pp. 1438–1457. doi:10.1080/09654313.2020.1867511.

Thung, I., Schouten, N., Dekker, G., and Papineau Salm, J. (2023) *Towards a circular economy in the built environment – Overcoming market, finance, and ownership challenges*. Amsterdam: Circular Buildings Coalition.

Tsui, T., Peck, D., Geldermans, B., and Van Timmeren, A. (2020) 'The role of urban manufacturing for a circular economy in cities,' *Sustainability*, *13*(1), 23. doi:10.3390/su13010023.

United Nations (2011) *Decoupling Natural Resource Use and Environmental Impacts from Economic Growth*. Nairobi: United Nations Environment Programme/Earthprint.

United Nations (2022) *World Population Prospects 2022, Summary of results*. United Nations Department of Economic and Social Affairs, Population Division. Available at: UN DESA/POP/2022/TR/NO. 3 (Accessed 25 August 2023).

United Nations (2022) 'Global trade hits record high of $28.5 trillion in 2021, but likely to be subdued in 2022'. UNCTAD. Available at: https://unctad.org/news/global-trade-hits-record-high-285-trillion-2021-likely-be-subdued-2022 (Accessed 25 June 2023).

United Nations (2022) *Global Status Report for Buildings and Construction: Towards a Zero-emission, Efficient and Resilient Buildings and Construction Sector.* Nairobi: United Nations Environment Programme.

Varju, V., Azizli, B., Wandl, A., Geldermans, B., and Acke, A. (2016) *Resource management in Peri-urban Areas: Going beyond Urban Metabolism – D3.9 Comparison report for policy makers*. REPAiR Project, Delft University of Technology.

Van Der Voet, E. (2022) *Imagining the future: building a knowledge base for a sustainable resource use*. Available at: https://hdl.handle.net/1887/3567350 (Accessed 12 July 2023).

Vogtländer, J., Peck, D., and Kurowicka, D. (2019) 'The Eco-Costs of Material Scarcity, a Resource Indicator for LCA, Derived from a Statistical Analysis on Excessive Price Peaks,' *Sustainability*, *11*(8), 2446. doi:10.3390/su11082446.

Walden, J., Steinbrecher, A., and Marinkovic, M. (2021) 'Digital product passports as enabler of the circular economy,' *Chemie-Ingenieur-Technik/Chemieingenieurtechnik*, *93*(11), pp. 1717–1727. doi:10.1002/cite.202100121.

Wang-Erlandsson, L. et al. (2022) 'A planetary boundary for green water,' *Nature Reviews. Earth & Environment*, *3*(6), pp. 380–392. doi:10.1038/s43017-022-00287-8.

Ward, C.P. and Reddy, C.M. (2020) 'We need better data about the environmental persistence of plastic goods,' *Proceedings of the National Academy of Sciences of the United States of America*, *117*(26), pp. 14618–14621. doi:10.1073/pnas.2008009117.

Weterings, R., et al. (2013) *Resources for our Future: Key issues and best practices in Resource Efficiency*. The Hague: Centre for Strategic Studies.

Williams, J. (2020) 'The role of spatial planning in transitioning to circular urban development', *Urban Geography*, *41*(6), pp. 915–919. doi:10.1080/02723638.2020.1796042.

Wolman, A. (1965) 'The metabolism of cities,' *Scientific American*, *213*(3), pp. 178–190. doi:10.1038/scientificamerican0965-178.

World Commission on Environment and Development (1987) *Our common future*. Oxford: Oxford University Press.

Xue, K., et al. (2021) 'BIM Integrated LCA for Promoting Circular Economy towards Sustainable Construction: An Analytical Review,' *Sustainability*, *13*(3), 1310. doi:10.3390/su13031310.

Zhang, L., et al. (2019) 'Investigating the constraints to building Information modeling (BIM) applications for sustainable building projects: A case of China,' *Sustainability*, *11*(7), 1896. doi:10.3390/su11071896.

CHAPTER 5

Adani, F., Genevini, P.L., Gasperi, F., and Tambone, F. (1999) 'Composting and Humification', *Compost Science & Utilization*, *7*(1), pp. 24–33. doi: 10.1080/1065657X.1999.10701949.

Anandhi, V., Belliraj, N., Ananthi, M., and Pirabu, J.V. (2020) 'Cloud computing and climate-smart agriculture: an efficient transfer of technology mechanism', *International Journal of Farm Sciences*, 10(1), pp. 59–60. doi:10.5958/2250-0499.2020.00012.9.

Atzberger, C. (2013) 'Advances in remote sensing of agriculture: context description, existing operational monitoring systems and major information needs', Remote Sensing, 5(8), 4124. doi:10.3390/rs5020949.

Azim, K., Soudi, B., Boukhari, S., Perissol, C., Roussos, S., and Thami Alami, I. (2018) 'Composting parameters and compost quality: a literature review', *Organic* Agriculture, 8, pp. 141–158. Doi:10.1007/s13165-017-0180-z.

Baccini, P. and Brunner, P.H. (2012) *Metabolism of the Anthroposphere – Analysis, Evaluation, Design*. Cambridge Mass: The MIT Press.

Baheri, N. (2015) 'The Built Environment in the Critical Zone: From Pre- to Postindustrial Cities', in Giardino, J.R. and Houser, C. (eds.) *Principles and Dynamics of the Critical Zone*. Amsterdam: Elsevier, pp. 563–578.

Batista, L.T., Franco, J.R.Q., Fakury, R.H., Porto, M.F., and Braga, C.M.P. (2022) 'Methodology for Determining Sustainable Water Consumption Indicators for Buildings', *Sustainability*, 14, 5695. doi:10.3390/su14095695.

Benis, K., Reinhart, C., and Ferrao, P. (2017) 'Development of a simulation-based decision support workflow for the implementation of building integrated agriculture (BIA) in urban contexts', Journal of Cleaner Production, 147, pp. 589–602. doi:10.1016/j.jclepro.2017.01.130.

Bill, R., Nash, E., and Grenzdörfer, G. (2011) 'GIS in Agriculture', in Kresse, W. and Danko, D. (eds.) *Springer Handbook of Geographic Information*. Berlin: Springer.

Bindreiter, S., Lorenz, W., Dengg, E., Pachauer, V., Grabuschnig, L., Wurzer, G., Ugljanin, N., and Rasper P. (2023, September 21). 'M-DAB2: The project', *eCAADe 2023 Education and Research in Computer Aided Architectural Design in Europe*, Graz, Austria, 21 September.

Boyle, T., Giurco, D., Mukheibir, P., Liu, A., Moy, C., White, S., and Stewart, R. (2013) 'Intelligent Metering for Urban Water: A Review', *Water*, 5, pp. 1052–1081. doi:10.3390/w5031052.

Bronson, K. and Knezevic, I. (2016) 'Big Data in food and agriculture', *Big Data & Society*, 3(1). doi:10.1177/2053951716648174.

Bui, E.N. (2016) 'Data-driven Critical Zone science: A new paradigm', *Science of The Total Environment*, 568, pp. 587–593. doi:10.1016/j.scitotenv.2016.01.202.

Castrignanó, A., Buttafuoco, G., Khosla, R., Mouazen, A.M., Moshou, D., and Naud, O. (eds.) (2020) *Agricultural Internet of Things and decision support for precision farming*. London: Academic Press Elsevier.

Chen, Y. and Aviad, T. (1990) 'Effect of humic substances on plant growth', in MacCarthy, P., Clapp, C.E., Malcolm, R.L., and Bloom PR (eds.) *Humic substances in soil and crop sciences: Selected readings*. Madison, WI, American Society of Agronomy, pp. 161–186.

Chen, Y., Magen, H., and Riov, J. (1994) 'Humic substances originating from rapidly decomposition organic matter: properties and effects on plant growth', in Senesi, N. and Miano, T.M. (eds.) *Humic substances in the global environment and implication on human Health*. London, Elsevier Science B.V, pp. 427–445.

Chokhachian, A., Hensel, M., and Perini, K. (eds.) (2022a) *Informed Urban Environments: Data-integrated Design for Human and Ecology-centered Perspectives*. The Urban Book Series. Cham: Springer. doi:10.1007/978-3-031-03803-7.

Chokhachian, A., Hensel, M., and Perini, K. (2022b) "Introduction to Informed Urban Environments", in Chokhachian, A., Hensel, M., and Perini, K. (eds.) *Informed Urban Environments: Data-integrated Design for Human and Ecology-centered Perspectives*. The Urban Book Series. Cham: Springer. doi.org/10.1007/978-3-031-03803-7_1.

Clarke, S. (2014) 'Las Vegas Food District: The Integration of Agricultural Urbanism and Regenerative Design', *Food Studies: An Interdisciplinary Journal*, 3(3): pp. 11–25. doi:10.18848/2160-1933/CGP/v03i03/40578.

Cossu, R. (2013) 'Editorial', *Waste Management*, 33(3), 497–498.

Cossu, R. and Williams, I.D. (2015) 'Urban mining: Concepts, terminology, challenges', *Waste Management*, 45, pp. 1–3, doi:10.1016/j.wasman.2015.09.040.

CZEN – Critical Zone Exploration Network (2024) Available at: www.czen.org/ (Accessed 24 July 2024).

De Wolf, C., Cetin, S., and Bocken, N.M.P. (2024) A Circular Built Environment in the Digital Age. Berlin: Springer.

ECOLOPES (2024) Available at: https://ecolopes.org/ (Accessed 14 August 2024).

ESDAC (2024) European Soil Bureau (ESBN). Available at: https://esdac.jrc.ec.europa.eu/esbn/Esbn_overview.html (Accessed 14 August 2024).

European Commission (2023) Eurostat report shows EU's progress on Sustainable Development Goals. Available at: https://ec.europa.eu/commission/presscorner/detail/en/ip_23_2887 (Accessed 24 July 2024).

European Commission, Directorate-General for Research and Innovation, Veerman, C., Pinto Correia, T., Bastioli, C., Biro, B., Bouma, J., Cienciala, E., Emmett, B., Frison, E.A., Grand, A., Hristov, L, Kriaučiūnienė, Z. Pogrzeba, M., Soussana, J.F., Vela, C., and Wittkowski, R. (2020) 'Caring for soil is caring for life – Ensure 75% of soils are healthy by 2030 for healthy food, people, nature and climate – Interim report of the mission board for soil health and food', Available at: https://data.europa.eu/doi/10.2777/918775 (Accessed 14 August 2024).

FAO – Harmonized World Soil Database (2024) Available at: www.fao.org/soils-portal/data-hub/soil-maps-and-databases/harmonized-world-soil-database-v20/en/ (Accessed 20 July 2024) Detailed Information available at: https://openknowledge.fao.org/server/api/core/bitstreams/149f1562-bf6a-439f-9d3a-eb93940f39cf/content (Accessed 20 July 2024).

Feng, S. (2024) 'Implementation of Decision Support System for Ecological Environment Planning of Urban Green Space', *Ecological Chemistry and Engineering*, 31(2), pp. 177–192. doi:10.2478/eces-2024-0012.

Finisdore, J., Rhodes, C., Haines-Young, R., Maynard, S., Wielgus, J., Dvarskas, A., Houdet, J., Quétier, F., Lamothe, K.A., Ding, H., Soulard, F., Van Houtven, G., and Rowcroft, P. (2020) 'The 18 benefits of using ecosystem services classification systems', *Ecosystem Services*, 45, doi:10.1016/j.ecoser.2020.101160.

Georgiadis, T., Barbera, G., Carotenuto, F., Lenzi, J., Motisi, A., and Rossi, F. (2014) 'How a traditional agricultural protection structure acts in conditioning the internal microclimate: A statistical analytical approach to Giardino Pantesco (Pantelleria Islan, Italy)', *Italian Journal of Agrometeorology*, 18, 41–58.

Gould, D. and Caplow, T. (2012) '8 – Building-integrated agriculture: a new approach to food production', in Zeman, F. (ed.) *Metropolitan Sustainability*. Sawston: Woodhead Publishing, pp. 147–170. doi:1533/9780857096463.2.147.

Green, L.Y., Mikhailova, E.A., Post, C.J., Darnault, C.J.G., Bridges, W.C., and Schlautman, M.A. (2016) 'A cloud-based spatial-temporal inventory for sustainable urban soil management', *Urban Ecosystems*, 19, pp. 811–822. doi:10.1007/s11252-015-0512-2.

Hagemann, S., Arpe, K., and Bengtsson, L. (2005) 'Validation of the hydrological cycle of ERA 40', *Berichte zur Erdsystemforschung, 10*. Available online: https://hdl.handle.net/11858/00-001M-0000-0011-FF56-A (Accessed 7 August 2024).

Heeren, N. and Hellweg, S. (2019) 'Tracking Construction Material over Space and Time: Prospective and Geo-referenced Modeling of Building Stocks and Construction Material Flows', *Journal of Industrial Ecology*, 23(1), pp. 253–267. doi:10.1111/jiec.12739.

Hensel, M. (2022) 'The Bigger Picture en Route to Informed Urban Environments – Initiating linkages between sustainability science, urban science, and architectural science through an inter- and transdisciplinary data-integrated approach', in Chokhachian A, Hensel M, Perini K (eds.) *Informed Urban Environments: Data-integrated Design for Human and Ecology-centered Perspectives*. Cham: Springer, pp. 11–26. doi:10.1007/978-3-031-03803-7_2.

Hensel, M. (2023) 'Geomorphic Tectonics', *Technology / Architecture + Design* 7(1), pp. 14–17. doi:10.1080/24751448.2023.2176132.

Hensel, M. and Sunguroğlu Hensel, D. (2023) 'Architectures of the Critical Zone: Designing Environments through Architecture and Environment Integration', in Hensel, M., Sunguroğlu Hensel, D., Binder, C.R. and Ludwig, F. (eds.) *Introduction to Designing Environments*. Cham: Springer, pp. 183–208. doi:10.1007/978-3-031-34378-0_10.

Hensel, M. and Sunguroğlu Hensel, D. (2024) 'En route to nature integrated design: opportunities and challenges', in Clements-Croome, D. (ed.) *Intelligent Buildings and Infrastructure with Sustainable and Social Values,* 3rd Edn. Bingley: Emerald ICE.

Hibbard, K., Janetos, A., van Vuuren, D.P., Pongratz, J., Rose, S.K., Betts, R., Herold, M., and Feddema, J.J. (2010) 'Research priorities in land use and land-cover change for the Earth system and integrated assessment modeling', *International Journal of Climatology*, 30, pp. 2118–2128. doi:10.1002/joc.2150.

Höpfl, L., Sunguroğlu Hensel, D., Hensel, M., and Ludwig, F. (2021) 'Hedges, Hedgerows and Hedgerow Networks and their Potential as Urban Green Systems', *Land*, 10(5), 529. doi:10.3390/land10050529.

Hong, Y., Chen, Y., Chen, S., Shen, R., Hu, B., Peng, J., Wang, N., Guo, L., Zhuo, Z., Yang, Y., Liu, Y., Mouazen, A.M., and Shi, Z. (2022)' Data mining of urban soil spectral library for estimating organic carbon', *Geoderma*, 426, 116102. doi:10.1016/j.geoderma.2022.116102.

Hossack, I., Robertson, D., Tucker, P., Hursthouse, A., and Fyfe, C. (2004) 'A GIS and Web-based Decision Support Tool for the Management of Urban Soils', Cybernetics & Systems, 35(5–6), pp. 499–509. doi:10.1080/0196972049045 1878.

Inglezakis, V.J, Poulopoulos, S.G., Arkhangelsky, E., Zorpas, A.A., and Menegaki, A.N. (2016)

'Chapter 3 – Aquatic Environment', in Poulopoulos, S.G and Inglezakis, V.J. (eds.) *Environment and Development*. Amsterdam: Elsevier, pp. 137–212. doi:10.1016/B978-0-444-62733-9.00003-4.

ISRIC World Soil Information (2024) *SoilWise – Knowledge & Data Flows*. Available at: www.isric.org/projects/soilwise (Accessed 14 August 2024).

Jónsson, J.Ö.G. and Davíðsdóttir, B. (2016) 'Classification and valuation of soil ecosystem services', *Agricultural Systems*, 145, pp. 24–38. doi:10.1016/j.agsy.2016.02.010.

Kalantari, F., Mohd Tahir, O., Mahmoudi Lahijani, A., and Kalantari, S. (2017) 'A Review of Vertical Farming Technology: A Guide for Implementation of Building Integrated Agriculture in Cities', *Advanced Engineering Forum*, 24, pp. 76–91. doi:10.4028/www.scientific.net/aef.24.76.

Kennedy, C., Cuddihy, J., and Engel-Yan, J. (2007) 'The changing metabolism of cities', *Journal of industrial ecology*, 11(2), pp. 43–59. doi:10.1162/jie.2007.1107.

Kennedy, C., Pincetl, S., and Bunje, P. (2011) 'The study of urban metabolism and its applications to urban planning and design', *Environmental Pollution*, 159(8–9), pp. 1965–1973. doi:10.1016/j.envpol.2010.10.022.

Khan, R., Aziz, Z., and Ahmed, V. (2018) 'Building integrated agriculture information modeling (BIAIM): An integrated approach towards urban agriculture', *Sustainable Cities and Society*, 37, pp. 594–607. doi:10.1016/j.scs.2017.10.027.

Köhler, T. and Schnitzer, B. (2014) 'Urban Mining Cadastre – A Geospatial Data Challenge', *International Federation of Surveyors (FIG) Congress Engaging the Challenges – Enhancing the Relevance*. Kuala Lumpur, Malaysia 16–21 June.

Komatsuzaki, M. and Ohta, H. (2007) 'Soil management practices for sustainable agro-ecosystems'. *Sustainability Science*, 2, pp. 103–120. doi:10.1007/s11625-006-0014-5.

Kovda, V.A. (1993) 'The Earth's Living Matter: Biosphere and Soils', *Environmental Conservation*, 20(3), pp. 199–204. doi:10.1017/S0376892900022979.

Lal, R., Bouma, J., Brevik, E., Dawson, L., Field, D.J., Glaser, B., Hatano, R., Hartemink, A.E., Kosaki, T., Lascelles, B., Monger, C., Muggler, C., Ndzana, G.M., Norra, S., Pan, X., Paradelo, R., Reyes-Sánchez, L.B., Sandén, T., Singh, B.R., Spiegel, H., Yanai, J., and Zhang, J. (2021)

'Soils and sustainable development goals of the United Nations: An International Union of Soil Sciences perspective', *Geoderma Regional*, 25, e00398. doi:10.1016/j.geodrs.2021.e00398.

Laureano, P. (1999) *Traditional Knowledge – The system of traditional knowledge in the Mediterranean and its classification with reference to different social groupings*. Report prepared www.unccd.int/sites/default/files/sessions/documents/ICCD_COP3_1/cstmiscleng.pdf (Accessed 24 July 2024).

Li, G., Sun, G.X., Ren, Y., Luo, X.S., and Zhu, Y.G. (2018) 'Urban soil and human health: a review', *European Journal of Soil Science*, 69, pp. 196–215. doi:10.1111/ejss.12518.

Li, X. and Feng, L. (2012) 'Multivariate and geostatistical analyses of metals in urban soil of Weinan industrial areas, Northwest of China', *Atmospheric Environment*, 47, pp. 58–65. doi:10.1016/j.atmosenv.2011.11.041.

Li, Y. Rahardjo, H., Satyanaga, A., Rangarajan, S., and Lee, D.T.T. (2022) 'Soil database development with the application of machine learning methods in soil properties prediction', *Engineering Geology*, 306, 106769. doi:10.1016/j.enggeo.2022.106769.

Ludwig, F., Hensel, M., and Weisser, W. (2021) 'ECOLOPES Gebäudehüllen als biodiverse Lebensräume', in Bundesinstitut für Bau-, Stadt- und Raumforschung', in BBSR (eds.) *Bauen von morgen – Zukunftsthemen und Szenarien*. Bundesamt für Bauwesen und Raumordnung, Bonn, pp 84–89.

Ludwig, F., Hensel, M., Rötzer, T., Ahmeti, A., Chen, X., Erdal, H.I., Reischel, A., Shu, Q., Tyc, J., and Yadi, H. (2024) 'Digital Workflow for Novel Urban Green System Design Derived from a Historical Role Model', *Journal of Digital Landscape Architecture*, 9, pp. 333–345.

Manea, D., Dumitrașcu, A., Marin, E., Mateescu, M., Gheorghe, G., and I. Dumitru, I. (2016) 'Study on irrigation systems in areas threatened by desertification – review', *International Symposium of ISB – INMA TEH. Agricultural and mechanical engineering*, 27–29 October 2016, Bucharest, Romania. Proceedings, 2016, pp. 803–812.

Mannan, M. and Al-Ghamdi, S.G. (2022) 'Water Consumption and Environmental Impact of Multifamily Residential Buildings: A Life Cycle Assessment Study', *Buildings*, 12, 48. doi:10.3390/buildings12010048.

Manny, L. (2023) 'Socio-technical challenges towards data-driven and integrated urban water management: A socio-technical network approach', *Sustainable Cities and Society*, 90, 104360. doi:10.1016/j.scs.2022.104360.

Mauser, W. and Bach, H. (2009) 'PROMET – large scale distributed hydrological modeling to study the impact of climate change on the water flows of mountain watersheds', *Journal of Hydrology*, 376, pp. 362–377. doi:10.1016/j.jhydrol.2009.07.046.

Morpurgo, J., Remme, R.P., and Van Bodegom, P.M. (2023) 'CUGIC: The Consolidated Urban Green Infrastructure Classification for assessing ecosystem services and biodiversity', *Landscape and Urban Planning*, 234, 104726. doi:10.1016/j.landurbplan.2023.104726.

Nallaperuma, B., Lin, Z.E., Wijesinghe, J., Abeynayaka, A., Rachid, S., and Karkour, S. (2023) 'Sustainable Water Consumption in Building Industry: A Review Focusing on Building Water Footprint', in Dissanayake, R., Mendis, P., Weerasekera, K., Silva, S. de, Fernando, S., and Konthesingha, C. (eds.) *12th International Conference on Structural Engineering and Construction Management. Lecture Notes in Civil Engineering*, vol 266. Springer, Singapore. doi:10.1007/978-981-19-2886-4_56.

National Research Council (2001) *Basic Research Opportunities in Earth Science*. Washington: The National Academies Press. doi:10.17226/9981.

Norra, S. and Stuben, D. (2003) 'Urban Soils', Journal of Soils and Sediments, 3(4), pp. 230–233. doi:10.1007/BF02988664.

Paltseva, A. (2024) Empowering Communities: The Future of Urban Soil Science Through Citizen Science, EGU General Assembly 2024, Vienna, Austria, 14–19 Apr 2024, EGU24-3217. doi:10.5194/egusphere-egu24-3217.

Pauleit, S., Gulsrud, N., Raum, S., Taubenböck, H., Leichtle, T., Erlwein, S., Rötzer, T., Rahman, M., and Moser-Reischl, A. (2022). 'Smart Urban Forestry: Is It the Future', in Chokhachian, A., Hensel, M., and Perini, K. (eds.) *Informed Urban Environments*. Cham: Springer.

Pehlken, A. and Baumann, S. (2020) 'Urban Mining: Applying Digital Twins for Sustainable Wolman, A. (1965) 'The Metabolism of Cities', *Scientific American*, 213(3), 178–193.

Pei, W., Biljecki, F., and Stouffs, R. (2024) 'Techniques and tools for integrating building material stock analysis and life cycle assessment at the urban scale: A systematic literature review', Building *and Environment*, 262, 111741. doi:10.1016/j.buildenv.2024.111741.

Pelizaro, C., Arentze, T., and Timmermans, H. (2009) '*GRAS*: A Spatial Decision Support System for Green Space Planning', in Geertman, S. and Stillwell, J. (eds.) *Planning Support Systems Best Practice and New Methods. The GeoJournal Library*, 95. Dordrecht: Springer. doi:10.1007/978-1-4020-8952-7_10.

Peña-Guzmán, C.A., Melgarejo, J., Prats, D., Torres, A., and Martínez, S. (2017) 'Urban Water Cycle Simulation/Management Models: A Review', *Water*, 9, 285. doi:10.3390/w9040285.

Perini, K. (2022). 'Urban Ecosystems and Nature-based Solutions: The Role of Data in Optimizing the Provision of Ecosystem Services', in Chokhachian, A., Hensel, M., and Perini, K. (eds.) *Informed Urban Environments*. Cham: Springer.

Product Cascade Use', *2020 IEEE International Conference on Engineering, Technology, and Innovation (ICE/ITMC)*, Cardiff, UK, 2020, pp. 1–7. doi:10.1109/ICE/ITMC49519.2020.9198462.

Rashed, R. (2018) 'Urban Agriculture: A Regenerative Urban Development Practice to Decrease the Ecological Footprints of Cities', *Environmental Science & Sustainable Development*, 2(2), pp. 85–98. doi:10.21625/essd.v2i2.170.

Rast, M., Johannessen, J., and Mauser, W. (2014) 'Review of Understanding of Earth's Hydrological Cycle: Observations, Theory and Modelling', *Surveys in Geophysics*, 35, pp. 491–513. doi:10.1007/s10712-014-9279-x.

Richthofen, A. von, Zeng, W., Asada, S., Burkhard, R., Heisel, F., Mueller, S., and Schubiger, S. (2017) 'Urban Mining: Visualizing the Availability of Construction Materials for Re-use in Future Cities', *2017 21st International Conference Information Visualization (IV)*, London, UK, pp. 306–311. doi:10.1109/iV.2017.34.

Schwilch, G., Lemann, T., Berglund, Ö., Camarotto, C., Cerdà, A., Daliakopoulos, I.N., Kohnová, S., Krzeminska, D., Marañón, T., Rietra, R., Siebielec, G., Thorsson, J., Tibbett, M., Valente, S., Van Delden, H., Van den Akker, J., Verzandvoort, S., Vrînceanu, N.O., Zoumides, C., and Hessel, R. (2018) 'Assessing Impacts of Soil Management Measures on Ecosystem Services', *Sustainability* 2018, 10, 4416. doi:10.3390/su10124416.

Stallone, R. (2011) What is Urban Mining? Available at: https://jessestallone.com/2011/04/20/what-is-urban-mining/ (Accessed 23 July 2024).

Stessens, P., Khan, A.Z., Huysmans, M., and Canters, F. (2017) 'Analysing urban green space accessibility and quality: A GIS-based model as spatial decision support for urban ecosystem services in Brussels', *Ecosystem Services*, 28, pp. 328–340. doi:10.1016/j.ecoser.2017.10.016.

Su, Z., Wen, J., and Wagner, W. (2010) 'Advances in land surface hydrological processes – field observations, modeling and data assimilation', *Hydrology and Earth Systems Science*, 14, pp. 365–367. doi:10.5194/hess-14-365-2010.

Sunguroğlu Hensel, D. (2020) 'Ecological Prototypes: Initiating Design Innovation in Green Construction', *Sustainability*, 12, 5865. doi:10.3390/su12145865.

Sunguroğlu Hensel, D. (2021) 'Data-driven research on ecological prototypes for green architecture: enabling urban intensification and restoration through agricultural hybrids', *Dimensions Journal of Architectural Knowledge*, 1, pp. 47–54. doi:10.14361/dak-2021-0106.

Sunguroğlu Hensel, D. (2022). 'Big Data and Decision Support in Rural and Urban Agriculture', in Chokhachian, A., Hensel, M., and Perini, K. (eds.) *Informed Urban Environments*. Cham: Springer. doi:10.1007/978-3-031-03803-7_11.

Sunguroğlu Hensel, D. (2022b). 'Ecological Prototypes for Green Construction – Linking Architecture and Ecological Engineering for Integrated Urban, Agricultural, and Ecological Use', in Kanaani, M. (ed.) *The Routledge Companion to Ecological Design Thinking*. New York: Routledge, pp. 26–37.

Sunguroğlu Hensel, D., Tyc, J., and Hensel, M. (2022) 'Data-driven Design for Architecture and Environment Integration: Convergence of data-integrated workflows for understanding and designing environments', *Spool*, 9(1), pp. 19–34. doi:10.47982/spool.2022.1.02.

The Nature Conservancy (2024) Urban Water Blueprint. Available at: https://water.nature.org/waterblueprint/#/intro=true (Accessed 10 August 2024).

Thiele-Bruhn, S., Bloem, J., Vries, F.T. de, Kalbitz, K., and Wagg, C. (2012) 'Linking soil biodiversity and agricultural soil management', *Current Opinion in Environmental Sustainability*, 4(5), pp. 523–528. doi:10.1016/j.cosust.2012.06.004.

Tyc, J., Sunguroğlu Hensel, D., Parisi, E.I., Tucci, G., and Hensel, M. (2021) 'Integration of remote sensing data into a composite voxel model for environmental performance analysis of terraced vineyards in Tuscany, Italy', *Remote Sensing*, 13(17), 3483. doi:10.3390/rs13173483.

Tyc, J., Parisi, E.I., Tucci, G., Sunguroğlu Hensel, D., and Hensel, M (2022) 'A Data-integrated and Performance-oriented Parametric Design Process for Terraced Vineyard', *Journal of Digital Landscape Architecture*, 7, pp. 504–521.

United Nations (2024a) *Transforming our world: the 2030 Agenda for Sustainable Development*. https://sdgs.un.org/2030agenda (Accessed 24 July 2024).

United Nations (2024b) *The 17 Goals*. Available at: https://sdgs.un.org/goals (Accessed 24 July 2024).

Verhagen, T.J., Sauer, M.L., van der Voet, E., and Sprecher, B. (2021) 'Matching Demolition and Construction Material Flows, an Urban Mining Case Study', *Sustainability*, 13, 653. doi:10.3390/su13020653.

Wolf, C. de, Sultan Çetin, S., and Bocken, N. (eds.) (2024) *A Circular Built Environment in the Digital Age*. Cham: Springer.

van Es, H. (2017) 'A New Definition of Soil', CSA News, 61(10), pp. 20–21. doi:10.2134/csa2017.62.1016.

Vanham, D. and Bidoglio, G. (2013) 'A review on the indicator water footprint for the EU28', *Ecological Indicators*, 26, pp. 61–75. doi:10.1016/j.ecolind.2012.10.021.

Wallace, K.J. (2007) 'Classification of ecosystem services: Problems and solutions', *Biological Conservation*, 139(3–4), pp. 235–246. doi:10.1016/j.biocon.2007.07.015.

Weisser, W., Hensel, M., Barath, S., Grobman, Y.J., Hauck, T.E., Joschinski, J., Ludwig, F., Mimet, A., Perini, K., Roccotiello, E., Schloter, M., Shwartz, A., Sunguroğlu Hensel, D., and Vogler, V. (2022) 'Creating ecologically sound buildings by integrating ecology, architecture, and computational design', *People & Nature*, 5(1), pp. 4–20. doi:10.1002/pan3.10411.

White, T., Brantley, S., Banwart, S., Chorover, J., Dietrich, W., Derry, L., Lohse, K., Anderson, S., Aufdendkampe, A., Bales, R., Kumar, P., Richter, D., and McDowell, B. (2015) 'The Role of Critical Zone Observatories in Critical Zone Science', in Giardino, J.R. and Houser, C. (eds.) *Principles and Dynamics of the Critical Zone*. Amsterdam: Elsevier, pp. 15–78. doi:10.1016/B978-0-444-63369-9.00002-1.

Wood, E.F., Roundy, J.K., Troy, T.J., van Beek, R., Bierkens, M., Blyth, E., Roo, A. de, Doell, P., Ek, M., Famiglietti, J., Gochis, D., van de Giesen, N., Houser, P., Jaffe, P., Kollet, S., Lehner, B., Lettenmaier, D.P., Peters-Lidard, C., Sivapalan, M., Sheffield, J., Wade, A., and Whitehead, P. (2011) 'Hyper-resolution global land surface modeling: meeting a grand challenge for monitoring Earth's terrestrial water', *Water Resources Research*, 47, W05301. doi:10.1029/2010WR010090.

Wu, P., Christidis, N., and Stott, P. (2013) 'Anthropogenic impact on Earth's hydrological cycle', *Nature Climate Change*, 3, pp. 807–810. doi:10.1038/nclimate1932.

Wurzer, G., Ugljanin, N., Bindreiter, S., and Lorenz, W. (2023) 'Material intensity of inner development', *SimAUD Symposium on Simulation for Architecture and Urban Design*. Hamilton, Ontario, Canada, 23 May. doi:10.34726/4322.

Yang, J.L. and Zhang, G.L. (2015) 'Formation, characteristics and eco-environmental implications of urban soils – A review', *Soil Science and Plant Nutrition*, 61, pp. 30–46. doi:10.1080/00380768.2015.1035622.

Yang, D., Yang, Y., and Xia, J. (2021) 'Hydrological cycle and water resources in a changing world: A review', *Geography and Sustainability*, 2(2), pp. 115–122. doi:10.1016/j.geosus.2021.05.003.

Yang, M., Zhou, X., Liu, Z., Li, P., Tang, J., Xie, B., and Peng, C. A (2022) 'Review of General Methods for Quantifying and Estimating Urban Trees and Biomass', *Forests*, 13, 616. doi:10.3390/f13040616.

Young, L.J., Hyman, M., and Rater, B.R. (2018) 'Exploring a Big Data Approach to Building a List Frame for Urban Agriculture: A Pilot Study in the City of Baltimore', *Journal of Official Statistics*, *34*(2), pp. 323–340. doi:10.2478/jos-2018-0015.

Zhang, H., Yin, S., Chen, Y., Shao, S., Wu, J., Fan, M., Chen, F., and Gao, C. (2020) 'Machine learning-based source identification and spatial prediction of heavy metals in soil in a rapid urbanization area, eastern China', *Journal of Cleaner Production*, 273, 122858. doi:10.1016/j.jclepro.2020.122858.

Zhang, Y., Xi, Y., Wang, H., and Zhang, Z.Z. (2023) 'Surfaces with modified morphology and wettability arrangement: a potential medium for water harvesting in desertification areas', *Water Supply*, 23(8): pp. 2972–2985. doi:10.2166/ws.2023.187

Zhu, X. (2014) 'GIS and Urban Mining', *Resources*, 3(1), pp. 235–247. doi:10.3390/resources3010235.

Zhu, S., Du, S., Li, Y., Wei, S., Jin, X., Zhou, X., and Shi, X. (2021) 'A 3D spatiotemporal morphological database for urban green infrastructure and its applications', Urban Forestry & Urban Greening, 58, 126935. doi:10.1016/j.ufug.2020.126935.

CHAPTER 6

Özdemir, V. and Hekim, N. (2018) 'Birth of industry 5.0: making sense of big data with artificial intelligence, 'the internet of things' and next-generation technology policy,' *Omics – A Journal of Integrative Biology*, 22(1), pp. 65–76. doi:10.1089/omi.2017.0194

Nahavandi, S. (2019) 'Industry 5.0 – A Human-Centric Solution,' *Sustainability*, 11, 4371. doi:10.3390/su11164371

Rosemann, M., Becker, J., and Chasin, F. (2021) 'City 5.0,' *Business & Information Systems Engineering*, 63, pp. 71–77. doi:10.1007/s12599-020-00674-9.

Siggelkow, N. and Terwiesch, C. (2019) *Connected Strategy: Building continuous customer relationships for competitive advantage*. Boston MA: Harvard Business Review Press.

Abdulali, A., Atadjanov, I.R, Lee, S., and Jeon, S. (2020) 'Realistic haptic rendering of hyper-elastic material via measurement-based FEM model identification and real-time simulation', *Computers & Graphics*, 89, pp. 38–49. doi:10.1016/j.cag.2020.04.004.

Abdulali, A. and Jeon, S. (2021) 'Data-driven Haptic Modeling of Plastic Flow via Inverse Reinforcement Learning', *2021 IEEE World Haptics Conference (WHC)*, Montreal, QC, Canada, 2021, pp. 115–120. doi:10.1109/WHC49131.2021.9517181.

Abt, C.C. (1987) *Serious Games*. Lanham MD: University Press of America.

Adams, P.C. (1998) 'Teaching and Learning with SimCity 2000', *Journal of Geography*, 97(2), pp. 47–55. doi:10.1080/00221349808978827.

Advanced Computational Design (2024) 'Large Scale haptic Feedback in Virtual Reality'. Available at: https://acd.tuwien.ac.at/sp5 (Accessed 28 August 2024).

Agrawal, A. and Choudhary, A. (2016) 'Perspective: Materials informatics and big data: Realization of the "fourth paradigm" of science in materials science', *APL Materials*, 4(5), 053208. doi:10.1063/1.4946894.

Alizadehsalehi, S., Hadavi, A., and Huang, J.C. (2020) 'From BIM to extended reality in AEC industry', Automation in Construction, 116, 103254. doi:10.1016/j.autcon.2020.103254.

Ammar, M., Haleem, A., Javaid, M., Bahl, S., Garg, S.B., Shamoon, A., and Garg, J. (2022) 'Significant applications of smart materials and Internet of Things (IoT) in the automotive industry,' *Materials Today: Proceedings*, 68(5), pp. 1542–1549. doi:10.1016/j.matpr.2022.07.180.

Arinez, J.F., Chang, Q., Gao, R.X., Xu, C., and Zhang, J. (2020) 'Artificial Intelligence in Advanced Manufacturing: Current Status and Future Outlook', *ASME – Journal of Manufacturing Science and Engineering*, 142(11), 110804. doi:10.1115/1.4047855.

Arnold, U., Söbke, H., and Reichelt, M. (2019) 'SimCity in Infrastructure Management Education', *Educational Science*, 9, 209. doi:10.3390/educsci9030209.

Aziza, B. (2018) 'Machine learning and data – where you'd least expect it'. *Forbes Magazine* Available at: www.forbes.com/sites/ciocentral/2018/10/30/machine-learning-data-where-youd-least-expect-it/#5c4fc16e9871 (Accessed 27 August 2024).

Barham, W., Preston, J., and Werner, J. (2012) 'Using a Virtual Gaming Environment in Strength of Materials Laboratory', *Computing in Civil Engineering*. doi:10.1061/9780784412343.0014.

Bereitschaft, B. (2015) 'Gods of the City? Reflecting on City Building Games as an Early Introduction to Urban Systems', *Journal of Geography*, 115(2), pp. 51–60. doi:10.1080/00221341.2015.1070366.

Berg, L.P. and Vance, J.M. (2017) 'Industry use of virtual reality in product design and manufacturing: a survey', *Virtual Reality*, 21, pp. 1–17. doi:10.1007/s10055-016-0293-9.

Biswas, S. and Visell, Y. (2021) 'Haptic Perception, Mechanics, and Material Technologies for Virtual Reality', Advanced Functional Materials 31(39), 2008186. Doi:10.1002/adfm.202008186.

Biswas, H.K., Sim, T.Y., and Lau, S.L. (2024) 'Impact of Building Information Modelling and Advanced Technologies in the AEC Industry: A Contemporary Review and Future Directions', *Journal of Building Engineering*, 82, 108165. doi:10.1016/j.jobe.2023.108165.

Cabero, J. and Barroso, J. (2016) 'The educational possibilities of augmented reality', *Journal of New Approaches in Educational Research*, 5(1), pp. 44–50. doi:10.7821/naer.2016.1.140.

Carayannis, E.G. (2023) 'GWU EMTECH lectures 2010–2022 and Dupont summit series lecture', Dec. 2023, Available at: www.youtube.com/watch?v=Q6j_qsWm_q0. (Accessed 1 September 2024).

Carayannis, E.G., Posselt, T., and Preissler, S. (2024) 'Toward Industry 6.0 and Society 6.0: The Quintuple Innovation Helix with Embedded AI Modalities as Enabler of Public Interest Technologies Strategic Technology Management and Road-Mapping', in *IEEE Transactions on Engineering Management*, 71, pp. 11238–11252. doi: 10.1109/TEM.2024.3406427.

Cárdenas-Robledo, L.A., Hernández-Uribe, O., Reta, C., and Jose Antonio Cantoral-Ceballos, J.A. (2020) 'Extended reality applications in industry 4.0. – A systematic literature review', *Telematics and Informatics*, 73, 101863. doi:10.1016/j.tele.2022.101863.

Cha, H., Bhardwaj, A., and Choi, S. (2022) 'Data-Driven Haptic Modeling and Rendering of Viscoelastic Behavior Using Fractional Derivatives', in *IEEE Access*, 10, pp. 130894–130907, 2022. doi: 10.1109/ACCESS.2022.3230065.

Chen, W., Liu, G., Zhang, Y., and Shirinzadeh, B. (2016) 'An artificial neural network based haptic rendering of contact with deformable bodies', *2016 IEEE International Conference on Mechatronics and Automation*, Harbin, China, 2016, pp. 2332–2337. doi: 10.1109/ICMA.2016.7558929.

Choudhury, A. (2021) 'The Role of Machine Learning Algorithms in Materials Science: A State of Art Review on Industry 4.0', *Archives in Computational Methods in Engineering*, 28, pp. 3361–3381. doi:10.1007/s11831-020-09503-4

Danieau, F., Lecuyer, A., Guillotel, P., Fleureau, J., Mollet, N., and M. Christie, M. (2013) 'Enhancing Audiovisual Experience with Haptic Feedback: A Survey on HAV', *IEEE Transactions on Haptics*, 6(2), pp. 193–205. doi: 10.1109/TOH.2012.70.

DeCost, B.L., Hattrick-Simpers, J.R., Trautt, Z., Kusne, A.G., Campo, E., and Green, M.L. (2020) 'Scientific AI in material science: a path to a sustainable and scalable paradigm', Machine Learning: Science and Technology, 1(3), 033001. doi:10.1088/2632-2153/ab9a20.

Deterding, S., Dixon, D., Khaled, R., and Nacke, L. (2011) 'From game design elements to gamefulness: defining" gamification"', in *Proceedings of the 15th international academic MindTrek conference: Envisioning future media environments*, pp. 9–15. doi:10.1145/2181037.2181040.

Duke, R.D. and Geurts, J.L.A. (2004) *Policy Games for Strategic Management*. Amsterdam: Dutch University Press.

European Commission – Research and Innovation (2024) 'What is Industry 5.0?' Available at: https://research-and-innovation.ec.europa.eu/research-area/industrial-research-and-innovation/industry-50_en (Accessed 30 August 2024).

Extremera, J., Vergara, D., Rodríguez, S., and Dávila, L.P. (2022) 'Reality-Virtuality Technologies in the Field of Materials Science and Engineering', *Applied Sciences*, 12, 4968. doi:10.3390/app12104968.

Fatima, S., Haleem, A., Bahl, S., Javaid, M., Mahla, S.K., and Singh, S. (2021) 'Exploring the significant applications of Internet of Things (IoT) with 3D printing using advanced materials in medical field,' *Materials Today: Proceedings*, 45(6), pp. 4844–4851. doi:10.1016/j.matpr.2021.01.305.

Fast-Berglund, A., Gong, L., and Dan Li, D. (2018) 'Testing and validating Extended Reality (xR) technologies in manufacturing', *Procedia Manufacturing*, 25, pp. 31–38. doi:10.1016/j.promfg.2018.06.054.

Federal Ministry for Economic Affairs and Climate Action – Platform Industry 4.0 (2024) What is Industry 4.0. Available at: www.plattform-i40.de/IP/Navigation/EN/Industrie40/WhatIsIndustrie40/what-is-industrie40.html (Accessed 24 August 2024).

Gaber, J. (2007). Simulating Planning: SimCity as a Pedagogical Tool. *Journal of Planning Education and Research*, *27*(2), 113–121. doi:10.1177/0739456×07305791.

Girvan, C. (2018) 'What is a virtual world? Definition and classification', *Education Tech Research Dev*, 66, pp. 1087–1100. doi:10.1007/s11423-018-9577-y.

Han, H.R. (2023) 'Hybrid Fiber Materials according to the Manufacturing Technology Methods and IOT Materials: A Systematic Review,' *Materials*, 16, 1351. doi:10.3390/ma16041351.

Han, B. and Leite, F. (2022) 'Generic extended reality and integrated development for visualization applications in architecture, engineering, and construction', *Automation in Construction*, 140, 104329. doi:10.1016/j.autcon.2022.104329.

Hajrasouliha, A.H. (2023) 'Applications, Approaches, and Ethics of the Extended Reality in Urban Design and Planning', *Journal of the American Planning Association*, *90*(3), pp. 551–567. doi:10.1080/01944363.2023.2275123.

Heckerman, D., Meek, C., and Cooper, G. (2006) 'A Bayesian Approach to Causal Discovery', in Holmes, D.E. and Jain, L.C. (eds.) *Innovations in Machine Learning. Studies in Fuzziness and Soft Computing, vol 194.* Berlin, Heidelberg: Springer. doi:10.1007/3-540-33486-6_1.

Hensel, M. and Menges, A. (2006) *Morpho-Ecologies.* London: AA Publications.

Hensel, M., Menges, A., and Weinstock, M. (2010) *Emergent Technologies and Design – Towards a biological paradigm for architecture.* Milton Park, New York: Routledge.

Hensel, M. and Sørensen, S.S. (2013) 'En route to Performance-oriented Architecture – The Research Centre for Architecture and Tectonics: Integrating Architectural Education with Research by Design along a practice-oriented Perspective', *SAJ Serbian Architecture Journal*, 5 (2), pp. 106–131.

Hensel, M. and Sørensen, S.S. (2014) 'Intersecting Knowledge Fields and Integrating Data-Driven Computational Design en Route to Performance-oriented and Intensely Local Architectures', *Footprint*, 15, pp. 59–74. doi:10.7480/footprint.8.2.812.

Höver, R., Harders, M., and Székely, G. (2008) 'Data-Driven Haptic Rendering of Visco-Elastic Effects', in *2008 Symposium on Haptic Interfaces for Virtual Environment and Teleoperator Systems*, pp. 201–208.

Höver, R., Di Luca, M., Székely, G., and M. Harders, M. (2009) 'Computationally efficient techniques for data-driven haptic rendering', *World Haptics 2009 – Third Joint EuroHaptics conference and Symposium on Haptic Interfaces for Virtual Environment and Teleoperator Systems*, Salt Lake City, UT, USA, 2009, pp. 39–44. doi: 10.1109/WHC.2009.4810814.

Holdren, J.P., et al. (2014) *Materials Genome Initiative Strategic Plan.* Washington DC: Office of Science and Technology Policy, 6. Available at: www.nist.gov/system/files/documents/2017/05/09/MGI-StrategicPlan-2014.pdf (Accessed 27 August 2024).

Hoon, M., Jabi, W., and Goldman, G., (2003) 'Immersion, interaction, and collaboration in architectural design using gaming engines', in *CAADRIA 2003 Proceedings of the 8th International Conference on Computer Aided Architectural Design Research in Asia,* Bangkok Thailand 18–20 October 2003, pp. 721–738. doi:10.52842/conf.caadria.2003.721.

Joolee, J.B. and S. Jeon, S. (2022) "Data-Driven Haptic Texture Modeling and Rendering Based on Deep Spatio-Temporal Networks," in *IEEE Transactions on Haptics*, vol. 15, no. 1, pp. 62–67, 1 Jan.–March 2022. doi: 10.1109/TOH.2021.3137936.

Kalidindi, S.R. (2020) 'Feature engineering of material structure for AI-based materials knowledge systems', *Journal of Applied Physics*, 28, 128(4), 041103. doi:10.1063/5.0011258.

Kharvari, F. and Kaiser, L.E. (2022) 'Impact of extended reality on architectural education and the design process', *Automation in Construction*, 141, 104393. doi:10.1016/j.autcon.2022.104393.

Kolhe, M.L., Karande, K.J., and Deshmukh, S.G. (eds.) (2022) *Artificial Intelligence, Internet of Things (IoT) and Smart Materials for Energy Applications.* Boca Raton FL: CRC Press.

Lin, L., Kollipara, P.S., and Zheng, Y. (2019) 'Digital manufacturing of advanced materials: Challenges and perspective', *Materials Today*, 28, pp. 49–62. doi:10.1016/j.mattod.2019.05.022.

Matthys, M., Cock, L. de, Mertens, L., Boussauw, K., Maeyer, P. de, and Van de Weghe, N. (2023) 'Rethinking the Public Space Design Process Using Extended Reality as a Game Changer for 3D Co-Design', *Applied Science*, 13, 8392. doi:10.3390/app13148392.

MacLean, K.E. (2000) 'Designing with haptic feedback', *Proceedings 2000 ICRA. Millennium Conference. IEEE International Conference on Robotics and Automation. Symposia Proceedings (Cat. No.00CH37065)*, San Francisco, CA, USA, 2000, pp. 783–788 vol.1, doi: 10.1109/ROBOT.2000.844146.

Materials Genome Initiative (2024) 'About the Materials Genome Initiative'. Available at: www.mgi.gov/about (Accessed 28 August 2024).

May, H.B. (1979) 'The Potentiality of Gaming-Simulation in Architecture. *Journal of Architectural Education'*, 33(1), pp. 7–11. doi:10.1080/10464883.1979.10758202.

Menges, A., Sheil, B., Glynn, R., and Skavara, M. (eds.) (2017) *Fabricate – Rethinking Design and Construction.* London: UCL Press.

Minami, T., Hikaru, N., Yuichi, T., and Yasuyoshi, Y. (2023) 'Effective haptic feedback type for robot-mediated material discrimination depending on target properties', Frontiers in Virtual Reality, 4. doi:10.3389/frvir.2023.1070739.

Monostori, L., Kádár, B., Bauernhansl, T., Kondoh, S., Kumara, S., Reinhart, G., Sauer, O., Schuh, G., Sihn, W., and Ueda, K. (2016) 'Cyber-Physical Systems in Manufacturing', *CIRP Annals*, 65(2), pp. 621–641. doi:10.1016/j.cirp.2016.06.005.

Morsi, R. and Jackson, E. (2007) 'Playing and learning? Educational gaming for engineering education', in *2007 37th Annual Frontiers in Education Conference – Global Engineering: Knowledge Without Borders, Opportunities Without Passports*, Milwaukee, WI, USA, 2007, pp.F2H-1-F2H-6. doi:10.1109/FIE.2007.4418179.

Ng, I.C.L. and Wakenshaw, S.Y.L. (2017) 'The Internet-of-Things: Review and research directions', *International Journal of Research in Marketing*, 34(1), pp. 3–21, doi:10.1016/j.ijresmar.2016.11.003.

Le, K.T. (2024) Materials World Magazine. Available at: www.iom3.org/materials-world-magazine/news/2017/mar/31/virtual-benefits-materials-science (Accessed 20 August 2024).

Li, J., Lim, K., Yang, H., Ren, Z., Raghavan, S., Chen, P.Y., Buonassisi, T., and Wang, X. (2020) 'AI applications through the whole life cycle of material discovery', *Matter*, *3*(2), pp. 393–432. doi:10.1016/j.matt.2020.06.011.

Lookman, T., Alexander, F.J., and Bishop, A.R. (2016) 'Perspective: Codesign for materials science: An optimal learning approach', *APL Materials*, 4, 053501. doi:10.1063/1.4944627.

Philbeck, T. and Davis, N. (2018) 'The Fourth Industrial Revolution: Shaping a New Era', *Journal of International Affairs*, *72*(1), pp. 17–22. Available at: www.jstor.org/stable/26588339 (Accessed 26 August 2024).

Qazi, A.M., Mahmood, S.M., Haleem, A., Bahl, S., Javaid, M., and Gopal, K. (2022) 'The impact of smart materials, digital twins (DTs) and Internet of things (IoT) in an industry 4.0 integrated automation industry', *Materials Today: Proceedings*, 62(1), pp. 18–25. doi:10.1016/j.matpr.2022.01.387.

Ramaiah, G.B. (2021) 'Theoretical analysis on applications aspects of smart materials and Internet of Things (IoT) in textile technology,' *Materials Today: Proceedings*, 45(6), pp. 4633–4638. doi:10.1016/j.matpr.2021.01.023.

Rane, N. (2023) '3D, 4D, and 5D printing in Architecture, Engineering, and Construction (AEC) Industry: Applications, Challenges, and Future Scope'. Available at http://dx.doi.org/10.2139/ssrn.4609912 (Accessed 1 September 2024).

Rane, N., Choudhary, S., and Rane, J. (2023) 'Artificial Intelligence (AI) and Internet of Things (IoT) – Based Sensors for Monitoring and Controlling in Architecture, Engineering, and Construction: Applications, Challenges, and Opportunities' (November 20, 2023). Available at http://dx.doi.org/10.2139/ssrn.4642197 (Accessed 1 September 2024).

Rangasamy, V. and Yang, J.-B. (2024) 'The convergence of BIM, AI and IoT: Reshaping the future of prefabricated construction', *Journal of Building Engineering*, 84, 108606. doi:10.1016/j.jobe.2024.108606.

Rathore, M.M., Ahmad, A., Paul, A., and Rho, S. (2016) 'Urban planning and building smart cities based on the Internet of Things using Big Data analytics', *Computer Networks*, 101, pp. 63–80. doi:10.1016/j.comnet.2015.12.023.

Romero, D., Bernus, P., Noran, O., Stahre, J., and Fast-Berglund, Å. (2016a) 'The Operator 4.0: Human Cyber-Physical Systems & Adaptive Automation Towards Human-Automation Symbiosis Work Systems', in Nääs, I., et al. Advances in Production Management Systems. Initiatives for a Sustainable World. APMS 2016. IFIP Advances in Information and Communication Technology, vol 488. Cham: Springer. doi:10.1007/978-3-319-51133-7_80.

Romero, D., Stahre, J., Wuest, T., Noran, O., Bernus, P., Fast-Berglund, Å., and Gorecky, D., (2016) 'Towards an operator 4.0 typology: a human-centric perspective on the fourth industrial revolution technologies', in *proceedings of the international conference on computers and industrial engineering (CIE46),* Tianjin, China, pp. 9–31.

Romero, D., Wuest, T., Stahre, J., and Gorecky, D. (2017) 'Social Factory Architecture: Social Networking Services and Production Scenarios Through the Social Internet of Things, Services and People for the Social Operator 4.0', in Lödding, H., Riedel, R., Thoben, KD., Cieminski, G. von, Kiritsis, D. (eds.) *Advances in Production Management Systems. The Path to Intelligent, Collaborative and Sustainable Manufacturing. APMS 2017. IFIP Advances in Information and Communication Technology*, 513. Cham, Springer. doi:10.1007/978-3-319-66923-6_31.

Sajid, S., Haleem, A., Bahl, S., Javaid, M., Goyal, T., and Mittal, M. (2021) 'Data science applications for predictive maintenance and materials science in context to Industry 4.0', *Materials Today: Proceedings*, 45(6), pp. 4898–4905. doi:10.1016/j.matpr.2021.01.357.

Salisbury, K., Conti, F., and Barbagli, F. (2004) 'Haptic rendering: introductory concepts', *IEEE Computer Graphics and Applications*, 24(2), pp. 24–32. doi: 10.1109/MCG.2004.1274058.

Schwab, K. (2015) 'The Fourth Industrial Revolution – What it Means and How to Respond', *Foreign Affairs*, Available at: www.foreignaffairs.com/world/fourth-industrial-revolution (Accessed 24 August 2024).

See, A.R., Choco, J.A.G., and Chandramohan, K. (2022) 'Touch, Texture and Haptic Feedback: A Review on How We Feel the World around Us', *Applied Sciences*, 12, 4686. doi:10.3390/app12094686.

Sisinni, W., Saifullah, A., Han, S., Jennehag, U., and Gidlund, M. (2018) 'Industrial Internet of Things: Challenges, Opportunities, and Directions,' *IEEE Transactions on Industrial Informatics*, 14(11), pp. 4724–4734. doi:10.1109/TII.2018.2852491.

Stanney, K.M., Nye, H., Haddad, S., Hale, K.S., Padron, C.K., and Cohn, J.V. (2021) 'Extended Reality (XR) Environments', in Salvendy, G. and Karwowski, W. (eds.) Handbook of Human Factors and Ergonomics 5th ed. Hoboken NJ: Wiley, pp. 782–815.

Stone, R.J. (2001) 'Haptic feedback: a brief history from telepresence to virtual reality', in Brewster, S. and Murray-Smith, R. (eds.) *Haptic Human-Computer Interaction. Haptic HCI 2000. Lecture Notes in Computer Science, vol 2058.* Berlin, Heidelberg: Springer, pp. 1–16 doi:10.1007/3-540-44589-7_1.

Tang, S., Shelden, D.R., Eastman, C.M., Pishdad-Bozorgi, P., and Gao, X. (2019) 'A review of building information modeling (BIM) and the internet of things (IoT) devices integration: Present status and future trends', *Automation in Construction*, 101, pp. 127–139. doi:10.1016/j.autcon.2019.01.020.

Tao, F., Qi, Q., Liu, A., and Kusiak, A. (2018) 'Data-driven smart manufacturing', *Journal of Manufacturing Systems*, 48, pp. 157–169. doi:10.1016/j.jmsy.2018.01.006.

Tian, C., Li, T., Bustillos, J., Bhattacharya, S., Turnham, T., Yeo, J., and Moridi, A. (2021) 'Data-Driven Approach Towards Smarter Additive Manufacturing', *Advanced Intelligent Systems*, 3(12), 2100014. doi:10.1002/aisy.202100014.

UBS (2023) 'How smart technologies are driving industry 6.0 and beyond' Available at: www.ubs.com/global/en/investment-bank/in-focus/2023/technology-driving-industry-6.html (Accessed 31 August 2024).

Vajda, S. (1972) *Probabilistic Programming*. New York: Academic Press.

Vasudevan, R.K., Choudhary, K., Mehta, A., Smith, R., Kusne, G., Tavazza, F., and Vlcek, L. (2019) 'Materials science in the artificial intelligence age: high-throughput library generation, machine learning, and a pathway from correlations to the underpinning physics', *MRS Communications*, 9(3), pp. 821–838. doi:10.1557/mrc.2019.95.

Vergara, D., Extremera, J., Rubio, M.P., and Dávila, L.P. (2019) 'Meaningful Learning through Virtual Reality Learning Environments: A Case Study in Materials Engineering', *Applied Sciences*, 9, 4625. doi:10.3390/app9214625.

Vergara, D., Rubio, M.P., and Lorenzo, M. (2017a) 'On the Design of Virtual Reality Learning Environments in Engineering', *Multimodal Technologies and Interaction*, 1(2), 11. doi:10.3390/mti1020011.

Vergara, D., Lorenzo, M., and Rubio, M.P. (2017b) 'Virtual environments in materials science and engineering: the students' opinion', in *Materials science and engineering: Concepts, methodologies, tools, and applications*. IGI Global, pp. 1465–1483.

Walsh, K. and Pawlowski, S. (2002) 'Virtual Reality: A Technology in Need of IS Research. Communications of the Association for Information Systems', 8(1), 20. doi:10.17705/1CAIS.00820.

Wang, K., Guo, F., Zhang, C., Hao, J., and Schaefer, D. (2022) 'Digital Technology in Architecture, Engineering, and Construction (AEC) Industry: Research Trends and Practical Status toward Construction 4.0', in Jazizadeh, F, Shealy, T. and Michael J. Garvin, M.J. (eds.) *Construction Research Congress 2022: Project Management and Delivery, Controls, and Design and Materials.* Arlington VA: ASCE Library.

Wang, M., Altaf, M.S., Al-Hussein, M., and Ma, Y. (2018) 'Framework for an IoT-based shop floor material management system for panelized homebuilding,' *International Journal of Construction Management*, 20(2), pp. 130–145. doi:10.1080/15623599.2018.14 84554.

Xia, P. (2018) 'New advances for haptic rendering: state of the art', *The Visual Computer*, 34, pp. 271–287. doi:10.1007/ s00371-016-1324-y.

Yan, W., Charles Culp, C., and Robert Graf, R. (2011) 'Integrating BIM and gaming for real-time interactive architectural visualization', *Automation in Construction*, 20(4), pp. 446–458. doi:10.1016/j. autcon.2010.11.013.

Yin, J., Hinchet, R., Shea, H., and Majidi C. (2021) 'Wearable Soft Technologies for Haptic Sensing and Feedback', *Advanced Functional Materials*, 31(39), 2007428. doi:10.1002/ adfm.202007428.

Yoo, Y., Boland Jr., R.J., Lyytinen, K., and Majchrzak, A. (2012) 'Organizing for innovation in the digitized world', *Organization Science*, 23(5), pp. 1398–1408. doi:10.1287/orsc.1120.0771.

Yuan, P.F. and Menges, A. (2019) Building Robotics: Technology, Craft and Methodology. Beijing: China Architecture & Building Press.

INDEX

IMAGE CREDITS

Fig. 1: Vincent et al. / The Royal Society, London

Fig. 2: Bob Geldermans

Fig. 3: Milica Vujovic

Fig. 4: Milica Vujovic

Fig. 5: Department for Digital Architecture, TU Wien & LamoLab Research Centre

Fig. 6: Bob Geldermans

Fig. 7: Bob Geldermans

Fig. 8: Bob Geldermans

Fig. 9: Milica Vujovic

Fig. 10: Milica Vujovic

Fig. 11: The Materials Project

Fig. 12: Crystallography Open Database

Fig. 13: ANSYS Inc.

Fig. 14: The Materials Project

Fig. 15: Crystallography Open Database

Fig. 16: Milica Vujovic

Fig. 17: Milica Vujovic

Fig. 18: Milica Vujovic

Fig. 19: Milica Vujovic

Fig. 20: Milica Vujovic

Fig. 21: Milica Vujovic

Fig. 22: Milica Vujovic

Fig. 23: Milica Vujovic

Fig. 24: Milica Vujovic

Fig. 25: Milica Vujovic

Fig. 26: Milica Vujovic

Fig. 27: Milica Vujovic

Fig. 28: Milica Vujovic

Fig. 29: Progressive Architecture

Fig. 30: Michael Hensel

Fig. 31: Milica Vujovic

Fig. 32: Defne Sunguroglu Hensel

Fig. 33: ANSYS Inc.

Fig. 34: ANSYS Inc.

Fig. 35: ANSYS Inc.

Fig. 36: ANSYS Inc.

Fig. 37: ANSYS Inc.

Fig. 38: Michael Hensel

Fig. 39: Milica Vujovic

Fig. 40: Milica Vujovic

Fig. 41: Wikimedia Commons, Creative Commons Attribution Share Alike 3.0 Unported Licence, Cmglee

Fig. 42: Milica Vujovic

Fig. 43: Department for Digital Architecture, TU Wien & LamoLab Research Centre

Fig. 44: Department for Digital Architecture, TU Wien & LamoLab Research Centre

Fig. 45: Michael Hensel / Sustainable Environment Association

Fig. 46: Michael Hensel et al / Sustainable Environment Association

Fig. 47: Michael Hensel et al / Sustainable Environment Association

Fig. 48: Michael Hensel et al / Sustainable Environment Association

Fig. 49: Wikimedia Commons public domain / Collection of the Yale Centre for British Art

Fig. 50: Wikimedia Commons, Licence CC-BY-3.0, Berthold Werner

Fig. 51: Michael Hensel

Fig. 52: Michael Hensel

Fig. 53: Daniel Coll i Capdevila / Photography: Michael Hensel

Fig. 54: Milica Vujovic

Fig. 55: Young Eun Choi / Oslo School of Architecture and Design

Fig. 56: Bob Geldermans

Fig. 57: Bob Geldermans

Fig. 58: Department for Digital Architecture, TU Wien & LamoLab Research Centre

Fig. 59: Arne Leibnitz & Veselin Dzhedzev, Department for Digital Architecture, TU Wien

Fig. 60: Jakub Tyc, Department for Digital Architecture, TU Wien

Fig. 61: Jakub Tyc, Department for Digital Architecture, TU Wien

Fig. 62: Jakub Tyc, Department for Digital Architecture, TU Wien

Fig. 63: Jakub Tyc, Department for Digital Architecture, TU Wien

Fig. 64: Milica Vujovic

Fig. 65: Milica Vujovic

Fig. 66: Bob Geldermans / wit.eu

Fig. 67: Bob Geldermans

Fig. 68: Bob Geldermans

Fig. 69: Bob Geldermans

Fig. 70: Bob Geldermans

Fig. 71: Circular Buildings Coalition

Fig. 72: Circular Buildings Coalition

Fig. 73: Department of Urbanism, Delft University of Technology

Fig. 74: Circular Buildings Coalition

Fig. 75: Bob Geldermans

Fig. 76: Bob Geldermans

Fig. 77: Bob Geldermans

Fig. 78: Bob Geldermans

Fig. 79: Michael Hensel

Fig. 80: CBE Hub, Delft University of Technology

Fig. 81: Bob Geldermans

Fig. 82: Bob Geldermans

Fig. 83: Bob Geldermans

Fig. 84: Bob Geldermans

Fig. 85: Bob Geldermans

Fig. 86: Bob Geldermans

Fig. 87: Bob Geldermans

Fig. 88: Milica Vujovic

Fig. 89: Milica Vujovic

Fig. 90: Milica Vujovic

Fig. 91: Milica Vujovic

Fig. 92: Michael Hensel

Fig. 93: Milica Vujovic

Fig. 94: Michael Hensel

Fig. 95: Michael Hensel

Fig. 96: Michael Hensel

Fig. 97: Michael Hensel

Fig. 98: Adobe Stock / Milko Vasa

Fig. 99: OCEAN net

Fig. 100: OCEAN net

Fig. 101: OCEAN net

Fig. 102: OCEAN net

Fig. 103: J.C. Volkamer, Public Domain, Licence CC BY-NC-ND 4.0

Fig. 104: Defne Sunguroglu Hensel

Fig. 105: Defne Sunguroglu Hensel

Fig. 106: Defne Sunguroglu Hensel

Fig. 107: Milica Vujovic

Fig. 108: OCEAN net

Fig. 109: OCEAN net

Fig. 110: OCEAN net

Fig. 111: OCEAN net

Fig. 112: OCEAN net

Fig. 113: OCEAN net

Fig. 114: OCEAN net

Fig. 115: Milica Vujovic

Fig. 116: Milica Vujovic

Fig. 117: Wikimedia Commons, Creative Commons Attribute Share Alike 3.0 Unported, Crystalclear

Fig. 118: Wikimedia Commons, National Archive Identifier: 5999807, Environmental Protection Agency

AUTHORS' BIOGRAPHIES

Michael U. Hensel is an architect and partner in the practice OCEAN Architecture | Environment. He is a professor at TU Wien where he leads the Research Department for Digital Architecture and Planning. He is also a board member of the Center for Geometry and Computational Design at TU Wien, and co-chair of the SIG *Knowledge Discovery in Architecture* at the Centre for Artificial Intelligence and Machine Learning. He is series editor of the book series *Designing Environments* (Springer Nature) and author and editor of numerous books including *Performance-oriented Architecture* (Wiley, 2013), *Grounds and Envelopes* (Routledge, 2015), *The Changing Shape of Practice* (Routledge, 2016) and *The Changing Shape of Architecture* (Routledge, 2019).

Bob Geldermans is an industrial ecologist and head of the Research & Innovation Department at WOOD.BE, the Belgium Knowledge Center for the wood and furniture industry. He is a guest professor at the University of Antwerp, focusing on materials, design, construction & sustainability from an integrated systems perspective.

Defne Sunguroğlu Hensel is an architect and partner in the practice OCEAN Architecture | Environment. She is Associate Professor of Urban Ecology and Landscape Architecture at Southeast University in Nanjing, China, and series editor of the book series *Designing Environments* (Springer Nature).

Milica Vujovic is an assistant professor at the Research Department for Digital Architecture and Planning at TU Wien, where she co-chairs the SIG *Knowledge Discovery in Architecture* at the Centre for Artificial Intelligence and Machine Learning. Her main interests lie in architecture, data-informed design, and using, processing, analyzing and visualizing data with the aim of extracting new knowledge that can support architectural design.

ACKNOWLEDGE-MENTS

We offer our sincere gratitude to the many great thinkers on whose shoulders we stood while writing this book. More specifically, we wish to specifically thank Julian Vincent and Birger Sevaldson, for sharing invaluable insights and illustrations, Ivan Thung, and Job Salm of the Metabolic/Circular Building Coalition, ANSYS Granta, the Sustainable Environment Association, OCEAN net, and the Department for Digital Architecture and Planning at TU Wien for sharing valuable illustrations, and Cecilia Furlan for reviewing. We also wish to thank the editorial and graphic design team at Birkhäuser for their dedicated and flawless work.

IMPRINT

Michael Hensel,
Vienna University of Technology, Austria
michael.hensel@tuwien.ac.at, ORCID 0000-0001-5899-5643

Bob Geldermans,
University of Antwerp, The Netherlands
bobgeldermans@gmail.com, ORCID 0000-0003-0897-5542

Defne Sunguroğlu Hensel,
Southeast University, Nanjing, China
defnesunguroglu@gmail.com, ORCID 0000-0003-2968-6432

Milica Vujovic,
Vienna University of Technology, Austria
milica.vujovic@tuwien.ac.at, ORCID 0000-0003-0963-7182

On behalf of the publisher
Acquisitions Editor: David Marold
Content Editor: Bettina R. Algieri
Production Editor: Anja Haering

Proofreading: Stephen Roche, Galway, Ireland
Layout and cover design: Floyd E. Schulze, Berlin, Germany
Typography: Sven Schrape, Berlin, Germany
Image editing: bildpunkt Druckvorstufen GmbH
Printing: Beltz Grafische Betriebe GmbH,
Bad Langensalza, Germany
Paper: Magno Natural, 120 g/m²
Typefaces: Exposure, Rapid ST

FSC www.fsc.org
MIX
Papier | Fördert gute Waldnutzung
FSC® C089473

Library of Congress Control Number: 2023936828

Bibliographic information published by the German National Library
The German National Library lists this publication in the Deutsche Nationalbibliografie; detailed bibliographic data are available on the Internet at http://dnb.dnb.de.

ISBN 978-3-0356-2637-7
e-ISBN (PDF) 978-3-0356-2638-4

Im Westfeld 8, 4055 Basel, Switzerland
Part of Walter de Gruyter GmbH, Berlin/Boston

www.birkhauser.com
Questions about General Product Safety Regulation:
productsafety@degruyterbrill.com

9 8 7 6 5 4 3 2 1